THE BIRDS AND THE BEES OF JOYFUL MONOGAMY

Nine Secrets to Hot Partnering

By Lynne E. Sheridan, L.M.F.T., Transformational Trainer

Foreword by New York Times Bestselling Author Raymond Aaron

Preface by New York Times Bestselling Author Marcia Weider

Here's to your Love Story,

Front Cover Image: Gene Jimenez
Publisher: Lynne E. Sheridan

Contents

To Gene Jimenez, who has patiently supported me in the full expression of who I am, and taught me how to be loved, allowing me to love him in the process; thank you for being my rock. I choose you again and again daily.

And to my children who found their way to me perfectly. Charlie, thank you for your integrity, courage and quiet commitment. Caroline, thank you for your exuberance, stories, creativity, and unabashed desire to be loved. You both continue to teach me much about love.

Foreword

Are you in the relationship you have always wanted? Do you feel it is as deep, connected, and passionate as you want it to be? Have you wondered if there are secrets to writing a love story that inspires others and rivals those written in history books?

You probably have your own stories of relationship struggles and, hopefully, successes. I have been married and divorced. I proposed to a lady a little over ten years ago, who turned me down when I was at the height of my career. I was sidestruck and devastated. And then I met the love of my life. In other words, I know a thing or two about what it takes to fail and then succeed in love.

That is why I am excited about *The Birds and Bees of Joyful Monogamy: Nine Secrets to Hot Partnering.* Author Lynne Sheridan has sifted through the predominant work on couples and relationships, and offered a solid manual for creating a deep, connected, and passionate partnership. With nearly three decades of transformational work around the world, Lynne has found a way to bring complicated concepts alive, and put them into very real and profound exercises for you to do at home. You are holding this book and reading my words because you undoubtedly want to write your own love story. The fact that you reached for this book says that you are ready to be privy to the secrets that make a relationship soar.

Whether you are married, considering marriage, in a long-standing relationship, or preparing yourself for relationship, *The Birds and Bees of Joyful Monogamy* is a guide for passionate monogamy. With notoriously monogamous birds as your guide, Lynne points out secrets that can illuminate your own partnership. Whether you are a woman or a man, this book is about you having a relationship that is more than satisfying in every way, with Lynne detangling traps that can often undermine that relationship.

Sometimes when it comes to relationship advice, authors have a way of getting caught in one perspective. Lynne has found a way to weave together cutting-edge research on relationships, and bring it to life with experiential processes for you to follow. At the same time, Lynne gives very real examples from others, as well as from her own life, with humbling vulnerability. You can count on Lynne being candid, clear, and saying it like it is, and giving you permission and ways to practice doing the same.

The Birds and Bees of Joyful Monogamy is not for the faint of heart. It is for you, who are ready to roll up your sleeves, dive in, and experience real intimacy and connection. Lynne provides you not only with Secrets to Hot Partnering; she gives you very real tools to practice with your partner, as well as ways to grow as an individual. After reading and actively engaging in the work at the end of each chapter, you will undoubtedly see the results in your unfolding romance. If you have the determination to continue and deepen the work, I am certain that you are undertaking an amazing journey that will change your relationships and your life.

Raymond Aaron
New York Times Bestselling Author

Preface

Given that you have *The Birds & Bees of Joyful Monogamy* in your hands, I know one powerful truth about you. Clearly, you are someone who values growth and wants to live your dreams. And since I have known Lynne Sheridan for over ten years and count her as one of my dearest friends, I can tell you that you have made an excellent decision to learn from one of the best teachers and guides on the planet.

Personally, I have been married, divorced, and like many, been blessed with both rewarding and challenging relationships in my life. Probably like you, I know they can sometimes be difficult as all of our 'stuff' tends to come up with the people closest to us.

Do any of these scenarios sound familiar? Do you find yourself loving and kind, calm and cool around most people, but you often or suddenly lose your temper or that sense of peace with your partner? Have you ever found yourself taking care of your partner at the expense of yourself? Have you been in a relationship, but still craved connection and real intimacy or even felt lonely? If so, then you'll be glad you picked up this valuable book.

Lynne has a way of making complicated material accessible and usable. She also has the unique ability to take what appears to be conflicting or differing perspectives and weave them together, showing patterns and similarities that allow for a deeper understanding of ourselves and significant others.

What that means is that not only will you glean fresh insights but also a real understanding of the inner workings of your relationships. And through the powerful exercises in each chapter, you will be able to immediately put in to use what you are learning. With Lynne's guidance, you will have more than a conceptual awareness of the material but also simple practices to live and embody this wisdom.

When I started my company, *Dream University(R)*, it was important to me that people produced real results that mattered to them, including accomplishing their most heartfelt personal and professional dreams and living a meaningful life.

That could be why Lynne and I instantly clicked. She feels exactly the same. Now, that being said, the tools are in your hands. I know that if you want the dream badly enough, then you will do whatever it takes to create it. Dig in. Enjoy. Relish every word and don't skip the priceless exercises at the end of the chapters.

Here's to *The Birds & Bees of Joyful Monogamy* supporting you in keeping, cherishing and growing with the love of your life.

Marcia Wieder
CEO, Dream University[R] and bestselling author

Acknowledgments

Even after all of these years, I still wake up in shock that I have had the privilege to work with tens of thousands of people around the world, in creating the lives that they want. I can't believe I have been so blessed! I want to start by acknowledging all of the individuals, couples, and families that I have had the honor of serving over the past 26 years as a transformational trainer and therapist. I have sometimes given volunteer staff, in transformational trainings, the analogy of a teaching hospital—we are *learning on people*. I have learned on people, sometimes through mistakes my mind wants to turn over and over, like a gem polisher; other times, through grace, serving them well. Thank you to every person that supported me in my growth in service.

Given that this is a book on couples, I am so grateful for the many couples who have shown me what it is to be in a real committed relationship. I have peppered this book with some of their stories, of course disguising their names and details to protect their confidentiality and privacy. At one point, when I was meeting with an elderly couple, interviewing them specifically for this book, they asked if their identities would be concealed. I told them I hadn't decided but imagined that was what I would do. The man, Hal (not his name), said, "I sure hope so. We lived through the 60s, and the statute of limitations hasn't run out for one or two things that I did." He went on to share that as a drug addict, he had robbed a pharmaceutical warehouse to take the goods back to the flophouse. He is since a leader in recovery, but before the evolution of his nearly forty-year marriage, there were some fireworks. Some of the stories I present are composites of many cases, altered enough to keep identities protected. To all of these lovers, I am grateful for every teaching moment I have been given through each couple or person. This book is a gift back to you, an attempt to save other people from pain, heartbreak, and divorce, and a chance for their hard lessons and wisdom to be passed forward.

In writing my Couples Retreats and this book, I have drawn upon the work of Dr. Harville Hendrix, John Gottman, Dr. David Schnarch, Dr. Sue Johnson, Thomas Moore, Dr. Brad Blanton, and a host of other wise teachers, who have paved the way for millions of couples to come to peace and passion. I am grateful to each of them, appreciative of their work, and I am both a hungry student and loyal and inventive teacher of the tenants. In this book, I will do my best to give a nod to anyone who developed certain material, and give you additional resources if you would like to explore a particular distinction further, or if you see that you want additional work done in a specific area. I am drawing from diverse material and theories rather than sticking rigidly to one, because I believe that there is a wealth of information available for people to utilize, and have picked what I believe to be the strongest for supporting committed couples in moving forward.

Thank you to my husband, my love, Gene Jimenez. Thank you for never wanting me to dim my light so that you could shine brighter. Thank you for every celebration that you walk into, with people raving about how much they love your wife. Thank you for not being threatened by my successes or that love, but wanting only for it to permeate my skin and sink in. You have been an artist, not only on canvas but in my life—you bring color and depth to every frame of my existence. I am the lucky one.

Thank you, Charlie Jimenez. When you came into my life, just over eighteen years ago, you gave me the chance to be a mother. Thank you for forgiving my mistakes, letting me learn how to love a child. When I first moved in with your dad, I actually used to wake you up because I was afraid you stopped breathing. I didn't know to let sleeping babies sleep. Thank you for teaching me about race cars, Star Wars, the Marvel Universe, and everything else I would never have had a clue about.

Thank you to Caroline Hayden; I always wanted a little girl. When we walked into stores when you were little, and people used to say that you must look like my husband, I'd just laugh, thinking, "Yep, but he's not my husband." You entering into my world was not an accident. Thank you for your humor, joy, and the way you light up any room you walk into. And thank you for being unapologetically you.

Thank you to my best friend and partner in transformation, Lisa Kalmin. Anyone who has spent time with us knows that we hold nothing back with each other. When I met you 26 years ago, I didn't know that my entire life was about to change. You believed in me like no one else in my life ever had. And you were the first person that I could really trust. If you said it, you did it. You showed up in your actions and not only in your words. I am forever grateful for our volatile, challenging, and soul-growing friendship.

Thank you to Denise Gobrecht. You serve as a constant example of generosity to me. Your love is inclusive, and you seem to always make more space in your heart for those you meet along the way, flooding all of us with little reminders of your love. You were there at the beginning of me waking up, and your love was a big reason why.

Thank you to Dannielle Harwood and Mic Heib, and Ron and Shellee Lazar. Dannielle, there are very few people I could stay with for days and never feel one bit of discord. We both resonate to the same chords. Mic, for the many ways you make all of us laugh, thank you. And for allowing me to have an ongoing love affair with your wife, knowing it exists with tea and long walks. Dannielle and Mic, as those who are close to you know, you are meant for each other and are an amazing example of love in action. Ron and Shellee, thank you for the moment I met you both, where you were in your own training but then got to jump into medical service, a steady calm in the midst of a damn challenging moment. You both have been a constant source of reassuring joy and love since then.

Gabriel Nossovitch, thank you for being my mentor, teacher, friend, and my mirror. I am incredibly grateful for you believing in me, and for all of what you have taught me about training, life, and loving someone. I will never betray you. You say that Lisa is like your sister, but you and I have often behaved more like siblings. Thank you for your patience and for reflecting back to me parts of myself that I resist. I love you.

Jeff Cosby, I am so thankful that when I had a short list of trainers I wanted to have coach me five years ago, you were the only one that felt right. I remember, 26 years ago, when I was in a training, you simply pulled my arms away from my heart and told me to stop covering up my heart but to let it in. You have been doing that since in many ways. Thank you for Mastery for every student who has grown exponentially through your creation, and thank you for training me on Masters. I am so appreciative of our growing partnership.

Thank you, Marcia Weider. I so appreciate our long-distance friendship. I knew the moment I met you that we would be friends. I love your honesty, directness, and pure loving heart. I also love that we can say what is true for each of us, hear each other, use the lessons for growth, and then move on. I so love you and appreciate your gift of the Foreword, and cheerleading of me. And yes, this book about love stories is to remind you that yours will unfold, and that man will be blessed.

My parents, John and Coral Sheridan, and Leigh Weil Shields, thank you for the lessons you each imparted on me. Dad, for the lessons of working hard, being committed, and living life fully. Mom, thank you for my love of language, of literature, and the arts. Thank you for your commitment to civil rights, and for marching with Dr. Martin Luther

King with me in your belly. It rubbed off on me. Leigh, for teaching me independence, strength, and to have a thick skin. I recently read Gail Godwin's *Grief Cottage*, and these words jumped out for me about you: *"After all the human noise and conflicts have stopped, the absent person has more room in your heart to spread out and be herself. My mother's been gone ten years and I know her much better now than when we saw each other every day."*

To my sisters, Shayne and Meg Vogt, and Leslie and Kelly Sheridan, from Lisa Wingate's *Before We Were Yours*: "But the love of sisters needs no words. It does not depend on memories, or mementos, or proof. It runs as deep as a heartbeat. It is as ever present as a pulse." Shayne and Meg, thank you for being that constant pulse of love for me. Leslie and Kelly, thank you for teaching me that love does not need proof, or depend on memories. And Elizabeth, you are always present for me.

To my brothers, Jeff and Jim Vogt, and Kevin Sheridan: Jeff, thank you for valuing me and seeing yourself in me. Jim, thank you for teaching me that everything is a lesson of my own creation, and for schooling me on empathy. Kevin, thank you for your exuberance for life, commitment to family, and for teaching me to let go of my attachments and to simply love.

Thank you to Tom, who enrolled me in the Lifespring trainings years ago. I don't even know your last name, but I sure am appreciative of your friendship to my father, and for your sharing of transformation with me. You may not know it, but you changed my life and many other lives in the process.

Thank you, Michael Strasner, for hiring me. I remember you giving me a heads up that I probably shouldn't be quite so honest in interviews, and looking past that anyway. I'm not sure I've gotten that lesson, but I am grateful for our continued work together and for you taking risks on me.

Thank you, John Hanley, for Lifespring. I was convinced that you never liked me during the entire time I worked for you. Thank you for your patience with me being more questioning and stubborn than you thought an enrollment person should be. I am eternally grateful for those years at Lifespring, and for all that I learned, and for my commitment to prove you wrong and get really good at enrollment. Being right about that has served me well.

Thank you, Joe Ross, for being my senior and an example of love. Thank you for the hour-long coaching calls on my commute, and for investing everything of yourself in me. It worked.

Thank you to every trainer who moved me, beginning with Charlene Aframo, who was a dead-ringer for my stepmom, and perfectly suited to unpack that. Thank you Lisa Creo, for zinging me out of superficial-land; Eleanor Hanouer, for our beautiful friendship and for your straight-forward wisdom; Jim Hellum, for being the St. Bernard of transformation; Terry Nelson, for nothing being a throw-away; Herb Tanzer, for your opening one-ness for me; Judith Rich, for lessons in standing in love in all situations; Ray Blanchard for your weaving of stories —and on and on to every trainer that touched me along the way.

And for my dogs—all of them, including my little pack who has been patiently working with me—Max, Nala, Brooks, and Chupiloo. Every dog I have rescued has rescued me and taught me more about love than any human being. As most of the world who knows me already knows, I want to be a dog.

With overwhelming gratitude and love to everyone who has shaped me along the way, whether or not you were specifically named, I carry you in every part of my being.

*"Love means to commit oneself without guarantee,
to give oneself completely in the hope that our love
will produce love in the loved person.
Love is an act of faith,
and whoever is of little faith is also of little love."*[1]
Erich Fromm

Prologue

Monogamy – It's Not Just for the Birds

Did you know that 90% of the bird kingdom is monogamous?[2] Not many people do. And more importantly, why should you care? You probably haven't even given the birds a second thought, beyond putting food in a backyard feeder, and maybe admiring a crow or robin in flight, or even when it comes to chicken, geese, or ducks—for many—by eating them. But you and I have a lot to learn from the birds, about the nature of monogamy and being in a long-term relationship. In this book, you'll hear a few spellbinding stories of just how far some birds will go for their mate, and possibly our winged friends will inspire you to do the same.

Please let me be clear; this isn't a book about birds. And it isn't a book about bees. But it is borrowing a play book from birds and bees, which could keep your marriage or partnership vibrant, sexy, passionate, and connected. Isn't that why you picked it up? If you want greater intimacy with your partner, you have the right book in your hands. If you want to have deeper connection with your partner, then continue reading. And if you want hot, passionate sex, then you get to discover how things can sizzle in the bedroom when you and your partner both feel seen and heard.

It's true that monogamy is a little different with the birds than with humans. Some species of birds cheat, and some "divorce," but at a far lower rate than humans. Some birds are socially monogamous, raising their young together and forming a bond, but then sexually stray.

Some are monogamous for a single breeding season, and most songbirds mate for seasons or even a lifetime.[3]

But as you'll see, there are some birds that are in it for the long haul. How far would you go for your partner? Would you be willing to go just to the point of careening full speed in an airplane towards the earth, nose down, tied together, only to let go in the last final moment? That would be like jumping off the Empire State building with a cord tying you and your partner together, but no other safety— only at the last minute having a cord attached just before you hit the sidewalk. That's a snapshot of the love life of bald eagles, who mate for life. Are you willing to go to extreme lengths to get your partner's attention? This goes well beyond a serenade underneath a balcony. Would you dance for hours in front of hundreds, screeching? Would you do it yearly? You and I could learn a lot from the Whooping Crane.

Where do bees come in? Well, most of this book is about who you are *BEEing* in your relationship. Here's the good news: This book doesn't involve a ton of different *doing* or actions. It isn't about you mastering new lovemaking techniques, no matter how much you may fancy yourself as a femme fatale or Casanova. It is about shifting how you are BEEing and showing up.

I have conducted transformational workshops for over a quarter of a century, traveling the world to work with tens of thousands of people on creating the results that they want. I have done scores of Couples Retreats, Intensives, and have worked with couples over the course of 13 years. And thankfully, I regularly witness miracles—miracles like people quadrupling their income, becoming millionaires seemingly overnight. I have had the joy of hearing story after story of women becoming pregnant, even though their doctors insisted that they could not. I have had the honor and joy of attending, or even officiating, weddings of people who met and fell deeply in love, even though they had a string of disasters and "dead" bodies behind them— relationships that they had demolished. I get the joy of seeing people start charities, dig wells in Africa, or set up schools in Haiti, doing work they had always dreamed of doing. All of this occurs because they have had a deep shift in their being. They were willing to look at their beliefs, and determine which ones were serving them and which ones may have been quietly undermining them. And most importantly, they showed up differently in their lives, and produced dramatically different results.

Most people take different actions when they want to achieve results. If you want more money, you work harder and log longer hours at the office, toiling away. If you are not getting pregnant, you see specialist after specialist, working on *in vitro fertilization*, taking hormones, and making sex into a chore that must be done a certain number of times during ovulation. Maybe you've wanted to do service work for a long time, but you just don't have the time. For many people, that only comes when they retire later in life, or they squeeze in an hour or two here and there, never really doing the heartwarming work that they want to do, or responding to a call within, which they had previously ignored. In other words, we do more and more work. Most people work longer hours and attempt to find mechanisms that will assist in making life easier. If the couple that wants a baby finds the right method of elevating her hips, or a different doctor with a new system, they then hope that she'll finally get pregnant. If a worker finds a new program on his computer, he will finally be able to present a report on time, and with the color graphs his colleague doesn't have. If a person finds the right funding mechanism, like GoFundMe, they will finally be able to have their trip funded, to build the well in Africa. All of these may be great actions and tools, or mechanisms to support, but often, the result doesn't occur.

This work will focus on who you are *BEEing*. Another way of saying that is *how you are showing up in the world*. Have you ever wondered what people say about you when you're not around? Would your family say the same things about you and your friends? Would your co-workers say the same thing or different things than your primary partner? What qualities or characteristics would they say that you possess? Those are ways of being. A great exercise is to ask the five people closest to you to describe you as honestly as they can. The trick is to have them be honest and not sugar coat their assessments. What do you think that they would say? What are qualities that are not available to you at this moment? Are you kind and loving, but not so courageous? Are you passionate, creative, and free, but not so hot at following through with the plans that you make and being on time? Are you a leader naturally excelling in business, in control, and confidently creating results, but not very good at opening your heart and being vulnerable, or sharing your tenderness with those that you love? Are you analytical, practical, logical, trustworthy, but not so great at being spontaneous, free, and fully expressed? What qualities are already fully expressed in you? And which ones are not fully expressed? Where can you grow? What qualities does your partner long to feel from you? What would support you in creating the life you envision? That is focusing on *being* rather than *doing*. If you have the courage to dive into the journal work and exercises at the end of each chapter, you may learn quite a bit about yourself and how you show up.

Then you will discover that when you access different ways of being, your results shift dramatically. You have different results without taking dramatically different actions. This is what impacts our relationships. So that is why the BEEs are the little stars of this book. If you give them a chance, they're pretty amazing at pollenating things to produce honey down the road. At the end of each chapter, there may be a section entitled THE BIRDS....giving you a chance to write down what plays you are borrowing from the birds to support you and your partner happily nesting. Some chapters may have a section entitled THE BEES, giving you a chance to make notes on some of the shifts in how you are showing up. There may also be assessment tools for you to see exactly where you are in this moment, and then a chance for you to TAKE FLIGHT, and exercises for you to implement what you are reading, and experience joy, passion, and full self-expression in your relationship. I am strongly encouraging you to do more than just go through the motions of reading this book. If you go through the motions, doing the minimum work to get you through, you will have results consistent with that. However, if you dig in, really challenge yourself to do the journal work and exercises, you will have results consistent with the amount of commitment and effort that you put in—just like being in a committed relationship.

This book is designed to provide you with important distinctions that will allow you to see your relationship and partner in a new light. I will provide stories of couples and how they utilized that particular learning, or the story of how they have evolved that teaching even further. The distinctions and stories are powerful, moving, and will hopefully provide illumination on your own relationship, as well as give you places where you can identify. But this book is not meant to be simply read and digested cognitively, but rather lived out loud. At the end of each chapter, you will find an exercise to support you in uncovering layers of the concept that has been explained. If you are anything like me, you often skip those exercises, thinking, "I'll do that later, once I've read a little bit more of where this is going." The vast majority of the time, I continue reading until the end of the book, doing a couple of the "shorter" exercises along the way, then completing the book, never to be returned to again, unless for a quick quote or to check some fact. Now is a time I am hoping that karma does not come into play. I am a big proponent of experiential learning, and have devoted my life to leading people into breakthrough, through the power of experience. My words may resonate, and the concepts may seem valuable or impactful, but they are meant to be combined with the use of the exercises, so that your learning occurs not just with your head but with your heart and body as well.

I recommend that you and your partner both read the book at the same time, setting aside a special date each week to discuss what is jumping out for both of you, share answers to questions and journal responses, as well as to do the exercises outlined at the end of the chapters. When my husband and I are working on new material, we sometimes set a special date in a restaurant, bringing our books and journals to the restaurant. In that way, we feel like we are still "getting out" and treating ourselves, but at the same time, we are deliberately forwarding our commitment and forwarding our relationship. I am guessing that I am not the only person who has a partner who does not like to read. I read voraciously, but my husband was raised on comic books and, aside from his master's program, doesn't want to read very much. Here is what we have come to thus far: When possible, I have books on tape, and when the book is not yet available in tape form, I highlight important distinctions, stories, or insights, and then read those to him, answering any questions he may have. Do whatever works for you and your relationship; email, text, or tweet the material if it supports. But please, then set aside a special time and space for you to complete the interactive part.

And before I write another word, let me make it clear that most often I do not pick a personal pronoun—like he or she—in this book. I do my best to say "partner," and sometimes I say "their" to refer to your partner. Forgive me this possible linguistic stretch, but I am not a fan of gender specific language, even alternating as has become fashion in recent years. I think we are all clear that there are partnerships where there are a he and a she; a she and a she; a he and a he; and even a he, she, and she; or a she, she, she, and he; or they and a she... In other words, pronouns are innately limiting with partnerships. Again, forgive me the plural of "their," and the generic of "your partner."

I also want to address some common misconceptions about monogamy before you read another word. Many people believe that when they make the commitment, they are in a prison, thinking it means shutting off other options, and being trapped without an exit door. That is often why many people are so reluctant to make a commitment to marriage or a long-term relationship, believing that they will no longer be free. For some, the idea of monogamy is terrifying. But monogamy is not prison, locking us off from other options or possibilities. Monogamy is a choice, and opening possibilities and options within that choice. I'm sure you know that when you ask some people what it's like to be married, they cringe and say that it is horrible, and recommend staying single as long as possible. But when you ask other people, they say it is the greatest blessing and honor of their lives, and an amazing adventure with their partners. Marriage is an institution. We can make it horrible or we can make it beautiful—it is how we are being within the marriage that can make it heaven or make it hell. Epictetus said, "A mind in and of itself can make a heaven of hell, a hell of Heaven."[4] That is a shift in how we are being, rather than focusing on what we are doing.

Monogamy is what you are choosing to make it, and I think you picked up this book looking to make it closer to heaven than hell.

In case you don't know some of the benefits of marriage, you can pull up many articles and research online. To get the ball rolling, here is a pretty good list: https://www.thelist.com/41041/surprising-benefits-married/.

Besides financial benefits on taxes and insurance, research shows you'll be richer, have lower stress, are less likely to be depressed, less likely to engage in risky behavior, achieve better results after surgery than your single counterparts, be more likely to survive cancer, sleep better, and live longer. Still, many people see marriage as outdated, and simply a societal construct. This book can even be successfully used by those folks, but it isn't my job to convince them of the benefits of being married. It's my job to stay in my marriage and choose it again every day.

In this book, you will learn how to have monogamy that is a heaven. I will share experiences of couples who have inspired me over the years. And as Sir Thomas Moore said in his book, *Soul Mates*, "I don't pretend to know all these things, and certainly I don't claim to do them all well myself. In fact, certain things I write about firsthand from outrageous failures and follies of my own."[5] In other words, this is a humbling book to write, because I get to share about some of my own failures and mistakes in my own marriage. Like you, and most human beings, I am far from perfect.

It's only fair that I give you the same window into my own relationship, and serve as my own *National Enquirer* for an expose of whether or not our marriage meets the muster, for me to offer this book. I have been married for seventeen years and had a year with my husband prior to our marrying. When I lead my Couples Retreats, I fully acknowledge that Gene and I are still newlyweds. I have been truly humbled by couples who have been together for forty or fifty years, and are still willing to throw themselves into Couples Retreats or development work. Gene and I are babes compared to the wisdom-keepers who have allowed us to learn from the missteps and grace of their journeys.

In fact, my third year of my marriage was hell. I bet that isn't what you imagined from the author of a book on relationship bliss, but it's the truth. And the truth sometimes is painful to acknowledge and even harder to admit. But I have also learned that once you acknowledge a painful truth, you can create something else. That year of hell became the compost for the development of incredible growth, over a decade of successful Couples Retreats and scores of couples knowing what's possible in their relationships. It makes sense—put any seed in total shit, and something amazing will blossom out of the dung. It isn't a pretty process, but the yield is amazing. There is no doubt about it; that year of hell was the beginning of the turning point for my marriage and our relationship. I didn't know it then, but it would have made it easier to get through if I would have known that somehow gems would be mined from the minefield that became a lot of our conversations. I would love to claim that some aspect of my *higher self* knew; but I didn't, and that made it that much harder to go through in the moment.

That third year was like my husband and I being on a medieval torture rack, stretched to the point that we both were begging to be untied. I remember the worst moment vividly. I was holding a fragile, glass antique angel in hand as I decorated the Christmas tree, and I spit words I never imagined would come out of my mouth. He said that I was a massive victim, a hypocrite, and the opposite of the work I claimed to be in the world. I said that he was perpetually depressed, insatiably needy, and draining every bit of energy from me. To one degree or another, we both were right. But in that moment of what has become known in infamy as the Christmas tree argument, neither of us would ever possibly admit that the other one was right. Even the angel was perfectly serving as a prop to underscore his accusation of my hypocrisy.

In that third year, I questioned why on earth anyone would marry. I wondered if there was something fundamentally wrong with me; I marveled at the fact that I could be a successful relationship coach for so many, and yet be reduced to childish behavior in my own marriage. If I imagined something was wrong with me, I was certain that there was something wrong with him. If I could just fix him, somehow make him see the error in his thinking, actions, and behavior, then everything would be just fine. I was shocked and embarrassed by my own thinking. I had coached hundreds of thousands of people on being responsible and choosing to engage with life, not blaming and resenting others. I was supposedly a victim to nothing and no one. Yet here I was, somehow thinking that it was my husband's fault that we were in our repetitive cycle of blame. If this was how I was being by year three, what was it like for other people?

To be clear, I would love to say that I listened to the horrifying string of insults, character assaults, and accusations that came out of his mouth, but I think that was one of the main problems: Neither of us was listening to the other. Yes, some doozies stand out. My husband Gene and I both said things that cut deeper than knives. We still carry bumpy scar tissue inside that is felt in moments of self-doubt. During that year, we would re-wound each other with those cuts, every couple of months. But the Christmas tree carnage was the worst.

What is our marriage? Well, after year three, it became a safe haven—not a place where we could hide from the assaults of the world, but a place where we could safely negotiate self-growth, and work on really reaching the other. Generally, we have an argument about every six months or so. It is a predictable argument, undoubtedly something where we could both give each other scripts and hold pretty close to what the other has written. It is unsolvable and has more to do with what is occurring internally with each of us than the other, but we take it out to ride the tired pony every now and then anyway. Most often, there is no screaming or the hurling of insanities, but rather just the same tired monologues that need to be heard. We usually pause for a while, after we enact the play, to do the real work within, then approach each other later with a stroking of the arm, asking about the kids or the day, or in the extreme case, speaking the most valuable words, "I'm sorry."

This is how this book emerged. After I wrote the Couples Retreats and began working with couples in an experiential way, I was daunted by what I witnessed. I was both inspired and horrified: inspired by couples who had been married over forty years, weathering adultery, moves from continent to continent, and tragedies; and horrified by what many couples were enduring as a "relationship," treating each other with contempt and spitting sarcastic responses to cover a lifetime of hurt. When I wrote my first Couples Retreat, I had no idea if any of it was really valuable, so I brought Gene with me to test it out while I simultaneously led the workshop. At the end of the weekend, we were closer, communicating with a more solid understanding of each other, and our arguments seemed to disintegrate. We agreed that it seemed to be effective for us, and we were receiving similar feedback from other participants. As I witnessed the success of the work, I began to get more and more motivated to have experiential work available to other couples—those who had great relationships but wanted to deepen their understanding of their partner, as well as those who were on the rocks, struggling to find the sweet spot of their relationships again.

Thankfully, I am aware that even our worst is the best for many couples. In my work since then, as a marriage and family therapist and transformational trainer, I have witnessed far worse. I see couples who cannot seem to interact with each other unless sarcasm and criticism laces every sentence. I work with couples who expect their partner to weather character attacks, slamming of doors, and yelling vicious derogatory derivatives on a daily basis. I have worked with women who endured decades of physical assaults by the person who supposedly loved them more than any other in this world. I have sat across from a woman who moved to thirteen different states to escape the man who loved her so much that he would not let her stay alive if he thought she would "belong" to another. Through it all, I have been amazed at the fire that is inspired in intimate relationships, and how, at times, our primary partnership brings out the absolute worst in us, and reveals any part of us that is still wounded and afraid.

Before I go any further, I want to clarify that this book is not meant to address domestic violence issues. If you are currently in a relationship where there is pushing, shoving, hitting, threats with weaponry, hair pulling, or forced sex (otherwise known as rape), then I am urging you to seek immediate help. These are not relationship issues; they are issues that have to do with the individual person, manifesting in your personal relationship. Sometimes people think that they have been so atrocious that they have deserved their partner hitting them. That is not the case. Research shows that domestic violence has nothing to do with the dynamic between two people, but is an issue within the person who batters, and therefore needs to be treated within that individual. It seems that batterers are adept at choosing people who will be the perfect recipient of horrifying behavior, and remain silent about the terrors that they endure, because it feels familiar from their own family of origin, or it matches their own feelings of worthlessness or self-doubt.[6] If you are currently hitting, throwing things, or otherwise using intimidation in your relationship, and justifying your behavior as what is needed to teach your partner a lesson, be clear that you need help. Your behavior is not loving, and if you want to have a fulfilling partnership, you need to get help from a therapist or mental health practitioner who has been trained to treat domestic violence. If you are on the receiving end of domestic violence, you also need to get help from a mental health practitioner who is qualified to assist you in ensuring your safety as well as working on your understanding of what a loving relationship looks and feels like.

I am writing this book for people who are willing to do the work to create a passionate relationship where intimacy is expressed and experienced. If you do not want to sleepwalk through your relationship, but are interested in creating *"a relationship that fosters the maximum psychological and spiritual growth of each partner."[7]* and if you want to deepen intimacy and connection, you picked up the right book. And if you have also been horrified by words you have spoken to your partner, as well as by your actions, then this book will offer another possibility for you. I know that if I struggled in my third year of marriage, after training transformational trainings for a decade, and living that work, there were probably others out there struggling.

It takes a certain amount of arrogance for someone to actually sit down and write a book on partnership and having a relationship thrive. I use the word, *arrogance*, but I really mean a mixture of stupidity and delusions—stupidity because it puts a great big X on my back, with people undoubtedly shining a spotlight on my own marriage, questioning whether we are happy enough, successful enough, or having enough wild, sensual, and crazy sex. Who am I to write a book on passionate partnerships if our home is not a constant state of bliss, connection, and intimacy? A part of me thinks that if I was not a licensed marriage and family therapist (LMFT), this book would not be published at all. Those letters give me some kind of an *expert* status to be preaching advice on successful coupling, and they edify my experience. But I can see that the critics have a point. That's where the delusions come into play. I believe that I do have something unique to provide to couples that are looking to deepen their intimacy, experience new depths to passion, and want to continue to grow together as they change and evolve.

For the past twenty-six years, I have been a transformational trainer, executive coach, and mentor, supporting people to have loving relationships, achieve goals, and live their purpose with freedom and joy. I have traveled to Russia, Chile, Mexico, China, Hong Kong, Taipei, Kuala Lumpur, and throughout the United States, training people. I have pushed admirals and bureaucrats, in Washington, D.C., outside their comfort zones, and demanded that super-aware Californians get below the jargon and translate concepts into tangible, measurable results. I became known as a type of relationship whisperer, who could work with singles and have a partner suddenly appear in their space after years of solitude. I was sought after to provide coaching for couples that had hit a tough spot in their relationships, and then I witnessed magic. Single people found "the one." Couples who were married for nearly fifty years were acting like newlyweds. Where there was discord in relationships, there was now peace.

In fact, I chose to become licensed as a marriage and family therapist, specifically because the emphasis in that field is on who we are in the expression of relationships. I love working with couples in a therapy session, even when anger erupts like a volcano. I have begun a session with one partner calling the other a "white, cracker slut," and the other hitting the ball back, with "selfish black bastard." By the time our work together was done, they had cried, laughed, and opened up to how the hurt became anger. I thrive on the energy that is created in a union, and marvel at being allowed through a window of intimacy in service to the relationship.

Why should you keep reading when you have a million other things to do? Unfortunately, most people spend more time thinking about their grocery list than they do on their relationship. In 2017, the top five New Year's resolutions were:

1. Get Healthy
2. Get Organized
3. Live Life to the Fullest
4. Learn New Hobbies
5. Spend Less/Save More[8]

What's missing from the list? Relationship. What else is missing? There are no tangible measurements to those declarations. "Fall in love" made #9, and "spend more time with family" made #10, but still!! We spend time and energy on health and fitness, glamour, parenting, home improvement, business strategies...but not on becoming the best partner that we can be, and having passionate relationships. We invest time and money into developing ourselves for our careers, and many of us are equally, if not more, invested in the raising of our children. But we seem to expect that our relationship will just keep ticking along without much more than a "Hi, honey, I'm home," and kisses. The results are abundantly clear that this strategy isn't working. The divorce rate in America, for first marriages, is estimated to be 50%[9]—so your marriage has a 50% chance of making it. If there are children involved, then two out of three of those marriages will end in divorce. If you are on a second marriage, it has about a 33% chance of lasting, meaning that overwhelmingly, we are not improving with even the second or third attempt.[10] Internationally, the news doesn't get much better, since there are at least 27 countries where at least one in four marriages end in divorce.[11]

I am encouraging you to stop having the past determine what is possible or should be expected in your partnership, and risk creating something new. In *The Birds and Bees of Joyful Monogamy,* you will:

- Stop pointing the finger and blaming your partner OR yourself for current breakdowns in your relationship.

- Clarify, explore, and expand your vision for your relationships and lives together.
- Illuminate patterns from your family of origin and where those patterns are supporting or getting in the way of intimacy, love, and connection.
- Experience profound compassion for where your partner carries wounds, and be able to recognize when that wound is touched and reactions occur.
- Learn how to fight fairly, expressing upset and anger without damaging your relationship, but rather forwarding it.
- Truly listen to each other to know the other person more deeply.
- Nurture and develop your capacity to like and respect your partner exactly for who they are.
* Solve the problems that can be solved, and surrender to those that are not solvable.
- Learn to read and understand your partners "signals" to avoid potential arguments and landmines.
- Give your partner what he or she has been yearning for and complaining about not getting.

If you are willing to invest yourself, not just reading but doing the exercises as well, you will find that your relationship can allow for the highest expression of who you are. It can be a refuge, and an exciting adventure and joy. Rainer Maria Rilke wrote, "For one human being to love another: that is the most difficult of all our tasks, the ultimate, the last test of proof, the work for which all other work is but preparation."[12] It is a beautiful, sometimes messy, often challenging and incredibly rewarding test of who we are. I believe that the rewards are beyond worth it, and that by virtue of the fact that this book is in your hands, you are prepared and ready for the journey. Head right into Chapter 1, where you'll learn the power of being all-in with back doors closed.

THE BEES

In order to have the BEES magically pollinate areas of your relationship, I recommend that both you and your partner get a beautiful little journal to record your progress, growth, and exercises as you move along your journey to Hot Partnering. The more you participate in life, the more value you create. You cannot sit and watch the exercise equipment and get in shape. You need to get on the equipment. Challenge yourself to actually do the work, and it will pay off. If you make excuses and have reasons why you don't make your relationship or this work important, then you will have results that match that level of commitment. Treat yourself—come on, you deserve a new journal, to have a record of your epic love story for your children and grandchildren.

How do you view yourself? How do others view you?

Write down a list of at least five qualities or characteristics that you believe you possess that are neutral or positive.

Now write down a list of at least five qualities or characteristics about yourself that you believe to be negative.

Ask at least three people to do the same. If possible, have one family member, or someone who is like family to you, complete these lists. Have your partner, or last intimate partner, complete these lists, as well as a close friend.

Here's the real trick: Don't argue with the feedback that they have given you. Don't use it as a bat to beat yourself up, only focusing on what you see to be negative. Simply take in the information, and see if you can see what each has written, from their vantage point.

Now, where do you want to grow? What qualities do you want to bring alive inside of you? What qualities or characteristics would support your relationship?

CHAPTER ONE

Fly Like an Eagle
Go BIG or Go Home Alone

*"Until one is committed, there is hesitancy, the chance to draw back,
always ineffectiveness. Concerning all acts of initiative
(and creation), there is one elementary truth,
the ignorance of which kills countless ideas and splendid plans:
that the moment one definitely commits oneself, the providence
moves too. A whole stream of events issues from the decision,
raising in one's favor all manner of unforeseen incidents, meetings,
and material assistance, which no man could have dreamt would
have come his way. I learned a deep respect for one of Goethe's
couplets: Whatever you can do or dream you can, begin it.
Boldness has genius, power, and magic in it!"*
W.H. Murray[1]

It's hard to find a better example of commitment than the North American Bald Eagle. Many people do not realize that Bald Eagles remain committed to their partner over the course of their entire lifetimes. They build nests together, which is no small undertaking, given that these nests often measure nine feet across, can be up to 12 feet high, and weigh about two tons. That's quite a symbol of commitment—a lot bigger than a ring on a finger. The male and female bald eagle both contribute equally in the nest building, but Dad's contributions go much further. He also supports in incubating the eggs and feeding the offspring.

During courtship, Bald Eagles engage in one of the most amazing displays of aerial gymnastics. They lock talons, twirling and careening in full dive, directly towards the earth, only letting go at the very last moment before impact. This aerial cartwheeling is widely photographed with wonder and amazement.[2] To me, it's quite the game of chicken. It's almost as though they are testing each other to see just how committed they really are to the relationship. If one were to let go of the other early, it would be an indication that they were not totally in. As human beings, we also test, but we often do not make those tests transparent, and we pull out of the free fall, way too early. With feelings of panic or fear, we sometimes let go of our partner, instead of holding on and staying connected.

The quote at the start of this chapter is by W.H. Murray, who also knows a thing or two about commitment. After all, he spent three years in prisoner of war camps, in Italy, Germany, and Czechoslovakia, during which time he wrote the book, *Mountaineering in Scotland*. The first draft was written on rough toilet paper because it was all that he had available. When the manuscript was found and destroyed by the Gestapo, Murray's response was to begin the manuscript again. At that point, he didn't know if he would climb a mountain ever again, as he was close to starvation and unsure if he would come out of the situation alive. He did, and he went on to climb many more mountains, and leave us a record of his passion. Perhaps you feel love-starved in your relationship, and like climbing a mountain would be easy compared to your fight for intimacy, but I think that we can all agree that Murray gives us a pretty good template for what will be required to make the summit. And the bald eagle gives us the chance to see that we need to be "all in."

I imagine that quite a few of you reading could tell me stories of where a lack of commitment killed a relationship. Think about it: Many people fight for years to avoid marriage. We even have a name for it now: commitment phobia. And it isn't only men that are commitment phobic, despite the common stereotype. Many people seem to believe that if they make a commitment, then they are not free. They drift from job to job, or date for six to ten years before they finally have the confidence to maybe risk it. But is it freedom to think that something could contain or limit us? Is it freedom to need to remain a tumbleweed in order to experience that we have choice? The philosopher, Jean Paul Sartre, said, "Man is condemned to be free; because once thrown into the world, he is responsible for everything he does. It is up to you to give [life] a meaning." [3] In other words, it's up to each of us. Wandering and not putting down roots cannot be confused with freedom, just as settling down and marrying is not commitment. They are whatever we make them to be.

If you are dating, and your partner says that they would maybe like to marry you someday, is it the same as your partner proposing and giving you a ring? No. Maybe someday is not the same as "this is happening." When the commitment is made, everything changes. Once a couple is engaged, a call from an ex-boyfriend or girlfriend isn't just a call from an ex; it is a much deeper conversation: "Do you guys still talk? Are you still close with her? How close are you?" And the house on the corner with the "For Sale" sign isn't just a house on the market; it is another discovery of the future: "Do you want to live in a house like that? Would you want our house to be here or in another place?" The entire world alters as a result of commitment.

Have you noticed that when you make a commitment to something, the growth begins as soon as the commitment is made? Sometimes when a couple enrolls in one of my Couples Retreats, I will hear about things altering the moment they enrolled. Perhaps the husband comes forward, saying that he wants a closer connection, or the wife gets pregnant after years of trying. There has been considerable research done on the energy of vibrations. From a perspective of sound and energy, everything that exists is putting out some level of vibration. Our words have vibrational energy as do our thoughts, meaning that the moment I commit myself and close all of my back doors, the energy of my thinking, speaking, and being alters. The energy of commitment is distinct and powerful.

There is another way in which commitment shows up, which is sometimes uncomfortable for us. Have you ever declared that you would work on a specific quality or characteristic, like patience or integrity, for instance? And then the very next moment, it seems that the universe seems to give you one situation after another where you get to practice patience: traffic jams, delays at the doctor's office, waiting for that check to arrive in the mail. This can be beyond frustrating; and it is often in those moments that people give up and think that their commitment is not being rewarded. But the opposite is occurring; you are working with the flow of the universe, and giving yourself the opportunity to see what was invisible to you before. Prior to making the commitment, perhaps you didn't see how impatient you were, and other people had been complaining about it. In making the commitment, it's like a spotlight suddenly was turned on that area of growth. This is another way in which commitment moves us. It's not always comfortable, but it is always valuable. It's like the old saying that "God doesn't give us what we ask for; he gives us the situations in which we have the chance to step into what we asked for: patience, power, gratitude, peace."

In the year 363 AD, Julian the Apostate, Emperor of Rome, invaded Persia, and after his army crossed the Tigris, he had all the pontoons and barges burned so that there would be no thought of going back. He is just one of many commanders who burned bridges, ships, and any escape route to make it clear to their troops that there was only one option: fight and triumph, or die.[4] For some of us, it takes that level of drastic action for us to finally commit. No, I am not advocating that you burn your car or any escape route, but rather that you find that commitment within yourself, so that all other options are closed off permanently.

I want to point out, not so delicately, that commitment is not a feeling. Ask yourself, honestly, are you committed to things only when it feels good and you are motivated? Or do you remain committed when you are hurt, angry, bored, frustrated, or whatever the emotion is that tends to hijack you? With Siri responding to our every question, Amazon supplying our latest want, we are a society of instant gratification. That's challenging with commitment because many of us only want to be committed if it is easy, comfortable, and yields a big reward. Think about the music videos that are shown—you sing and get a recording contract, and then you instantly get fame, fortune, girls, boys, yachts, mansions, and whatever your heart desires. In a recent survey, MonsterTRAK had noted that college respondents said that "they expected to be compensated highly in their first job, and to become millionaires very early in their careers." But most successful older people were willing to pay their dues. The year I got out of college, my roommate started a job as an engineer at McDonnell Douglas, making over $55,000 a year. I was happy to land a job writing circulars for home improvement stores, at $18,000. I survived on Top Ramen, and stepped over a man who slept in the entrance of my apartment building in Minneapolis. I didn't have the funds that winter to repair my VW Bug when it broke down, so I trekked about 20 blocks to work in the Minneapolis snow for a while until I save up the funds. Yep, I know it sounds like the story parents always tell about walking for miles in the snow to school, but there is something to be said for those stories. Being willing to pay dues means that it isn't always going to be instant gratification or the Hollywood romance; to yield gold, you've got to do a lot of alchemy.

This is a pretty good example of what has occurred with commitment in all areas of our society. If you have been married for any length of time, you know well that commitment is not a feeling. If you are a parent, you have a great example of commitment. When your toddler wakes up in the night, peeing their bed or throwing up, most of us would rather be sleeping than changing the sheets and our toddler's clothing. But we get up anyway, clean up the mess, change the sheets, and then go back to bed. This is an example of commitment, despite feelings, thoughts, and how desperately our body wants to get back in bed again.

Many of us have elaborate wedding ceremonies, agonizing over the dress and the shoes, and inviting the people who matter the most to us to witness the making of a commitment. Have you ever been to a wedding ceremony where the minister asked the congregation if they would support the couple in keeping their commitment, and the congregation dutifully answers, "I will?" But do we really? No. We do, on good days when things are going well, and it feels romantic. But most of the time, as a culture, we do not. When things get difficult, and one partner or another calls buddies for sympathy and agreement that the other person is the problem, often the responses are along the lines of, "I told you she was a prima donna," or "He's a jerk; I can't believe he doesn't realize how lucky he is to have you." Or, "It's her problem—how hard is it to just have sex and be a good wife?" Or, "He doesn't do shit around the house, and expects you to do everything—you should leave." Whether people actually say that the person should leave, they are only adding gasoline to a fire that is raging out of control.

How do you feel when you think about commitment? Do you have a healthy relationship with it, or an antagonistic one? For example, do you feel that commitment calls parts of you forth that would not have otherwise been called forth—asks you to be a better person than you are right now? Or do you see it as a prison? Do you feel like you will fail? Do you worry that you don't have what it takes?

Let me give you an example. Nathanial had it all—a moderately successful career, a beautiful girlfriend, a loving family—and yet he could never bring himself to settle down. When I asked him if he was in a relationship, his response was, "What do you mean by that?" When I asked again, he said, "I don't think so." I questioned further, and he said, "I don't know what she thinks, but to me, no, I am not in a relationship." When I explored a little further about what did matter to Nathanial, with every answer he gave, there were disclaimers, like, "I guess I'd like to try to be a better man." I guess I'd like to try?! Guessing has no conviction. And trying means that I am going to put forth some kind of work or effort, but I won't deliver on it. These are conditional forms of language. And our language always reveals our paradigm, or belief system. In other words, how we say it IS how we mean it. Internally, Nathanial had it wired that if the conditions worked out, he'd deliver; but if there was traffic, an unforeseen incident or obstacle, then he wouldn't deliver. Nathanial, and many of us, are operating like a pinball being shot in the machine—wherever the next paddle sends us is where we go. When we talked a little more about whether or not Nathanial makes commitments in his career, he confessed that he would always say things like, "I'll see what I can do," or "I'll see you around ten." Can you hear the lack of commitment that a common thread was weaving through Nathanial's entire life? He was a kind and loving man, and yet, up until now, he has related to commitment like it were some kind of prison that would strip him of his freedom. It doesn't even matter the commitment—it could be to his girlfriend, to being a "better" man, or to his career—he was hesitant to commit to ANYTHING.

With commitment, there is an opportunity for you to call greatness forth and reinvent yourself. When Dr. Martin Luther King declared equality, it was far from guaranteed. Dr. Martin Luther King wasn't naturally outgoing. In fact, he reportedly used to get embarrassed as a child when he'd go to church and hear people singing, dancing, or calling out Amen when the Pastor would give the sermon. But through the power of his commitment, and his willingness to reinvent himself for that commitment, he became a different man: passionate about civil rights, and vocal and willing to do just about anything in service of that commitment. That is the power of commitment.

For you to have significant results in using *The Birds and Bees of Joyful Monogamy*, you get to make a commitment. Sure, you could read this book casually. You can pick up whatever you pick up, and work at it a little bit. You could do it half-heartedly or without a commitment to completing it, but then you will get half-assed results, and I am imagining from the fact that you have even selected this book, *you do not want mediocre results.*

GROUND RULES

Yes, this book has ground rules. There are rules for just about everything we do. Life has a set of ground rules that goes with it. For example, you cannot stand in front of a speeding train and expect to remain in the game of life. Gravity is one of the rules of life. If I step off the top of a building, I will fall down. We can resist the rules, but in the end, it really doesn't serve us, and the end may come far sooner than we would have wanted it to come. If you want a beautiful garden of succulent fruits and vegetables, you have got to be willing to water, weed, and give the garden some work. The hardest work you will be asked to do, in participating fully in *The Birds and Bees of Joyful Monogamy,* will be internally, with a genuine willingness to look at yourself honestly, and then openly share and reveal your realizations with your partner. There will be weeding of the garden, and with commitment, that weeding will come from you.

If you notice you are resistant to following through with an exercise, write about it, talk about it, but do it. Dig underneath any resistance that may arise, attempting to sabotage your commitment. And keep the vision you have for your relationship at the forefront of your thinking. None of this is about simply doing exercises in a book. It is about you having the relationship that you've always wanted and dreamed of, and being willing to put the work in to yield the gold.

Make a commitment to your relationship. Use completing this book as a metaphor for your relationship. In other words, remain committed to your work with each other through these exercises, no matter what challenges may arise.

Be on time for your dates with each other, and for times you set aside to work on the exercises in this book. Be willing to show yourself that you can succeed in a commitment, and show your partner that you are making them important and that nothing else will become "more important" during the process. Many people operate in "either/or" thinking, meaning that they can have one thing occur or another— they can meditate, or get breakfast ready for the kids—but not both. If we engage in this thinking, then things that matter will always be falling off the list. How can you reinvent yourself to have ALL of it occur? This may mean being uncomfortable, rigorous, and disciplined, and it will pay off in the end.

When you complete the exercises in this book, do not use alcohol, marijuana, or other mood-altering substances. Part of the work outlined in *The Birds and the Bees of Joyful Monogamy* is to become more conscious of hidden aspects of how you are being. The use of mood-altering substances undermines that purpose. Of course, if you have been prescribed a mood-altering substance, take your prescription as instructed. Should you choose to alter a prescription, speak to your doctor. This being said, sometimes we use alcohol or other substances (this is being written in California, where we now have marijuana outlets just about everywhere) to mask feelings of anxiety and fear, or give us permission to be more risking or passionate. For example, people sometimes have a couple of drinks before they can really be passionate with sex, instead of allowing themselves to go through the anxiety or fear with their partner. I am encouraging you to feel whatever comes up for you in this work, without dulling it with drugs.

When you are doing the exercises outlined, and concentrating on your work with your partner, turn off any cell phones and electronic devices. Yes, I know that as a society, we have become quite dependent, but you can let go of it and give your partner your full focus for at least that set time period.

Give of yourself fully. You probably realize that the more fully you participate in anything, the more value you create for yourself and for others. Be willing to give of yourself fully, while on dates and doing any of the exercises. Use the process as a mirror for your willingness to give fully in your relationship.

You were promised "Nine Secrets to Hot Partnering." In case it isn't clear yet, **SECRET #1 TO HOT PARTNERING IS: BE COMMITTED.** Everything comes out of commitment.

Now another secret, about Bald Eagles: The birds fly alone during the winter months and migration, reconnecting with their mates during breeding season. Think about it; Bald Eagles thrive in long-distance relationships. Sometimes when girls are in high school or college, or in their twenties, they abandon their friends as soon as they are in a relationship. They spend every waking minute with their partner. If their boyfriend is in a bad mood, they are in a bad mood. But this goes well beyond high-schoolers.

Many of us seem to absorb whatever is occurring with our partner, taking on moods, feelings, and attitudes. If one partner likes football, then suddenly the other partner is sporting jerseys and watching football every weekend. If one partner is upset about something, then the other partner can no longer be happy. This represents a type of enmeshment, where the two seem to be operating as one, a type of synchronized water ballet. That may seem romantic, but it is incredibly limiting, because you are not your partner. You have your own moods, feelings, thoughts, and desires. You are not supposed to be your partner, and they are not meant to be you. Monogamy works when both partners have their own interests, drives, and desires.

Think about it. People say, "She's my better half," or "He completes me," and we think, "How romantic." Is it really romantic to be incomplete? Imagine someone coming up to you and saying, "I am missing some fundamental aspects of myself; do you want to be in a relationship?" I wouldn't think, "How romantic." I would run screaming from the building. When we think of the movie, *Jerry McGuire*, one of the iconic lines that is remembered is, "You complete me." That definitely plays into the part of each one of us that doesn't feel like we are enough or complete. Do you think you would really find it romantic if someone came up to you and said, "I am missing some key parts of myself?" And, "I feel as though I'm inadequate, and like I'll never have enough power to do the things that I want to do. Do you want to be in a relationship with me?" Would you find that romantic? Would you want to date that person? I don't think so. Most of us would run as fast as we could away from the person. But that's the ideal that Hollywood, fairy tales, and society often gives us: that we are incomplete and need a partner to complete us. But you are complete in and of yourself. You get to have different opinions, thoughts, likes and dislikes, and interests than your partner. In Chapter 10, we'll cover quite a bit more about what it is to have your own interests, friends, passion, and life, while at the same time connecting with your partner and sharing deep intimacy. Many couples lose themselves in their partner, looking to their partnership to make them happy and give them fulfillment. That is an inside job, left for each of us to do ourselves—not for anyone else.

You will find that when you make a commitment, not only to your partner but also to yourself and what matters to you, your relationship will be enriched and become more fulfilling. You can then come together and share your interests, feelings, and thoughts with each other. This is intimacy. The word *Intimacy* comes from Latin, meaning, "profoundly within," or the *"within-est"* place inside of each one of us. If you are reflecting back what your partner thinks and feels, you are not sharing that *within-est* place within yourself. When you share your own genuine thoughts and feelings, even if they are wildly different than your partner's, you are showing your authentic self, giving your partner a chance to truly know you.

Now, another interesting fact about bald eagles is they are not sexually loyal to one single mate, even if they are socially monogamous. However, they only two-time when things are good with their primary partner. Why do I include this in a book about monogamy? Because when I initially began doing "Couples" Retreats, I thought I was being inclusive to heterosexual, homosexual, gay, transgender, and all relationships. I quickly learned that wasn't the case, when a polyamorous triad approached me about attending the retreat. I said that it would be no problem. In fact, I said that I found it hard enough to be in a relationship with one person and communicate successfully; and if they could do it with three, that was pretty amazing, and I wanted to assist in any way that I could. I later learned that with partnerships where there is not sexual monogamy, there needs to be strong communication, deep connection, and trust, for them to be willing to have another person enter the relationship. In other words, like the eagle, if the bond is solid and unshakable, they can then choose to include other sexual liaisons, if both partners agree to it, but without that agreement and strength within the relationship, it doesn't work. And when I say "both partners agree to it," that needs to come from free choice, not manipulation, threat, or coercion. I have seen relationships where the partners had a candid conversation about what they wanted sexually and emotionally, and it included having another partner for both of them. And I have also seen relationships where one partner really wants an open relationship or other sexual partners, but the other partner adamantly doesn't. At times, there is the threat of losing the partnership unless the one agrees to have other partners. At other times, there is the manipulation of "you knew this about me when you got in a relationship with me," instead of recognizing that since it hadn't been occurring, the partner assumed it was no longer a priority. These are dicey waters to navigate. The bottom line is that both partners assumed that the other person would change and eventually come around to their perspective, but that didn't happen. For now, I want to give you an example of commitment from a couple who used the three levels of Couples Retreats that I do quite beautifully.

BIRD'S EYE VIEW: HAL & KAT

When Hal, age 70, and Kat, age 64, came to the first Couples Retreat, they had resigned themselves to peacefully co-existing. They had been married fifteen years and were deeply disappointed with the level of intimacy, but they both thought, "This must be as good as it gets. This is life; get over it." To Kat, he was the "typical man," and to Hal, she was a woman with kids, and then, when the kids left, "a roommate with benefits."

Hal and Kat actually met in a hippie commune, a "crash pad," in 1971, in Albuquerque, New Mexico. They briefly shared that same crash pad, and then they did not see each other again until seventeen years later. Kat's mom was a stay-at-home mom, and her dad was stoic, silent, and detached. She had a middle sister who was jealous and abusive. Kat grew up tremendously fearful of making a mistake, since her father was incredibly critical, and her sister would chide her about possible failure. In school, she felt ugly, stupid, too skinny (see, there is such a thing!), and inadequate, since she didn't make the cheerleading squad. When she went off to college, and with the advent of the Vietnam War, Kat became a popular girl with hippie guys. She had a master's degree in psychology, but was more content with the free-love lifestyle. She moved into a commune, where she met her first husband, a rage-oholic, to whom she was married for 22 years. David "took her hostage," and the yelling continued for most of the 22 years, with extensive emotional abuse through the birth of two children.

When Kat and her husband, David, heard about a commune in New Mexico, where there were no drugs, they decided to move there. That was her first encounter with Hal. Kat was wandering, exploring Children of God, Hari Krishna—looking for something to dedicate herself to. Eventually, she found that in Christian faith. David went back to college to become a minister in the Seventh Day Adventist Church, whose members were conscientious objectors to the war at the time. Since David believed that Jesus was coming soon, Kat and David put off having children for ten years. She had her first child at age 36, and remained clean and sober ever since. They homeschooled the children, ate vegetarian, and lived a clean lifestyle. Kat had her second child a few years later. Kat and David moved to Arkansas, where, by coincidence, they were just 30 miles from where Hal had moved.

Hal was an only child to an affluent family in the Midwest. His mother was a successful real estate agent, who had been the oldest child of 13, with a mother who died early. Hal's mom married a man who beat her and, although she already had a son, she left and moved to Great Falls, Montana, where she met a soldier who had just returned from the front lines in Germany. When Hal was born, he felt that he did not belong—his mother was cool and uncaring, and he felt he needed to raise himself. He was a lonely boy who felt there was no love in the world. Although he was a talented athlete, winning track awards, he became suicidal in high school. His answer came when a friend gave him some beers. In high school, Hal would "get the shakes from drinking," but no one saw the signs of his distress. His parents decided to buy a restaurant in Billings, and he was not invited. In high school, he was left to fend for himself, making money to survive while he lived alone in what had been his family's home. It isn't surprising that he wanted to join the military to die, but in the winter of 1967, he was in a car accident that left him close to dead, in a hospital in rehabilitation, for close to two years. He missed Vietnam by two years, and then was left with survivor's guilt. Hal came out of the hospital addicted to Demerol, and with the burden of a doctor's decree that he would never walk again. He quickly proved the doctors wrong, walking and then hitchhiking and jumping from town to town, from one hippie pad to another, getting temporary jobs and raiding pharmaceutical warehouses in the depths of his addiction. He married a nice "hippie chic," and was eventually given an ultimatum from his boss at work, making it clear that if he didn't get clean, he'd lose the job. Hal found Alcoholics Anonymous, got clean, and felt he had finally found the family he'd been lacking all those years.

Kat and Hal were friends for a while before they dated for two and a half years. When they did marry, Hal was suicidal by the end of the first year, and had devised a plan to get out of it, since "things had not gone as planned." There was tension between Hal and Kat's youngest children, and when the children moved out, they were left with little more than stalemates and compatibility.

At 62 years old, Kat participated in the WorldWorks trainings, a type of intense transformational education, and began to get back her idealism. Since Hal had significant physical ailments at the time, he did not participate, but they gratefully jumped when the Couples Retreat was offered. Until that point, Kat didn't realize that Hal also had wanted more than what their relationship was. Through the work at Couples, Hal was "laughing out loud," realizing how perfect his partner actually was for him, that Kat was busy and at times felt like his mother, cold and distant, and that he had been pulling away from her when he felt that she was too busy for him. Kat was vulnerable for the first time about her needs, and realized "no one was ever there to hold her" in her childhood, and that she had been repeating that pattern with Hal. She finally let Hal comfort and hold her. Hal said that he wanted to have a better relationship all those years, but didn't know how to "be a good dog."

Hal and Kat have become superstars, utilizing the work in incredibly successful ways. They participated in the first two Couples Retreats, and followed up with additional coaching sessions to hold themselves accountable to what they had learned. They both participated in "just about every experiential thing out there, including the original scream therapy, Fritz Perls, encounter groups, and everything else." To them, the Couples Retreats pulled everything together. They now set Monday mornings as their "turn off the phone" and focus-on-each-other date time. Now, instead of getting into arguments, they laugh with each other. They know the cycle of their arguments: "Kat stabs me (not physically), I stab back, then we stab a little back and forth, then I withdraw and she walks away loudly, occupying herself but making sure I know that she's pissed. I happily shut everything off and move on to the next event, which pisses her off even more. Then we don't talk."

Now, they do not get past stabbing each other, and instead laugh, realizing that they are lashing out because of fear, hurt, or old wounds of the past. They do not blame each other for the emotions they are feeling. When Kat comes home from work, she often sits with Hal, cuddling to talk about the day. They consistently read a book together, and discuss new ways of approaching things and how to continue to grow the relationship, challenging themselves individually and together. (As I interview them, they have a tendency to finish each other's sentences because they know so well where the other is going.)

Kat: "Recently, I woke up in a bad mood, went into the kitchen, and Hal said something pretty neutral, but I felt stabbed, and I stabbed back. I stopped and saw what I was doing. I went back into the bedroom, lay down, regrouped, got back up, and walked in the kitchen and said, "Okay, let's start over."

After the Couples Retreats, they had new motivation to work on healing Hal's old injuries, and pursued different avenues of treatments.

Hal is now off all narcotics, and he jokes that he "wore Kat out on Monday." Since the Couples Retreat, Monday morning dates include tantric sex, which they began exploring through the second Retreat. They have found that spending concentrated time connecting is far better than "fitting in a quickie." Kat, in her 60s, and Hal, in his 70s, describe sex as "off the charts," because there is now a wonderful atmosphere for sex, preparation of the external space, as well as internal space. They say that sex is now "more connected and spiritual, and the two of us become one in the sexual encounter." Kat says she was shocked when she discovered that only 30% of women have vaginal orgasms, since she has "always been a multiple orgasm person, and it occurs through intercourse—I thought it was that way for everyone." The highest praise comes from Hal, now in recovery for over twenty years, who says, "Sex to me is an LSD trip." That says it all.

Before you go on to the next chapter, you get to do a check-in with yourself on commitment. When you have completed your journal work, and worked with your partner to Take Flight, then you'll be ready to find out the second secret for hot partnering. Let me warn you, it isn't for the faint of heart, but it will be well worth embracing. Most human beings go their whole lives without confronting this sad fact. But for those who have the courage to dive in and do the work, the rewards are lasting. You'll need to be fully committed before you dive into the next chapter.

If you are reading this book with your partner, and I encourage you to do so, then each of you should have a journal to record your growth and work throughout this process. If you are reading it on your own, good for you. Your work will yield results even if your partner isn't yet on board. If your partner doesn't like to read, I can relate. My husband doesn't like to read, so when we are working on a book to grow our relationship, we set aside a date night, where I read sections to my husband. Then we work on our homework and share our responses at dinner with each other.

THE BIRDS

Please take out a journal now, and answer the following questions:

1. You now know that eagles do cartwheels, locking talons and dive bombing towards earth with their partner. Do you stay holding your partner even through challenges, or do you pull away? When you are frightened, do you hold your partner closer or push them away? How could you continue to hold them even through your fear or upset? What would you need from your partner to feel safe enough to hold on?

2. Eagles fly solo on migration and during the winter months, then come back together for breeding, nesting, and care of the off-spring. Do you give yourself enough time to fly solo? What are interests that you have that your partner doesn't share? Do you allow your partner to have their own emotions and feelings, or do you find yourself taking on whatever emotions and feelings they have?

3. Bald eagles are in it for the long haul, monogamous for life, building the nest together, incubating the eggs together, and caring for the young. How committed have you been to your partner? What are the actions you do that show your partner commitment?

THE BEES

Please take out a journal now, and answer the following questions:

1. How have you related to commitment in the past? Especially the commitment you have made to your partner and relationship? Has it been a burden? An obligation? Is it something that inspires you and calls you to reinvent yourself?

2. Have you avoided being fully committed in your relationship? Why? (Fear of losing your freedom? Fear of being controlled by someone else? Fear of being hurt by the other person, etc.?)

3. On a scale of 1–10, 1 being NEVER, 10 being ALWAYS, where would you rank yourself in terms of keeping the commitments you make with your partner? (I'll call you back in an hour...I'll meet you for dinner at 8:00 pm....I'll do the laundry tomorrow...I'll pick it up at the hardware store this week...etc.)

TAKE FLIGHT

1. Share with each other your answers, simply listening to each other. Do not listen to each other to "be right" about your point of view, but rather to understand and know your partner better. Ask other questions to support in exploring more about what they are saying.

2. Turn to each other and agree to give your word on the ground rules that have been outlined. Commit to each other that you will use *The Birds and Bees of Joyful Monogamy* to revitalize your partnership and create greater intimacy, deeper connection, and love.

3. Acknowledge the commitment you have made to each other and the process by setting your first three or four dates, with journals and space to complete the exercises. Plan on completing at least one exercise per week, to keep momentum in moving forward.

CHAPTER TWO

Be Happy or Be Right...

"We do not see things as they are; we see them as we are. We do not hear things as they are; we hear them as we are."
The Talmud[1]

The California Condor is one of the largest birds in North America, with a wingspan that nears ten feet. This giant bird once dominated the skies, but in recent years it took drastic measures to save them from extinction. They are the cleaning crew of the animal world, cleaning the carcasses of deer, cattle, and sheep. They cower to almost no one, and are dominant in making sure the remains are all for them. There is one exception to this: When a Golden Eagle comes to graze on the feast with the Condor, the Condor, usually dominant and much bigger, steps back and allows the Eagle to feast. Keep in mind that the wingspan of a Golden Eagle is about 26 to 40 inches; in other words, just shy of four feet, less than half the size of the Condor. Why back down from a fight when you clearly have an advantage? Because the Condor knows that the Eagle's talons are far stronger and could rip him to shreds. Smart. The Condor could be right that it is the bigger and stronger bird, or can happily eat once the Eagle is done.

In case I'm not making my point, when California Condors court, they fly together over great expanses of territory, doing aerial acrobatics. They are searching for their potential nest site. Together, they explore the options, but it is the female who has the final say in the location of the nest. The male Condor is content to keep the peace and let her decide. And yes, once Condors mate, they are usually together for life.[2]

Condors have learned that they can be right about proving that they are bigger and stronger, or they can be happy, which is more than I can say about most human beings. Month after month, in the transformational workshops that I do, I ask people, "What do human beings want to be more than anything else?" People yell out, "Loved." "Happy." "Valued." "Successful." For each of their answers, I respond, "I wish; I really do." Gradually, it dawns on someone, and then a few people, and eventually, there are shouts, "TO BE RIGHT." Yep. All of us want to be right. If we boil down the geopolitical or economic situation, what war amounts to is one side saying, "We're right about the way that we see it; it should be this way," and the other side saying the exact same thing, except about whatever is their point of view. Think about politics. The debate consistently boils down to, "We're right the way we see it, and you should see it this way," from all sides. At sporting events, people argue that their team is the superior team, and why they are better than the opposition. If you think about the last argument that you had with your significant other, in simple terms, it was, "I'm right; you're wrong." Here is a sample:

Partner A: "I told you to buy dog food this morning; where is it?"

Partner B: "You did not. You never said anything about dog food."

Partner A: "I told you four times before you left this morning: once when we were getting dressed, then at breakfast, and twice when I said what kind I wanted—and again when you were heading out the door."

Partner B: "I wish I had a videotape—I swear you never said that. And I was listening because you told me that stupid story about your sister."

Partner A: "You never listen. It won't get done unless I write it down."

Partner B: "Why is it always my fault? You have conversations in your head and just think you say it out loud."

Does that sound familiar? Substitute whatever topic you argue about, for the dog food. It doesn't really matter what the content of the argument is; both partners just want to be right in that the way they see it is the way that it is. They swear that it is TRUE—with a capital T—and that the other person is wrong. But the tricky point with arguments is that each person has their own truth, or point of view. Carl Jung wrote, "Whether or not the stories are "true" is not the problem. The only question is whether what I tell is my truth."[3] In other words, we only have *our* truth. We see things, hear things, and experience things through the filter we have of that person or the situation, then the moment is colored to fit our perception. In fact, you are probably so good at your arguments and knowing the filter that you and your partner view life through, you could both write scripts for the next argument, and you would be pretty close to accurate.

In Seattle's love lab, John Gottman has amassed information to show just how little we process and can think when the heart is racing, the blood pressure is sky rocketing, and we are intent on making our next point to be right. In actuality, Gottman discovered that when we are emotional, our neurons aren't firing like they usually do. We are not quite thinking clearly, even though we feel like we are. In that moment, it would serve us to remember that the brilliant point that I am about to make is really pretty stupid. It may seem in my own mind to cinch my argument, but in actuality, it's pointless.[4]

Where did this all start? When we are born, we all enter into the world with a wide array of qualities and characteristics, and are quite varied. But within a matter of a few years, there gradually is a little set personality. If you have children, you have witnessed this transformation firsthand. If you have nieces, nephews, or grandchildren, you probably remember when it occurred. Within that first eight years of life, our paradigm, or world view, is being shaped and influenced by just about everything in our world: our family, peers, education, socio-economic situation, race, gender, religion, ethnicity, experiences...on and on. By the time we are eight years old, that paradigm is pretty well formed. For example, an eight-year-old Caucasian boy, raised by wealthy horse ranchers in Kentucky, with a doting mom and dad, walks into a store very differently than an American Indian girl raised by a single mother on a remote Indian reservation, with her grandparents living in her home. Each child has a very different perspective based on the experiences that have shaped them. Likewise, they have different beliefs about the world, themselves, others, and what they think is possible.

When that paradigm is set, we then begin to collect evidence to validate it. We look for situations to be right about the way that we see it, whatever the "it" is. We want to be right that our framework for the world is true or accurate. For example, if I was raised by a hard-working father who could never get ahead no matter what he did, I may have a belief that no matter what I do and how hard I work, I just won't get ahead, witnessing firsthand my father. In my life, I may then end up in situation after situation where I am working tremendously hard, but then get laid off or passed over for a promotion or a raise. Let's say that I came from the same situation of a hard-working, blue-collar dad who could never get ahead. Instead of believing I will never get ahead, I may create a belief that I am going to prove how worthwhile I am, and that no one will ever disrespect me like my father. I then constantly climb ladders, win awards and achievements, only to still feel disrespected inside. Both frameworks and paradigms were set in reaction to the set of conditions and experiences the child had—they are opposite sides of the same coin.

It doesn't make sense that we would want to be right about things that do not necessarily serve us, but it's what we all do. After all, it is how we made sense of our world, and if that is suddenly lost, we may feel lost. I can think of countless examples of women and men that I have coached, who have been looking for their soul mate. When we begin to dig a little bit, there are beliefs like, "I can't trust men;" "I can't trust women;" "If I were to open up to a man, he would leave me;" "Women only want money;" "Men only want sex." If these are the real beliefs that are being held at the core as true, then it doesn't matter what kind of affirmations the person does to attract Mr. or Ms. Right. In other words, there could be 100 people in a room—98 of them absolutely amazing, trusting, and loving potential mates, and two total losers. If you have a belief like some of the ones above, then inevitably, you will be attracted to the two losers, who will allow you to be right about your belief about men or women. It is an exhaustive process for anyone who has ever been mired in the cycle.

Think of what you witnessed with your parents as well. If you watched your mother acquiesce to your father, giving in to whatever his wishes or demands were, you may have a belief that you need to sacrifice yourself to be in relationship. Or, on the flip side of that exact same coin, you may have a belief that you will never allow a man to tell you what to do, but instead will maintain control at all costs. If you watched your father be the tender caregiver, and your mom was cool and aloof, you may believe that men are more nurturing, and automatically have a chip on your shoulder towards women, hearing every comment that is made as cold or aloof. Or you may attempt to make up for your mother, by going out of your way for everyone else around you in your life. If you had a mother who left your father for another woman, and was in a loving relationship but kept hiding it from others, you may end up in a relationship where hiding of some sort is required—hiding alcoholism, hiding your choice of sexual orientation, hiding your real feelings. Conversely, you may feel that it is essential to live your life out loud, hiding absolutely nothing—even when it may serve you to keep some things to yourself.

All of what I am outlining above may be conscious to you, or something that you are perhaps partially aware of, or things that you have done quite a bit of work to illuminate. If so, congratulations; you can see some of the froth in the churning waves of the ocean. But underneath the ocean, there is a massive iceberg that is the unconscious—for all of us. Really, I say that very little of us are conscious when put in the framework of the unconscious. The unconscious is not just your own unconscious but also of the collective. It is everything on every continent and in every culture that has ever been known, as well as the unknown and mystical throughout all of time. So as you become aware of beliefs that you are holding that you were unaware of, be prepared, because there may be layer upon layer of those beliefs that come to light gradually over the course of your lifetime. Your beliefs about partnership, relationship, or who you are when you are in relationship, may be illuminated over the course of many years. Usually by the time people are in their forties, they have had the assistance of a track record in relationship that clarifies their beliefs.

I have a perfect story of one of my own foibles and follies, which may help clarify the need to be right and how it creeps into conversation after conversation. As I write this, I am looking out on a beautiful golf course in Escondido, about 75 miles from my home. With three full-time careers, two children, and some volunteer work, I wasn't setting aside much time to sit down and work on *The Birds and Bees of Joyful Monogamy*. I finally arranged to go to a little resort for some quiet writing time with minimal interruptions. A couple of days ago, my husband and I were talking on the phone about how it was going. I said that I was a little restless and hadn't been out, and I asked him if he would like to come down to spend the night. We volleyed back and forth about the schedules and when he could or couldn't come down. I hung up the phone and had heard that he was coming down for a few hours that very night for dinner, and then headed back home again.

I was expecting Gene by 5:00 p.m. at the latest, but closer to 4:15 if he was driving from where he was teaching. Five o'clock came and went, and by 6:30, I was alarmed. I called his cell phone and text messaged. No response, which for my husband, he'd just about have to be dead not to be texting or tuned in to his cell phone. I grew more and more fearful that something had happened to him. I began calling every hospital within a 75-mile radius, California Highway Patrol, and even the school where he taught, to verify that he had left and wasn't caught up in an emergency on campus. As the clock neared 8:00 p.m., I called the police department. At some point, the current husband of my husband's ex-wife (I'll let you read that again—it's a full story for later) told her to call our home, and he answered the phone. She simply said, "Call your wife, NOW."

I imagine it is a similar feeling for any parent who has waited up for a late teenager after curfew, with the hours ticking by and the mind traipsing out images of car crashes, abductions, or worse horrors. I was unbelievably relieved and also unbelievably angry. Our phone call dissolved into a screaming match, which boiled down to the same point for both of us. Gene felt that I always needed to be right about whatever way he didn't do what he was supposed to do, and I felt that he needed to be right that he did everything fine and it was all me. No matter what our argument, that is the crux of it.

In this case, Gene said that he thought he was clear that he was coming the following night for a few hours and heading home. I thought he was coming that night. I acknowledged that I sometimes do not hear things in our conversation. I have hearing aids from some hearing loss in the higher register, and at times I don't want to say "what?" again when I am not hearing. Gene acknowledged that he doesn't listen very well sometimes, and sometimes what he classifies as "just talking," doesn't register. Not the best combination in that moment. We eventually both felt heard, and that each of us was willing to be responsible, but in the midst of it, we both wanted to be right about all that we said or how the conversation really went. In any moment where there is tension or discord, I look to "what belief am I being right about?"

There is a parable that was written by John Godfrey Saxe, in the mid-1800s, which crosses religious traditions and is well-known to illustrate that the way that we "see" it, isn't necessarily the way that it is.

It was six men of Indostan,
To learning much inclined,
Who went to see the Elephant
(Though all of them were blind),
That each by observation
Might satisfy his mind.

The *First* approached the Elephant,
And happening to fall
Against his broad and sturdy side,
At once began to bawl:
"God bless me! but the Elephant
Is very like a wall!"

The *Second*, feeling of the tusk,
Cried, "Ho, what have we here,
So very round and smooth and sharp?
To me 'tis mighty clear,
This wonder of an Elephant
Is very like a spear!"

The *Third* approached the animal,
And happening to take
The squirming trunk within his hands,
Thus boldly up and spake:
"I see," quoth he, "the Elephant
Is very like a snake!"

The *Fourth* reached out an eager hand,
And felt about the knee
"What most this wondrous beast is like
Is mighty plain," quoth he,
"Tis clear enough the Elephant
Is very like a tree!"

The *Fifth*, who chanced to touch the ear,
Said, "E'en the blindest man
Can tell what this resembles most;
Deny the fact who can,
This marvel of an Elephant
Is very like a fan!"

The *Sixth* no sooner had begun
About the beast to grope,
Then, seizing on the swinging tail
That fell within his scope,
"I see," quoth he, "the Elephant
Is very like a rope!"
And so these men of Indostan
Disputed loud and long,
Each in his own opinion
Exceeding stiff and strong,
Though each was partly in the right,
And all were in the wrong!

MORAL,

So, oft in theologic wars
The disputants, I ween,'
Rail on in utter ignorance
Of what each other mean;
And prate about an Elephant
Not one of them has seen![5]

In some versions of the parable that has been told throughout the ages, the king explains that all of them are right because each of them touched a different part of the elephant, and the animal has all of the features that were mentioned. Likewise, when we are in disagreements, it is helpful to remember that each of us may have a different interpretation of what is occurring, or has occurred. Each of us may be interpreting the situation through a different lens or filter, and each of us may be touching a different part of the whole.

Clearly, this is easier said than done. Perhaps it is a lifelong process. But if we are in a relationship to understand and know our partner, then we get to be interested in their viewpoint and perspective. In writing about couples therapy, Tony and Norman Bobes say, "Not knowing is an attitude and belief 'that the therapist does not have access to privileged information, can never fully understand another person, [and] always needs to be in a state of being informed by the other.'"[6] We can always think we know who someone is, without really knowing. There are countless personality profiles we can take, and psychological profiles we could study, but the other person is still a mystery. Even from day to day, the subtleties that change our character mean that my partner is very different on this day than they were yesterday, perhaps not even in words that they can yet explain. I sometimes say that it is helpful to view your partner as another country. Each of you come from different lands, where there are different customs and languages. The objective is to continually be in an inquiry of those customs and your partner's languages. Your love may be speaking English, but it might as well be a foreign language at times. If we are attached to being right about our perspective, and making them wrong about theirs, then there is an indication that we don't really want a passport to their nation, and also want to stay only in our own little world. I am inviting you to let go of your world and what you hold as "the truth," to understand your partner's reality.

Henry Ford is attributed as saying, "If there is one secret to success, it lies in the ability to get to the other person's point of view and see things from his angle as well as from your own."

Are you willing to let go of being right? If you are, be prepared, because you may begin to notice that the process of letting go of being right about the way you see things will work, not just with your partner, but also at work, with your mother and father, and throughout every area of your life. Remember the elephant.

Let's revisit the California condor. They can soar to heights of 15,000 feet, and travel up to 150 miles in one day, in search of their next meal. Vultures often circle for entire days, overhead, waiting for the animal to die. But sometimes the vulture is left empty-handed because whatever animal they left up for dead, rallied and made a full recovery. Condors move on. They let go of what could be, and travel to the next location for a certain meal. If your position or point of view isn't getting you fed, move on.

How do you move on? How do you let go of being right in the moment? John Gottman calls *repair attempts* a couple's secret weapon, and describes a repair attempt as "a statement or action—silly or otherwise—that prevents negativity from spiraling out of control." According to Gottman's research, he can learn if a couple's relationship will last or end, based solely on repair attempts. Essentially, our job in a relationship is to make repair attempts, and to take a repair attempt when our partner makes it. A repair attempt doesn't need to be rocket science. In the middle of a circular argument that is going nowhere, my husband will sometimes imitate one of our dogs, making a face that looks exactly like one of our loved little beings—it used to be a Labrador-Rottweiler face, but now he does an impeccable Brussels Griffon. It is a simple repair attempt that always diffuses the tension and takes it down a notch or two.

In making repair attempts, it's helpful to know if your partner is more kinesthetic (oriented to touch), auditory (geared to really hear everything), or visual (what they see really impacts). Sometimes we are a combination of orientations, but usually there is one that is predominant. I've had couples explain that one partner literally cannot hear anything, and simply needs the other to wrap their arms around them. Touch works for that person. For some of us, including myself, the idea of being hugged or held in an argument is torturous. No way. Obviously, I am not kinesthetic. Others of us need the other partner to clearly say what they were seeing, where the trigger was, or how they were responsible in the situation. Words matter, with the other person processing and having insight into their actions. For someone more visual, making a funny face or imitating the under bite of a little dog does the trick to shift the energy. Gene thankfully knows that he needs to go visual and auditory. And yes, you guessed it: I've got to reach towards him and touch—that is how he is shifted. I'll explain more clearly in Chapter Five, about how we are perfectly matched to grow undeveloped areas of ourselves.

You are already at the **SECRET #2 TO HOT PARTNERING: BE RIGHT OR BE HAPPY. CHOOSE HAPPY.** A little warning with this one: It is easy to read about and understand, but much more challenging to put into practice. So as you work on this one, every time you let go of your point of view, position, and holding on to your interpretation, give yourself an internal high five. Celebrate when you make little gains. And think about it: If nations were willing to do diplomacy with this principle at the forefront of their thinking, we would have a very different world than the one we have now.

Take out your journal, and be willing to scavenge through the bones of past arguments to find the meat of the matter. When you have uncovered what you have been being right about, and are clear on what it is costing, then you are ready to move on and learn that you really don't have anything to complain about. Did you read that sentence twice? In Chapter Three, you'll discover the key to happiness, not only with your partner but in your entire life. I'm not overstating it, I promise. Do your homework, and then head into a single distinction that could, if you choose, alter your life forever.

THE BIRDS

1. The California Condor allows the smaller Golden Eagle to the feast rather than being dominant and chasing that bird away. What "feast" have you been keeping for yourself instead of allowing your partner in? Where have you been continually being right, refusing to back down rather than being happy?

2. The condor travels up to 150 miles in a day for its next meal. Where do you circle over and over, waiting for something to change instead of moving on?

THE BEES

1. Think of your last argument with your partner. What were you being right about? Think of most of your arguments and the primary point you are making. Is it that you are not being heard? Not valued? Discounted? What is the point your partner keeps coming back to, again and again? That he is not capable? That she was wronged? That he is powerless to change things? Write.

2. What do you remember about the relationship between your parents? How did they interact? How did they treat each other?

Did they show affection freely and openly? What were the messages that were conveyed to you about sexuality and romance?

3. What are your own beliefs about the expression of anger, sadness, fear, affection, pride, and love? Which do you feel competent at expressing, and in which areas, if any, do you feel a sense of repression?

4. In what areas do you notice differences between you and your partner in the expression of emotions? What do you believe about the differences?

5. How did your family express the following emotions when you were a child?

   - Anger
   - Sadness
   - Fear
   - Affection/Love
   - Attraction

6. How do you defend yourself in your relationship from feeling the pain, hurt, or upset you felt as a child?

TAKE FLIGHT

1. Share with each other what you have written to the questions above, and continue to explore each other's world—not to be right about what you think you know about your partner, but rather to understand and know your partner more fully.

2. Support each other in identifying what the fundamental belief is that you are being right about when you argue. Think of a

fundamental belief that we each have about ourselves as being like an ice cream store—it is all ice cream, but there are differences in flavors. A fundamental disempowering belief is along the lines of:

- I am not enough.
- I'm alone.
- No one gets me.
- I am too much.
- I'm not valuable.
- I'm not capable.I'm worthless.
- I'll always be alone.
- I'm worthless.
- I'm not good enough.
- I'm powerless.
- I'm a failure.

These are beliefs that most of us do not operate out of in the majority of our lives, but when we are fearful, threatened, doubting ourselves, or defending, they are always just under the surface.

3. Be gentle with each other, and after your conversation, spend some time simply cuddling and acknowledging your partner for being so courageous to reveal and be in self-inquiry, as well as for being committed to knowing and understanding you.

CHAPTER THREE

Bring It On: Be Prepared to be Challenged
Lessons from the Black Vulture

"It is my daily mood that makes the weather. I possess tremendous power to make life miserable or joyous. I can be a tool of torture or an instrument of inspiration; I can humiliate or humor, hurt or heal. In all situations, it is my response that decides whether a crisis is escalated or de-escalated, and a person is humanized or de-humanized. If we treat people as they are, we make them worse. If we treat people as they ought to be, we help them become what they are capable of becoming."
– J.W. Goethe[1]

I could wax poetic on this, and do, in some of the upcoming chapters. If we see people as worthless, trouble, angry, or whatever interpretation we have made of them, they will live into that perspective. If we see them as loving, bright, and magnificent, they will live into that perspective—maybe not in an instant, BUT sometimes the shift is instantaneous. Sometimes it takes place over time. There are countless movies where we love depicting that very transformation, and whether it is Ebenezer Scrooge in *A Christmas Carol*, or the Beast (Adam) from *Beauty and the Beast*, this is the stuff that inspires. And the good news is that it is true. If we shift how we view and relate to someone, they have space to show up in a different way. But it means rolling our sleeves up and doing the work, focusing on giving patience, compassion, and space to our partner rather than what we think we should be getting from them.

Eric Fromme was on to something when he noted that most people spent most of their time in bookstores in the self-help section, looking for books on how to feel more loved, appreciated, and valued. He aptly pointed out that the focus of love is not on getting more or arriving at some peaceful place of Nirvana. He wrote:

"Love, experienced thus, is a constant challenge; it is not a resting place, but moving, growing, working together; even when there is harmony or conflict, joy or sadness, is secondary to the fundamental fact that two people experience themselves, rather than by fleeing from themselves. There is only one proof for the presence of love: the depth of the relationship, and the aliveness and strength in each person concerned; this is the fruit by which love is recognized."[2]

As Fromme was adept at noting, we spend an extraordinary amount of time thinking about being loved and falling in love. The focus is on love as a noun, rather than love being a verb. Most people focus on the receiving rather than the giving of love. And we expect it to be carefree.

But, as Fromme noted, that is not real love.

Most of us are willing to work on our relationships, if our partner is the person who does the changing. Are you blaming the discord in your relationship on your partner? Do you insist that it is their shortcomings that are setting you back? Are you happy when your partner agrees with you and goes along with your wants and desires, and then unhappy when you are challenged?

Time to consider the Black Vulture. You were expecting only Lovebirds in a book about joyful monogamy, and instead, I give you vultures— sounds a lot like relationships, expecting one thing and being given another. But there is much to be gained from the vulture, and it isn't an easy lesson; but once learned, it is a sure way to grow yourself for the rest of your life. As part of the mating ritual, one vulture, presumed to be the male, dive bombs at the female repeatedly. Does this sound a little like middle school, where a young boy will often mercilessly tease the girl he has a crush on? It's a little like that, except the vulture dive bombs their intended, attacking with a sharp beak repeatedly. But this definitely isn't middle school taunting or name calling. This is a serious test of the partner's mettle, and I think the vulture is on to something. The Vulture wants to repeatedly challenge their partner to verify that they are strong enough to protect their territory and their young. They are *testing their mettle*. Let's be clear that whoever it is we choose, we will challenge in ways that are unfathomable to them, and they will challenge us sometimes beyond our breaking point.

When your partner challenges you, you could continue pointing at them, a victim to their attacks, resenting and blaming them for your unhappiness. If that is what you choose, then you are in for a lifetime of misery. Or you can accept the biggest challenge of all: being willing to be responsible for everything—every word out of their mouth, every one of their actions, every moment in time. This is the challenge of a lifetime, and should you choose it, you are in for a lifetime of surprises, and the experience of power and genuine joy. To move any relationship forward, it is important, and even essential, for each person to be willing to be responsible. This has been the biggest challenge of my lifetime, and it has changed everything in my life. Let me explain what I mean by *responsible*, because I feel quite certain that it is *not what passes for responsibility as defined in societal terms.* This is the transformational definition of responsibility.

This is the absolute key between running for the hills when your partner challenges you, or being willing to strip yourself down and face the parts of you that may not be so fun to face, then returning with humility and vulnerability. This is the difference between the partner who consistently calls their mom or a friend, and complains when you do something, and someone who takes the upset directly to you. This chapter begins one of the most important distinctions of a person's life, and certainly my own.

The Etymological Online Dictionary defines victim as a "living creature killed and offered as a sacrifice to a deity or supernatural power," from Latin *victima* "person or animal killed as a sacrifice." "Person oppressed by some power or situation," is from 1718. Weaker sense of "person taken advantage of," is recorded from 1781.[3]

An ancient Sanskrit definition shows the root of the word as coming from, "one who separates," which brings quite a bit of meaning and importance to the work of partnership. When I ask many people to define the word *victim*, generally the words that emerge are: helpless, powerless, and the idea that someone has done something to them, or something happened to them that was beyond their control. Perhaps there was a time in your life when you experienced being a victim, where you were taken advantage of or hurt in some way. I imagine that all of us have experienced times when we felt powerless. You may still feel like you were powerless to impact what occurred— perhaps someone you loved died, or you were robbed, and you feel like it was completely out of your control. This is not about control.

You may feel like you are no longer a victim. Perhaps in hindsight, you now see that you made choices that led to this event occurring. Either way, it's okay. Use any event where you felt like a victim at the time, for the purpose of opening up the distinction that you are about to open.

Sometimes there may be a traumatic event—perhaps one partner has an affair. In that case, it is very easy for the partner who did not stray from the marriage to believe that they are a victim. After all, they are the one who supposedly kept to their vows and remained faithful. I have worked with many couples who have dealt with infidelity. Let's take Eric and Joni. When the affair was finally revealed, there was an unwillingness on the part of Joni to see that she had anything to do with what had occurred. Eric was the one who had the "wandering eyes" and "flirted," and "couldn't live up to his word or keep a promise." Believe me, I am not siding with Eric either. I cannot fathom the amount of pain that occurs when there is infidelity. I have witnessed it again and again, and can only guess at the gut-wrenching questioning and hurt; but just as people go to funerals and give inane advice, saying, "I remember how I felt when X died, and here's how I got through," none of us can really know the pain of another. This is not a book about infidelity, although there are many good ones, including *After the Affair,* by Janis Abrahms Spring and Michael Spring.[4] My point is that we can be a victim of a specific event.

We can all put ourselves in the role of the victim at the drop of a hat. If you've ever been fired, perhaps you felt it was unfair and that you were wronged. If someone robbed you, or lied about you, maybe you felt like you were a victim in that moment.

Each of us can be a victim of our partners for far less than an affair. You can be a victim in general as you move through life. It isn't random that as I was writing this section, my phone rang from a potential new client. Nigel began the call by saying that his wife, Laura, had told him that it was okay to call, and he was frustrated. "Laura won't have sex with me anymore. I mean, we've gone about six months, and I'm about to burst. It's been this way ever since our son was born. She has been totally focused on motherhood for the past eleven years. It isn't normal. Every man needs sex, and she has a real breakdown when it comes to expressing intimacy. I am a good husband, and there is nothing else that is wrong with our relationship—it's just that she will not be intimate with me." Nigel is looking entirely for Laura to change. If Laura would just begin to have sex with him again, everything would be fine. From Laura's perspective, she lost connection with Nigel a long time ago. She no longer feels any attraction towards him, and sees him as controlling her, ordering her around, and dominating her every move. If Nigel would change, then perhaps....

Both partners are pointing to the other person as being the problem, and they are a victim to what is occurring. Both partners genuinely see that they are in the right, and it is their partner who is not empathetic, and is wrong. And both partners are stuck in a stalemate. They are not moving forward, and cannot move forward because it would mean that they would need to give up some of their own ground. Both partners are blaming and resenting the other, thinking that the burden of change rests solely on their partner. And neither partner is owning their own power, but rather giving it to their partner. According to each of them, their partner is the one who has them trapped in a prison. From this position, nothing can occur. And yet I am sure that many of us can see ourselves in Nigel and Laura. I know that when we are at our worst, my husband, Gene, and I can easily slip into the blaming and finger pointing.

Let's take it to some other examples. Do you know someone who can never manage to get anywhere on time, and they always have an excuse of the traffic or the babysitter being late? Do you know someone who thinks he is limited and can only do so much to get ahead before the "man" stops him? Do you know someone who can't do their project or go out socially because their kids are just "too much to handle?" These are all examples of victim thinking. Perhaps you are not a victim to any specific event or to what you do or not do, but you may feel powerless over the conditions, obstacles, and circumstances of life.

So often, when people participate in transformational work, they want those closest to them to participate as well. It would be like finding a money tree, where the money grew back the moment it was picked off the tree. If you found that tree, you'd want to share it with those you love—heck, EVERYONE! Or if for your entire life there were monsters living in your closet and under your bed, interrupting everything you wanted, and then those monsters suddenly vanished. You'd be excited and would want to vanquish that for others. Here's the challenge. Quite often, when others are told about the training, they want to participate—especially if they are close to the person who did the work, and they trust that person. But they have the normal circumstances of life: kids at home, needing to work, time out of their existing schedule and money. Often, people think that they can't possibly be bigger than those conditions or circumstances of life. They can either care for their kids OR go after their dream of going back to school. They can either pay the mortgage and afford a vacation in a few months OR participate in the trainings. It is EITHER/OR thinking. And it is the feeling that they cannot be bigger than the conditions of life. They are a victim to the kids, their bank account, and their schedule. At times, all of us may feel that we don't have the power to alter whatever is occurring. The joy is that we can. It may mean making different choices, getting assistance, or coming up with about a million options to give ourselves space. It involves reinvention, and is often uncomfortable. After all, our children certainly don't want to be the excuse as to why we didn't accomplish our goals. We get to live our own lives with power, knowing we are not a victim to anyone or anything. In doing so, perhaps we'll teach our kids the same.

The victim generally views things as outside of their *control*, and the predominate experience of life is regret, hopelessness, powerlessness, and resignation. There is always an explanation as to why things don't turn out, and it usually involves blaming someone else and resenting them for what they did or did not do.

BIRD'S EYE VIEW: SAM & TAMMY

The best way I can think to illustrate what I mean by responsibility instead of victimhood is by telling the story of Sam and Tammy.

Sam and Tammy, both 47, met and fell in love in their freshman year of college. Tammy wanted to go out with another guy, Steve, but like so many other women who discovered the *ideal* guy, later found out that he was gay. Tammy's friend, Sheila, kept insisting that she go out with a mutual cute friend in their group, Sam. Sam and Tammy dated off and on in the beginning, not because they didn't realize that the other one was right for them, but because they were both young and were strongly encouraged by their families to not settle down too quickly. Sam is of Welsh, German, English, and Yugoslavian decent, and Tammy is Korean and Japanese. Both were raised in the Christian Scientist faith. To date, they have been married 30 years and have been together as a couple for 34 years. They have a girl and two boys, and began having children seven years after they were married.

Since his father left at an early age, Sam was raised primarily by his mother. On visitations with his father, he quickly learned that his father was an alcoholic, with gambling problems. Sam's mother was a teacher and expected him to excel in school; if he got anything less than an A, his mother would say that he could do better, and that he was "smart enough to be a lawyer." With his father leaving early, and his mother with high expectations, Sam's core negative belief about himself is that he is not good enough—nothing he does will be good enough. Yes, Sam did become a lawyer, but for all of us, no amount of evidence will ever convince us that our core wounding is not really real. There is a lot of energy expended in actually proving "I am good enough," and the echoes of the conversation from childhood continue to echo, no matter how many degrees, how big the house, how respected by the community. Sam also made a vow that he would never divorce like his parents did, and cause that kind of pain. Tammy felt abandoned by her father and didn't want anyone to ever leave her, which fit pretty well with Sam's promise that he would NEVER leave.

Tammy was raised by a father who was Chinese, and a mother who was Vietnamese. She felt like she was supposed to do what she was supposed to do—"be a good girl and get good grades,"—and that everything would be fine. Her father left her mom at some point, and Tammy learned that she couldn't trust men to be there for her. Her mom, of course, was handling their lives as a single parent, and gave Tammy little emotional connection or affection. In other words, all that Tammy wanted was to have a partner to be there for her, giving her the emotional attention that she was longing for deep inside instead of relating to her as her accomplishments.

All of this came to a head when Sam began working late hours on cases, coming home exhausted, and paying little attention to Tammy. Although she knew that Sam loved her, she felt abandoned emotionally—just like what occurred with her father. Tammy then began pushing Sam away, out of the fear that he would leave her. The more she opened her heart to Sam, the more vulnerable she became to his hurting her. Tammy then began pushing Sam away, wanting intimacy but being absolutely terrified of it, so she unconsciously began testing to see if Sam would leave her. She began an affair with a co-worker, and even as she was in the affair, there was an internal knowing that she was settling for fool's gold versus the real thing. She convinced herself that she was in love with a person who was her personal trainer, because he was paying attention to her. With Sam setting up his career as a lawyer, and working incredible hours, she had been feeling unacknowledged and unappreciated, and the personal trainer was filling that void. Meanwhile, Sam was working incredibly hard for his family, and feeling unacknowledged and unappreciated because Tammy didn't seem to see that he was doing everything for them as a couple. When Sam found an email on Tammy's phone, he was clear what was occurring. The next day, they were supposed to have a major party, with a bunch of friends coming over. Sam got through it but felt like he needed to put on a show— the entire time, his heart was breaking. To that end, everything blew up that night, and the affair came to light. During the time period of finding out about the affair, Sam had been ordering a new setting for Tammy's ring, to surprise her on their anniversary. Two days after Sam found out about the affair, he went to pick up that new setting on the ring he had ordered. When he talks about making that drive to pick up the ring, there are tears in his eyes even now. He said that he was standing in faith and was trusting, and the ring was a sign of that faith. When Sam gave it to Tammy on their anniversary, she made a promise that she would not change the ring or wear it until all of her back doors were completely closed, and she meant it for the rest of their lives. The ring remained in her jewelry box for a couple of months.

A dear friend, of both Tammy and Sam, told them about transformational trainings that she had attended, and urged both to attend. Two and a half months later, they both created the time to attend the WorldWorks Introductory Course (for more information, go to www.worldworkstrainings.com). They had been seeing a marriage therapist, and he was having both of them begin by being in the inquiry as to how they were responsible for what had occurred; but when I met them, their relationship was still up in the air, and they were not clear if they were choosing to continue their marriage. By the end of the training, they both chose their marriage and each other in a way that they had not done previously.

Both Tammy and Sam believe that the work they have done on their partnership, through the Couples Retreats, has opened up a new level of depth and intimacy in their relationship. A large part of the first Couples Retreat is to be honest, revealing, and transparent. (www.inspirecoachingworkshops.com has more information on how you can attend). When Neale Donald Walsch talks about love in *Friendship with God*, he writes:

"What else does it mean to be totally loving? It means to be fully present in every single moment; to be fully aware, to be fully willing to express the love that is in your heart full out, without hidden motivations, hidden agendas—without hidden anything. It means to be fully naked, transparent.[5]

Tammy found real freedom in being totally honest and letting go of all of the fears of what would occur if she told the complete and uncensored truth to Sam. During their first retreat, Tammy revealed that about three or four years into their relationship, she had been raped. Tammy had not told Sam, or anyone else for that matter, and had spent many years in self-blame and attempting to repress the memory. In letting down her walls, Tammy discovered that there was new space for Sam to be compassionate, comfort her, and really know her deeply. Sam has discovered that he can be there for Tammy, more than just physically or as a financial provider, but be intimately connected and available to her.

They have begun to see that there are layers to their wounding and the "dance" that they do as a couple when they argue. They have established a strong sense of togetherness, intimacy, and connection, but they are also standing firmly in their own power, and following their own passions, knowing it will enrich the partnership in the long run. This is the legacy they want to pass to their three kids as they venture into the world and fall in love—showing that they can have their own lives, passion, interests, and power, but also remain deeply connected and intimate, not from a sense of need, but also with gratitude.

In choosing the framework of responsibility, both see how they managed to play into each other's lessons. It would be easy for Sam to be a "victim" of Tammy's affair, and place the blame squarely on her shoulders, but he does not. It would be easy for Tammy to carry shame, and continue to consciously and unconsciously push Sam away to continue to be right that all men will leave her, but she does not. Sam is responsible and chooses the interpretation that he unconsciously generated Tammy having the affair, for him to once again not feel good enough. But he doesn't need to choose that interpretation. Instead, Sam chooses to see that this is his journey—he will consistently create places where he can feel not good enough, and then he gets to remind himself that he is good enough. He is valued and loved. That is his internal work to do.

Tammy is responsible and chooses the interpretation that she created the affair and the feeling of being abandoned by Sam, attempting to push him away so that she could be right about men leaving her, just like her father. Then she could continue to distance herself emotionally, rather than allowing her full heart to come out. She doesn't choose that. Instead, she knows that when she is looking to push Sam away, she gets to lean in, open up to him, and share her vulnerability.

Responsibility may or may not be about actions we did or events that occurred. It is choosing to look at life through the glasses that we are the author of what is occurring, not from fault, blame, guilt, or shame, but as a way to see a bigger perspective. Perhaps it is choosing to see our soul's growth or the lessons we are here to learn. Maybe it is choosing to acknowledge what we instinctively knew or sensed, but also denied. It may be about seeing the road that we paved that led to that final moment.

Responsibility is an interpretation in which I declare that I am fully the cause of what happens in my life, including my thoughts, feelings, actions, interpretations, and resulting events. This isn't a question of fact, but rather an interpretation that is made. This is the only place from which you can access your power; otherwise, things are happening *to you*. Responsibility has nothing to do with duty, burden, or obligation. It is a privilege to look through the filter of responsibility, not something that you are forced to do.

In viewing things from a responsible perspective, there is no moral judgment that is being made—it isn't good or bad, or right or wrong. It's looking at it, thinking, "So what...Now what?" When you look at the world from this perspective, it is acknowledging that your existence matters, and that you impact others and the world. The locus of control is on *I*, rather than *they*.

When someone is telling a story from the victim perspective, there is a lot of talking about people or a person outside of them, and little about them. There is a lot of input from others as to how that event occurred, and little from themselves. In being responsible, your input is the majority of the conversation, not from blaming yourself, but rather acknowledging how you generated it.

Responsibility is not about *control*. Sometimes when people are learning responsibility from this transformational framework, they put it in the context of what they think they can control and what they cannot control. Etymologically, the word, *control*, comes from late Middle English, "to check or verify accounts," or Latin, contrarotulare, "a copy of a roll." So it is related to checking or verifying something, AFTERWARDS. In other words, it is looking afterwards and keeping record. Interesting. The word, *power*, whether in Middle English, Anglo, or French, all relates to the Latin *posse*, "be able." So, in responsibility, you are looking at yourself as very able—able to move yourself consciously through your life and lessons of your life.

Sam and Tammy are a good example because now when they argue, they say that "it goes pretty fast because no one is wanting to be right or remain stuck." They acknowledge how the other person views the situation, and have a deep compassion for each other's core wounds from childhood, and the many ways that wound is inadvertently exposed through their partnership. They have mentored other struggling couples and have become a resolute stand for the importance of putting your relationship first, knowing that investment will show up in every other area of life. For years, they had the lives that others dreamed of—both high-powered lawyers, having a beautiful house, healthy children, snazzy cars, and adventurous vacations. But now they have found their bliss in realizing who lies next to them nightly, and becoming invested in discovering that person fully.

When one partner is challenged, both are challenged. Let me be clear; this is not about challenging just for the sake of challenge. This is about healing a part of our partner that needs to be healed. When Tammy had the affair, it challenged Sam to confront his belief that he would never be good enough. And when Sam leaned in to support Tammy emotionally, it challenged her beliefs that men would leave her. Sam still gets busy and caught up in his routine, and Tammy occasionally gets lonely and feels like she isn't getting enough attention. But instead of looking elsewhere, now Tammy vulnerably reveals her hurt and fear, even though it is terrifying for her to show how much she loves and needs Sam. When Sam feels that nothing he does is ever enough for Tammy, he reveals his fear and self-doubt, even though a part of him says that if he does, she will leave him. Instead, she loves him. This is what I mean by challenge.

Elizabeth Gilbert, the author of *Eat, Pray, Love,* puts it beautifully when she says:

"People think a soul mate is a perfect fit, and that's what everyone wants. But a true soul mate is a mirror, the person who shows you everything that's holding you back, the person who brings you to your own attention so you can change your life. A true soul mate is probably the most important person you'll ever meet, because they tear down your walls and smack you awake...soul mates, they come into your life just to reveal another layer of yourself to you."[6]

And the real challenge is to be responsible, to view whatever challenge your partner is bringing to you as not being done to you or outside of you, but instead authored by you unconsciously for you and your partner's growth. This isn't about playing God, or about a narcissistic perspective that we control everything. It is about interpreting that things are not outside of us.

Now, there are many different levels of jumping into the distinction of responsibility. I think the first level of responsibility is, "It's not me; it's you." This is the thinking of someone who is not even conscious of responsibility. There is finger-pointing, blame, anger, and resentment. Dr. Sue Johnson describes a type of dance that partners do in relationships, called "find the bad guy," with both partners continually pointing fingers at the other, sending a message of *"it's not me; it's you"* who is the problem. In that endless cycle, both partners feel wrong. Obviously, this doesn't work, even though we all duck into this dance periodically.

Another flavor of this is, "I am not responsible." Let's look at the bright side with this thinking. At least there is an awareness that responsibility exists. But it is also clear that in this thinking, the person is a victim of the circumstances and conditions of their life. Things occur or do not occur as a result of something or someone else, not them. In a relationship, this thinking can become dire, incredibly quickly.

The second level of responsibility is very common in the world. It is, "I take responsibility." In this type of thinking, the person is acknowledging responsibility for something that has occurred or been done. The focus is on an action that has occurred or not occurred. There is also a feeling of fault, blame, guilt, and shame. This thinking is head-bowed-down acknowledgment that the person did something wrong, something they shouldn't have done, or failed to do something that they were supposed to do. From a linguistic perspective, the word *take* indicates that it is not inside of the person. We don't take things from inside of ourselves; we take things that are outside of ourselves. For example, we can take something off of that shelf, but we don't take awareness or anger. Rather, we would say, "I am angry" or "I am aware," not "I take anger" or "I take awareness."

The third level of responsibility is, "I am responsible for how I relate to the event." This is where possibility actually begins. For example, if someone rear-ends my car on the highway, I know that I can choose how I respond to the event. I could choose to be angry, getting explosive with the other driver or blaming them for not looking where they were going. I could choose to be patient, understanding that we all sometimes look away for a moment, for the radio, and unfortunately, our phones. I could choose to be jaded, thinking that the person undoubtedly doesn't have insurance, and that I'll have to pay for it myself. I could choose to be compassionate, knowing that I have a chance to impact this person in a positive way, and help them to calm down and not be so anxious about what has occurred. I am the chooser of my response to the event.

First, it is a present tense awareness of what is occurring. The focus is not on the past or the future, but is instead on this moment; I am the chooser of how I relate to whatever has occurred. The focus may be, "How can I relate to this event in a positive or forwarding way for my life?" or, "How can I focus on my role in the event?" or "How can I influence the situation?" There is power and authority in focusing on my attitude in influencing, so that things can be changed through me.

The fourth level of responsibility is, "I am responsible for ALL aspects of my life." I don't think I need to point out that most human beings don't come close to this way of thinking. This is foreign, and by foreign I don't just mean another country—I mean another world. Being responsible for all aspects of our lives is being responsible for our attitude, our actions, our future, our reactions, our emotions—everything—the whole shebang. This is the key and focus of living a life of transformation. In this thinking, I am proactive and conscious of my contribution in any and all situations. Life is not only about me but also includes everything that is occurring around me. That means I have a choice as to how I relate to every moment, to all people, places, and events. Sometimes when people begin to play with responsibility, they often begin blaming themselves for everything that occurred or did not occur. In that way, they then become the victim and the perpetrator. Responsibility is NO FAULT, NO BLAME, NO GUILT, NO SHAME. Besides sounding like a great Bob Marley rift, it is a catchy way to remind ourselves that responsibility is not about blaming ourselves. It is simply looking at whatever occurred, interpreting our contribution, and then moving forward.

Taking that deeper, level four is, "I am responsible for everything." Being responsible for everything means everything—not just things in my immediate surroundings. I am responsible for famine, war, hunger, every government on this earth, the planes hitting the World Trade Center and Pentagon in 2001, celebrations, the results of every race in the Olympics, the weather—everything.

What that means is a willingness to view everything that is occurring, through a filter or a lens of "I am not separate from that." This is extreme and incredibly radical. This has nothing to do with controlling anything, or what we think we can exert influence over. This is simply viewing whatever is occurring in the moment within inquiry as to our contribution or inter-relatedness in that moment. Responsibility is viewing the event, not from blame or fault or guilt, but rather with a perspective of how our thinking, beliefs, attitude, and emotions may have played into that moment. So, going back to September 11, 2001, from a view of responsibility, there would be an inquiry as to how my own thinking could have created that occurring in the world. Did I have an illusion of security, living in a bubble, such that I unconsciously manifested a break in that bubble? Did I have a lack of recognition and understanding of other cultures, such that I manifested a chance to learn other perspectives and cultures? Was I dug in with my own positions and point of view, being right so much that I manifested an extreme example of that? It is a WILLINGNESS to interpret that we are responsible for everything.

Level four thinking with responsibility is viewing that we are not separate from anything else. From a quantum physical perspective, everything is energy, swirling in motion. Nothing is actually separate from anything else. That includes thoughts and emotions. Our thoughts and emotions have energy. Have you ever walked into a room, and you could immediately tell that someone was angry? They didn't say anything, but you could feel it. Or, have you been on the phone and felt that someone shifted their attention to their keyboard and off of the conversation? You could feel that a part of their energy was missing. In viewing responsibility through this framework, it is being willing to interpret that I am not operating separately from anything else, but rather, I am interconnected.

Let me be clear: I am not saying that anyone consciously wanted that event to occur. This is not about our conscious mind but our unconscious. It is sometimes estimated that only 4 to 6% of us are driven by the conscious mind, and 90+ percent of us come from our unconscious. So, if I am unconsciously judging other people, digging in and being self-righteous, then that can be manifested externally in people around me. If I am angry when I set out for work, I may then end up with someone cutting me off in road rage. If I believe that "traffic stinks on Fridays," then I may end up in heavier traffic on Fridays. For all we know, there is someone else who doesn't think traffic is bad on Fridays, and they sing and laugh on their drive home, so that any traffic isn't really a bother. This is simply a perspective.

When your partner lashes out and makes a sharp comment, instead of getting angry back, accusing them of "always picking a fight," from the perspective of being responsible, you would look inward and ask what was occurring with you, such that you heard your partner the way that you did. Were you in a bad mood? Were you angry at something else, and now your ears are tuned for anger? Let's pick the dog food conversation back up from the last chapter. If your partner forgot to buy dog food, and you were both being level four responsible, the conversation would sound more like this:

> PARTNER A: Did you pick up the dog food?
>
> PARTNER B: No, did you want me to?
>
> PARTNER A: Yep, I told you three times this morning.
>
> PARTNER B: I never heard you say that.

PARTNER A: Oh, I must not have been clear. I was doing so many other things, I probably didn't say it clearly; I was everywhere this morning.

PARTNER B: No, it was probably me. I had my head on other things, and I don't think that I really was paying attention. I'm sorry about the dog food.

PARTNER A: No sweat. I needed to go out and get deodorant anyway; I'll pick some up.

PARTNER B: I can go if you want to start dinner; it's no trouble.

You can hear that this is a very different conversation than most couples have. It gives you an idea of what's possible when both partners are being responsible at level four. But even if only one person is being responsible, it still can create magic:

PARTNER A: Did you pick up the dog food?

PARTNER B: No, did you want me to?

PARTNER A: Yep, I told you three times this morning.

PARTNER B: I never heard you say that.

PARTNER A: Oh, I must not have been clear. I was doing so many other things, I probably didn't say it clearly; I was everywhere this morning.

PARTNER B: I didn't think that you told me.

PARTNER A: I can see that. I get to work on being clearer, or getting your attention so that things aren't missed.

PARTNER B: OK. Well, what do you want to do about the dog food? Do you want me to go, or will you?

PARTNER A: I can go before I start dinner if you want.

PARTNER B: Or you can start dinner and I'll go.

You get the idea. There isn't a lot of arm wrestling. Now, what it does take is a willingness to let go of being right. Partner A would need to let go of being right that she told him to get it three times, and that he just never listens to anything. The choice is being right about him not listening to anything, or to love in that moment. If it occurs again and again, then maybe she can sit down and talk about how she doesn't really feel as though their communication is going well, and ask for possible suggestions and input. Her partner is more likely to respond favorably than if she has been arguing with him consistently over dog food!

That's **SECRET #3 TO HOT PARTNERING: BE RESPONSIBLE FOR EVERYTHING.**

In fact, if there were a secret in this book that was like magic for your entire life—like the golden ticket in *Willie Wonka and the Chocolate Factory*—it is this one. Choose to put on the glasses that let you see that you brought the challenge to yourself, for your greater growth.

Remember, being responsible isn't blaming yourself, or feeling guilty or ashamed. It is choosing to see through the lens that whatever is occurring is happening as part of some cosmic dance, and your role in the dance is not random or accidental, but rich with lessons for your growth and development. Is this true, as in a fact? I would like to believe so, and could wax poetic on indications that this could be "reality," but this isn't the book for that. For this moment, it is merely trying it on, like a new coat in a store that you realize has tremendous magical powers.

There is a lot of support for looking at the world through the lens of a victim. Turn on the news today, and I promise you, the bulk of what you'll hear is that framework. "He did that to me." "She hurt me." "That corporation should be sued because the coffee was too hot and I burned my leg when I spilled it, coming out of the drive-through." You get the idea. And most of the conversation at offices around the water cooler is more of the same: "Can you believe that the boss put yet another project on me?" "I was passed up for a promotion because that guy kisses the boss's ass." "I would be able to meet my deadlines if it weren't for...."

Perhaps that is the sleek coat of black plumage that the Black Vulture wears. It could be that the Black Vulture dive bombs at the potential mate to bring out the strength that she has. Maybe that challenge makes the partnership stronger. And when the pair is stronger, the entire wake is stronger. In fact, Black Vultures have such a strong bond, they remain together year round, not just during the mating ritual. And the entire committee of vultures sticks together. In other words, you are fighting FOR your partner, not AGAINST them. You are on the same team. In moments when you believe your partner is on the opposite side of the ring, you get to remember the Black Vulture: They are in your corner. It may not feel like they are in your corner at that moment—dive bombing you in whatever way that they are—but trust that you are on the same team, and they are fighting for your growth; even if it is painful, there is some gold in there.

Remember, this book will not work itself. This is like gym equipment: If you are using it, you will see results. If you are just reading stories about other people, conceptualizing in your head but not doing the exercises or sharing with your partner, you will yield the equivalent results. I am encouraging you to build a strong foundation underneath you, each chapter and secret building on each other. So when you have dug your teeth into responsibility and are ready, I am incredibly excited about what's next. It's the key to actually going somewhere with your partner instead of staying stalled.

THE BIRDS

Take out your journal, which is quickly becoming packed with beautiful lessons, and then answer the following for the Birds and for the Bees:

1. The black vulture challenges their mate repeatedly as a way to grow the relationship and bond. Where has your partner been challenging you to grow?

2. Where have you been challenging your partner to grow? How does your partner respond to your challenges and calling forth?

3. How would you like to respond to each other's challenges to grow?

THE BEES

1. Where I am most often a victim in my life is... (my partner not following through with things, my doing the dishes and cleaning, the traffic, my boss...)

2. What do I get out of being a victim? (sympathy, irresponsibility, excuses, manipulation, covert control...)

3. If I were to choose the interpretation that I am author of whatever is occurring, not from fault or blame, but for a greater purpose or life lesson, what would be possible would be...

4. How this would alter my relationship, and all of my relationships, would be...

TAKE FLIGHT

1. Share your journal responses with your partner. Remember, do not be defensive, but hear the ways in which your partner has been in your corner, supporting you in larger life lessons and wanting you to grow.

2. Each of you pick a story from your life, of a time that you felt like a victim, helpless, and powerless. Tell each other that story from the perspective of a victim. Now tell the same story from the perspective of responsibility, without blaming yourself, and without shame, fault, or guilt. Simply explore the bigger reason for that in your life, and what was learned from what occurred. Remember, in the moment, it may feel horrible, difficult, and sad, but you are the one who determines if it remains that, or becomes a growth opportunity and lesson for your life.

3. Find a way to acknowledge each other whenever EITHER of you is being responsible in the moment, rather than viewing whatever is occurring through the filter of victim.

CHAPTER FOUR

Have Great Vision

"A dream you dream alone is only a dream.
A dream you dream together is reality."
– John Lennon, quoting Yoko Ono[1]

If you've ever seen an Atlantic Puffin, the first thing you'll notice is that they are absolutely adorable. They are often called the "clowns of the sea," with Technicolor bills and matching orange feet, during the breeding season. Their Latin name, *Fratercula,* comes from the words, *little brother*, referring to the black and white plumage, said to resemble robes that monks once wore.[2] They are small birds, especially considering the fact that they live in incredibly challenging conditions. They are barely a foot tall, weighing about the same as a can of soda, but they can fly as fast as 55 mph, with wings beating at around 400 times per minute.[3]

These little birds chatter like crazy when they are breeding, talking to each other constantly, but they remain perfectly silent while at sea. Puffins have thick, downy feathers, making them look like little puff balls, and they can puff up their feathers even more when intruders are around. Besides being adorable, what can we learn from Puffins? Puffins have amazing vision, hunting their prey by diving, then staying under water for up to a minute searching for fish. They can usually catch and hold about 10 fish in their beak per hunt, but the highest number recorded was 62. I like to imagine the ornithologist who was lucky enough to have the job of removing them from the beak and counting. Even more amazing, Puffins return to the same nesting place each year, with the same mate, and then they proceed to make elaborate cozy homes for their newborn chicks. These homes have long passageways and are burrows about three feet long. The egg is laid at the very end of the tunnel, and there is a separate bathroom area at the first bend of the tunnel, allowing the baby chicks to learn how to stay neat and clean, with a separate place to relieve themselves. If their feathers are dirty, the Puffin's waterproofing could be compromised, so this isn't just a matter of cleanliness; it is survival.[4]

What is the Puffin teaching us, besides "cleanliness is next to godliness?" First, let's start with vision. The Puffin has impeccable vision since they spend most of their lives at sea, either in flight or resting on the ocean. Their survival depends on their vision, for spotting schools of fish in the water and knowing exactly when to dive in. But in addition to a practical vision to catch their own meal, they have a shared vision with their partner: establishing elaborate homes for their young, with designated "bathrooms," and sleeping and eating areas all distinct from each other for cleanliness.[5]

Where are you going? What do you want? How are you getting there, and are you enjoying the journey along the way? For years, athletes have used the power of envisioning to enhance their performance and improve their ability. In fact, new research shows that when an athlete is hooked up to electrodes, and they visualize the race that is about to be run, their brain and entire body respond as though the race is actually being run. Each time that they visualize the race being run well, they are conditioning their brain, body, and entire being to actually run that race when the starting gun is really fired.[6] This is commonplace for Olympic athletes, and in the last twenty years, corporations have also begun to use the power of visualization to achieve greater results.

Multi-gold medal winner, Michael Phelps' swimming coach, Bob Bowman, thinks that vision and mental rehearsal are two sides of the same coin. He said that "for months before a race, Michael gets into a relaxed state. He mentally rehearses for two hours a day in the pool. He sees himself winning. He smells the air, tastes the water, hears the sounds, and sees the clock." In fact, he goes even further out than that, seeing himself as a spectator in the stands, watching the meet. He visualizes overcoming obstacles, like being further behind in a race than he expected to be, practicing every possible scenario repeatedly. This mental rehearsal is a well-established technique employed to high performers in every aspect of life, because "the brain cannot distinguish between something that's vividly imagined and something that's real."[7]

Far too often, couples are headed in some kind of direction, but it is often the opposite direction. A good example was Laura and Nigel earlier. Nigel is a homebody and wants quiet nights at home with his wife curled up in his arms. He values predictability, likes planting roots and investing in forwarding his career, and continuing to improve his home. He is practical and doesn't put much faith in religion or spiritual pursuits. For years, Laura has studied Buddhism and has been lured by the call of the East. She dreams of moving to India, living in an Ashram, and doing work supporting the children of the streets. Laura wants to expose her son to different cultures, thinking, and beliefs, including a deep spiritual practice. For Laura, staying at home with Nigel is suffocating, and she feels that her spirit is being crushed. Neither one of them talk much about what they want with each other;

instead, they continue to drift further and further apart, because Laura feels no attraction towards Nigel, and is thinking, "All he wants is sex and for me to be a good little wife, staying at home."

Both Laura and Nigel have clear ideas about their visions for the future, but those visions are very separate. And upon first examination, it may seem that those visions are in opposition. But Laura and Nigel have not even attempted to come up with a shared vision that they both can live into. They have not attempted to explore ways in which they can compromise. Do you think that if Nigel was willing to take a trip to India with Laura, exploring her vision, that Laura would be more attracted to him? Do you think that if Laura was willing to curl up on the couch with Nigel, being affectionate, that Nigel might be more content to support her soul's wanderings?

As individuals, it is important to know where we are going. Many people are sleepwalking through their lives. They go to college because it was what their parents expected them to do. After college, they meet and marry the person that their parents would approve of, and settle down, working towards the house and the 2.5 children. Each day, they wake up, putting one foot in front of the other, marching off to a job and a career that they ended up in, coming home to a partner and children and the "life" that they created. Far too many people are robotically moving through their lives, resigned that this is "all there is."

If you ask a child what they want to be when they grow up, you will notice that their answers change. When I first asked my son, he said he wanted to be "the guy that cleans up the big buildings." My husband and I were fine with our aspiring janitor, if that was what made him happy. The next time I asked, it was a baseball player, and then "the guy that drives around in those big buses, with beds and televisions on them. I would live there and move all the time—definitely not married." His answers continue to change as he grows and changes; and currently, he is heading towards race car driver. I wasn't so excited about that one in terms of safety, but this is his life to live. The point is that when we are children, we believe that we can be whatever we want. Then gradually, as we set forth in the world, and there are failures or challenges, we begin to pull our vision in. We are told to "be more practical or realistic," and we adapt and adapt and adapt...until we are in a job that is fine, but certainly doesn't make our hearts sing or delight us.

Have you let the expectations of other people alter your choices? I think of my husband, the youngest of five children, with two older brothers who were avid football players and much more physical. The year he went out for football was one of the worst of his life. He thought that his father would be proud of him and that he could follow in the steps of his older brothers. Instead, he felt incompetent, small, and weak, and like he was a disappointment to everyone. At some point, he began running track, which no one in his family had ever done, and it was a sport unfamiliar to his family. Gene still laughs that his father attended every track meet in college, even though he had no idea how the scoring worked. Likewise, when Gene was a child, he began to draw, and teachers began to notice that his drawings were amazing. He continued to draw through high school, but instead of encouraging his drawing and artist abilities, his family wanted him to go to work in the family olive-tree business. His mom was the lone supporter of his ambitions towards art. Gene's career counselor, at Mater Dei High School, asked him to look towards careers like becoming a mechanic, or some trade school, rather than going to college. Thankfully, Gene did not follow any other advice than the small, still voice within himself, and he was the first person in his family to enroll in college to focus on fine art. He now has an art gallery in the Santa Ana Arts District, and has had exhibits of his work, around the country (artofgene.com).

Sometimes it is challenging to hear that small, still voice (or shouting, fanatic voice for some of us) within us above the din of other people's expectations and our own fears. To create a successful shared vision, first there must be a connection to your own passion and purpose. Sometimes in a relationship, one person sacrifices their vision and adopts or hijacks the vision of the other person. Like a sailboat, the one person believes that they can ride the wind that fills their partner's sails. But inevitably, the ride isn't what was expected.

Do you know what you want? What is your purpose for being on this earth? Why are you here? What is your legacy? Are these questions inspiring to you? Paralyzing? In my work as a transformational trainer, I have been able to ask tens of thousands of people what they want. Most often, where the conversation begins is with what the person doesn't want. They may not have clarity about where they are going, but they are certain they don't want some of what has already been. There is an old expression coined by Carl Jung, "What you resist, persists." In other words, I can put my energy into what I do not want, and not move any closer to what I really do want. If I am focused on what has occurred in my life, thinking I want "more money, better relationships, different opportunities, and less stress," than what has occurred before, I end up with just that: pretty much what I had before but a little more, less, different, or better.

Perhaps you have seen that with a friend or family member. They wanted the next boyfriend or girlfriend (or husband or wife) to be better or different than the last one, and they ended up with pretty much a slightly different version of what they had before. It is looking at the past to determine the future. Recycling is great for our planet but not so hot for our relationships and lives. If I am using what has come before as a template for the future, looking to the past, then I will end up with some variation of that past. It may feel a little safer since I have some idea of what will or will not be required of me, and since I have done it before. But true creation is being willing to declare it out of thin air, or from the depths of your being, without regard to what has occurred in the past or what you think you are or are not capable of—declaring a vision from nothing. There is *no-thingness*— no reference to a *thing* or idea from the past to determine what will or will not be in the future.

Where is your ship, as a couple, sailing? Again, if you are focused on the back of the boat and the wake of what has come before, the ship may be stalled; it may be going in circles, drifting off course, and you will not know until much later, since the wake pretty much looks the same. The sun continues to rise and set each day, and sometimes it takes years to realize we've been sailing in circles. You can be the ones who chart the course for the ship, or let whatever current comes to carry you. Sometimes I hear people say, "I want to be organic and be responsive to what presents itself." Wonderful, but that doesn't mean that there is not a course that has been charted internally, whether or not we are conscious of it. At the same time, if I map out my direction and then ignore everything along the way, in pursuit of reaching that goal, the journey will not be very enjoyable, and I will have missed some important signals along the way. There is a balance of being clear on what it is that I want and where I am going, but at the same time, listening to the signals that present themselves, because what may seem like a diversion, may actually be a profound route to fulfillment.

Like Nigel and Laura, do you sometimes believe that you and your partner are too different to have a successful relationship and shared vision? I want to give you a few examples of people who could have given up hope of loving their partner, but came up with creative solutions instead. *O Magazine* recently inspired me with the story of Marisol, 45, a chef and author, and Rob, 55, a new-media entrepreneur. They fell in love but didn't necessarily want to join their households since they had both gotten pretty used to their routines, and Rob had two children, who really didn't want the households joined either. What have they chosen to do? In over seven years since they were married, they have maintained separate homes, having sleepovers every now and then. Rob said, "When I thought about marriage, I pictured all four of us living together, but the truth is, that was my dream. It wasn't Marisol's dream, and it wasn't the kids' dream... During our dating days, I would stay at her place when I wasn't with the kids. I was happy, she was happy. There was nothing broken, so I thought: "Why don't we just continue that but be married?[8]

Another couple, highlighted in the same article, have lived together for over a decade and have recently married. Andrea, 34, and Scott, 44, opened an art gallery recently with two employees: the both of them. They are together at work and at home—nearly all of the time. Andrea explains one way in which it works, "We used to split domestic chores down the middle, and each person always felt like they were doing more. But when we tried that at work, we saw how silly it was. We're each better at different things: I do the books, and Scott does the shipping. So we carried that idea into our home life—I never walk the dog; Scott never vacuums—and things got so much better. We negotiate in a really healthy way."[9]

Philosophers, Simone de Beauvoir and Jean-Paul Sartre, maintained a close friendship and romantic relationship throughout their lives, but both were not proponents of monogamy, and they rejected the social standards set for them for relationships at the time. Simone had a long-standing affair with Bianca Lamblin, a student, and at one time, there was a love affair between the three. Simone used Sartre's love affairs as fodder for her fiction, and Sartre reportedly never submitted material to a publisher without her input. The two remained irreplaceable to each other throughout their lives, with an arrangement that worked for them.

A little closer to home, my friend, Bianca, was in a long-term relationship with Ethan, who had two children from a previous marriage. It was a frustrating relationship for both, and eventually Bianca left. A couple of years later, she began a friendship with Chris and Tamara, who had always been interested in Bianca as a possible third partner in their relationship. Taking her by surprise, Bianca fell in love with both of them, and although they are no longer in partnership, they are co-parenting and maintain a deep commitment to loving each other.

I am not advocating adding a partner into your relationship, or even living in separate houses or having affairs. I simply am pointing out that your shared vision is just that: yours. I am first using these couples to illustrate that all of them could have thrown in the towel, thinking that the differences of their individual visions couldn't possibly be compromised or reconciled. They didn't give up; instead, they created a solution that worked for them. I am also using these inspiring examples as reminders that your relationship, and how you choose to manifest your love, is your choice. It's beyond annoying that as I am writing this paragraph, there is a voice in the back of my head saying that there needs to be some legal disclaimer. So, here it is: Obviously, it is within the laws as set forth in your nation and state.

If you have not given heartfelt thought to where you are headed in your life as an individual, now is the time. Do it as though you were finger-painting as a child—just keep exploring, possibly through writing, dreaming, and drawing, and continue to be in possibility, without the words, *I can't,* slipping in. If you decide you do not like the vision that is unfolding, or that there is something you want out of the picture, you can simply start again. Take it bite by bite. If it is easier for you to think of what life would be like five years in the future, how you would wake up, where you would live...going step by step, then do so. The main objective is that this works for you to begin to uncover the life that you envision.

Once you have gotten some clarity around what matters to you, then you have an opportunity to come together with your partner to share. In sharing with each other, and designing your shared vision, please listen to each other well. Sometimes we do not give what is needed most, which is space for the person to explore, discover, and refine the vision that they are sculpting. In this process, there is only possibility—you do not get to say NO, or argue as to why that isn't possible or could never occur. As Emily Dickenson wrote, "I dwell in possibility."[10]

Puffins have impeccable vision for the immediate moment, diving for their food and coming back with a big haul in their tiny beaks. But they also have a shared vision, building an incredibly cozy little home, often in freezing conditions. As the clowns of the sea, they often inspire laughter in human beings, looking almost like a colorful cartoon during breeding season, when their beaks change into a bright Technicolor rainbow. Think about it; they put on a great display of color for the one that they love, almost like dressing up for a yearly date.

Remember, our visions may be changing from year to year, and sometimes in times of intense change, they may alter daily. You get to set aside time to share with each other how you are changing. I was thinking the other day that I hadn't really looked at my husband when I kissed him at the airport. We were simply going through a typical day, but I hadn't really looked at him. I think that as human beings, we do that a lot. We relate to our partner through the lens of who they were yesterday, last week, last year, or when we met that person. Each of us is constantly changing, growing, learning, and discovering new parts of ourselves. I am therefore encouraging you to set weekly dates with your partner, where you are actually looking at that person, talking about who they are in this moment, and who you are in this moment.

Before we turn away from the Puffin, I want to talk about another aspect of their vision. The puffin returns to the same breeding ground year after year, excavating the burrow for use again. It is unclear how they navigate their way back to breeding grounds, not to mention the exact same burrow—but somehow, they do. Also, ornithologists believe that the Puffin leads a solitary existence while at sea. Think about it; this little bird makes the frigid North Atlantic its home and, most of the time, bobs around on the waves with no land in sight. But that little bird somehow knows exactly how to find the way back home to its mate.

Sometimes in the hectic whirlwind of today, we sometimes lead very separate lives from our partners. We have different jobs, different friends; sometimes travel is involved, with a long time away from each other, and it's easy to lose sight of our partner. I'm sure you've heard stories of someone who felt disconnected from their partner at home, and then began a romance in the office with a coworker. How do we keep our focus on our partner even while we are very much in our own world, the world that our partner may not be a part of or even understand?

I think it requires a unique balance to be able to share our different worlds with each other and not lose sight of our partner in the process. But that means making time and space to share not only what we're doing, or the experiences that we're having, but also how we are feeling about whatever's occurring in our life. This means making time to check in with our partner about their world and whatever is occurring for them, and sharing our own world. This doesn't mean constantly talking about the kids or what someone did today. It is taking the conversation deeper to be in an inquiry about what our partner is feeling about their life.

I travel quite a bit, doing trainings in different locations in the world. I am away from my husband for weeks at a time. When we were first married, Gene used to ask me if I missed him while I was away. I said I didn't. I didn't miss him because I didn't feel as though he was away from me. Just because we were physically separate from each other didn't mean that he was away. I felt as though he were with me, in my heart and in my thoughts, so much that it didn't feel like he was away from me. He used to tease me about it. Now he understands it.

However, I do notice that in the first couple days that I am gone, there is an adjustment period. Our first or second conversation on the phone is not always so great; it's as though we need time adjusting to the idea that we are in different locations. We also need to take the conversation deeper deliberately, into what each of us is really feeling like wherever we are. This is, to me, not losing sight of our partner. I get to envision what is occurring at home, what pressures are on my husband, and also be aware that it is much easier to be the partner that leaves and is in a new location, than the partner that is left at home with the same routine. The same routine gives reminders that our partner is not present.

I think the challenge is to be authentic—really authentic. Sometimes we censure ourselves from those we are the closest to. I hear people say that they're afraid to tell a partner about something that happened, maybe a flirtation, or someone asking them out on a date because they didn't see the wedding ring. We're afraid of admitting certain feelings—loneliness, neediness, fear, doubt— so we end up talking about the superficial. It takes courage to be completely honest with wherever we are with our partners. In other words, I am in this relationship for the long haul. That means that I am interested in everything that he is feeling and thinking. I really want to know the real him, even if that means a messy conversation.

Think about it; sometimes people don't want to tell their partner that they find another person attractive. They're afraid that the partner will become jealous or insecure. But it is absolute insanity to think that just because we are married or in a long-term relationship, we won't find other people attractive. It would be like walking through a magnificent garden and only being allowed to say that one flower was beautiful. Of course, we're going to notice other people and find them attractive. It doesn't mean that we're going to break our commitment or vow. Often, my husband will complement a celebrity or woman on the street, saying that she's beautiful, and I'll agree with him. In fact, as an artist, he paints many naked women and will often share with me how beautiful they were, and aspects of their beauty. I love that he sees the world through this lens and appreciates the human form.

If I am interested in growing for the rest of my life, then I become very interested in what my husband finds attractive. There are deeper conversations, like conversations about certain qualities that a person may possess. I may say that I admire someone's commitment and resolve, and that I find it attractive. My husband then gets to be in an inquiry about his own commitment and resolve. If we're committed to growing with each other for the rest of our lives, then he is making note of the fact that I find commitment attractive. And if he feels like he is coming up short in commitment and resolve, then he would get to further develop and strengthen those qualities. Or he may feel like he is very committed and resolute when he decides something, and then he will simply note that I find it attractive. In other words, if I am growing with someone for the rest of my life, I want to know what they find attractive so that I can continue to grow and develop those aspects of myself, whatever they are. What that means is that I get to see my partner as capable of handling information, and I also get to be compassionate if insecurity emerges, and then there is a chance to talk about that.

These are all ways that I think you cannot lose sight of your partner. So, the puffin is teaching us about vision—seeing for our own survival, sharing a joint vision, keeping sight of our partner, and knowing how to find our way home, no matter what.

What is the opportunity? Have your own vision to sustain you, not expecting your partner's vision to fuel you for the long solitary times at sea. Then create a shared vision and get creative, no matter how many obstacles that may seem to be blocking that vision. Then put on your most vibrant colors, showing your partner the brightest parts of you, instead of just barely going through the motions of life robotically. Show what makes you uniquely you.

SECRET # 4 TO HOT PARTNERING – HAVE YOUR OWN VISION AND A SHARED VISION WITH YOUR PARTNER.

Once you have clarified your own vision and a shared vision with your partner, you'll be ready to go on to Chapter 5, where you'll finally have the answer to a fundamental question that each of us asks at one time or another. The answer may give you some peace and, at the same time, be a little unsettling, but you're ready for it; otherwise, you wouldn't have picked up *The Birds and the Bees to Joyful Monogamy.*

THE BIRDS

1. In your journal, giving yourself time for reflection, write down your responses to the following self-inquires before sharing with your partner.

2. The Atlantic Puffin has sharp vision to take in their daily feed, but also an elaborate shared vision for their nest and caring for their young. What is your own personal vision for your life? What are you passionate about? What is the legacy you want to leave? What moves and inspires you? How do you envision incorporating that daily in your life, if you are not already?

3. Have you been attaching your dingy, expecting your partner's boat and sails to be enough to keep you contented? Have you given up aspects of yourself because you thought they didn't match your partner's vision? If so, what?

THE BEES

1. Describe your personal vision of a deeply satisfying love relationship, using the following series of short sentences to respond. Make sure that every sentence is phrased positively, rather than about what you do not want. Include qualities that are already present that you appreciate, as well as those you would like to develop. For example, "We enjoy each other's

company;" "We have passionate and creative sex;" "We are loving and patient parents to our children." Avoid one-word answers, and elaborate as much as possible, feeling free to add additional areas of importance.

How do you feel about your partner?

What do you find attractive about your partner?

What activities do you do together?

What is the experience when you are together and engaging in activities?

How do you relate to each other and what are your conversations like?

Do you live where you currently live, or somewhere else?

What is your sex life like?

What do you do for recreation and enjoyment?

How do you spend your free time? Television? Reading? Socializing?

How do you support each other in your careers?

How do you talk about money? Spend money? Save money?

If you have children, what is their role in your partnership or household? Who does what with the children, and how do you support each other in this commitment?

If you do not have children, do you want them? When? When would you choose to have a child? How many children? Would you adopt? Would you have foster children?

How are tasks/chores around the house handled?

How do you relate to mutual friends as a couple?

Do you each have friends of the opposite sex (or same sex and transgender with those partnerships), and how do you relate with each other about trust?

How do you handle conflict when it arises?

What is your relationship to each other's families of origin?

How healthy are you physically?

2. What words would friends use to describe your qualities/characteristics as a couple?

3. What would you like to inspire in others when they are with you?

4. What is the experience you want others to have when they are a guest in your home?

TAKE FLIGHT

1. Choose a Partner A and a Partner B. Partner A, take out your journal of the questions that you answered above. Speak from your heart, and share your vision with your partner, taking at least ten minutes, using your responses as a guideline but simply speaking freely and in detail about your vision for your relationship.

One of the greatest gifts that you can give your partner is listening—simply listening without interjecting your opinion, or contradicting or adding in additional details. It is generous and caring, and it works well when either of you has a lot on your mind or is upset in some way.

Partner B, you are generously listening to Partner A, nodding and occasionally saying, "Mmmm" or "Ahhh," or giving your partner some indication that you are connected to the words that they are speaking.

When they are complete, acknowledge your partner with a hug, and thank them for opening up and sharing with you.

2. Partner B, it's your turn. Using your journal notes of the questions pertaining to your vision, as a guideline, you are to communicate for ten minutes, adding detail and sharing your vision for your relationship and lives together.

   Partner A, you are generously listening, nodding when something moves you, or giving a heartfelt noise to indicate that you are with your partner as they communicate.

3. Now you are going to have the opportunity to work together on your vision. Hand your journal to your partner. You are going to review their list and place check marks next to the items that you have in common. If the thought is the same but the words are slightly different, give it a check mark. If your partner included things that you did not but you would enjoy as well, give them check marks.

4. How important to you are the items that you checked on both lists? If they are essential, you will give that statement a 10; if they are not important at all, a 0, using numbers in between to reflect the importance to you. Both of you review both lists, and

give each statement your own personal ranking as to importance to you.

5. Beginning with the items that are most important to BOTH OF YOU, write those items on a separate sheet of paper entitled "OUR VISION." So your list will begin with statements that you both ranked with a 10, and will end with the statements you both gave a 2 or 3. If there is a statement that one person ranked a 10, and the other a 2, see if you can come up with a compromise to satisfy both of you. If you cannot right now, leave it off the list. Remember to write this list in the affirmative, present tense. For example, "We are respectful to each other and listen without interrupting.

6. Read your shared vision aloud to each other, really noticing if you read it and believed that it is actually possible, or if you are reading it thinking that it is a fantasy. Notice, as you read it, if you believe your partner is not committed to this vision but you are. Notice, as you read it, if you are inspired or excited. In other words, notice what your mind is making up and what you are feeling.

CHAPTER FIVE

WARNING: DO NOT NEGLECT YOUR PARTNER!

The Scarlet Macaw

"Did I pick the right person? This question inverts the starting and ending points. We do not pick our perfect match because we ourselves are not perfect. The universe hands us a flawed diamond—in the rough. Only if we are willing to polish off every part of ourselves that cannot join do we end up with a soul mate."[1]
– David Schnarch

Most of the world is convinced that their partners need to change for things to be ideal, but thankfully, in Chapter Three, you learned about responsibility, and have begun the journey of polishing off the parts of you that do not join, to create your soul mate. Brushing off the parts of yourself begins with understanding how important it is to give love and attention to your partner. When you do, you create a type of invincibility in them. And when you don't, it can wreak havoc on everything.

Case in point: the Scarlet Macaw. The Scarlet Macaw has a white face and brilliant bright red plumage, with highlights of orange, yellow, green, and bright blue. Maybe you have seen one in a pet store, or in the home of a bird lover, and if you are lucky enough to live in the tropics, perhaps you see them with regularity in the wild. A type of parrot, these birds are incredibly intelligent, learning a vast vocabulary of words and tricks, and can live to be 70 or 80 years old.[2]

They are serially monogamous but also may change mates after several seasons. They are affectionate and loving, and they come with a powerful warning: If they are neglected, they become noisy, destructive, and aggressive. Are you getting one of the most important lessons of the Scarlet Macaw? Don't neglect your partner. In other words, they require plenty of exercise outside of the cage, and constant socialization to remain bonded with their owners. Another interesting fact, because they consume large amounts of clay in the wild, they can eat fruit that is toxic to other animals and birds. They have a type of invincibility.[3]

Have you ever looked at your partner and wondered why that person? Of all the people in the world, how did you end up with this one? Perhaps you and your partner are total opposites, and everything he or she does drives you crazy. Or perhaps you are so alike that you feel absolutely no separation between the two of you. Maybe there is a middle ground—times where you feel that you are with the perfect person to compliment you, and times when you wonder if your union was a cosmic joke. After all, there are some unusual pairings that have occurred throughout time—especially from the outside looking in on another relationship.

There are partnerships where the sole desire of both parties is to not be alone, and they join to journey through life without feeling loneliness. There are relationships where the sole purpose is to have fun and experience as much together as is possible on this earth. They are adventurers, always looking for the next place to go or experience to try. There are unions that focus primarily on keeping peace, and conflict is avoided at all costs, with upsets swept under bulging rugs. There are couples who want to protect and shield each other from the outside negative energies of the world, from any hurt or challenge. There are couples whose primary goal is to be comfortable, focused on creature comforts, food, drink, and ease. Undoubtedly, we could go through countless reasons why couples come together, and how they choose to go through their lives with each other. For the purpose of the work that you are doing, I'm going to offer another option—an option for partnership—clarified beautifully in *Getting the Love You Want,* by Harville Hendrix. Hendrix so beautifully describes another possibility: a *conscious* marriage, which he defines as a "marriage that fosters maximum psychological and spiritual growth" for both partners.[4] Whether or not you are married, this is a higher possibility for your partnership, one that is incredibly rewarding but definitely not always easy.

When all of us initially fall in love, we are in a state of bliss. There is nothing that our partner can do that is wrong, and they are ideal for us. If friends or loved ones offer anything but total support, there is defensiveness and denial. This is the person—THE ONE. Teenagers epitomize the total abandon and elation of new love very well, but to one extent or another, that is how all of us are when we "fall in love." Dr. Lucy Brown, and her colleague, Dr. Helen Fischer, in the department of neurology and neuroscience, at the Albert Einstein College of Medicine, in New York, and her colleagues, did MRI brain scans on college students looking at photographs of their new loves, and here is what they discovered:

"When a person falls in love, the ventral tegmental area in the brain floods the caudate nucleus with dopamine. The caudate then signals for more dopamine; the more dopamine, the higher a person feels. The same system becomes activated when someone takes cocaine."[5]

So, when we fall in love, it is as though we are drugged. Did you ever have nights of talking on the phone for six or eight hours and not needing sleep? Did you ever experience days of endless texting and counting the minutes until you could be together again? Have you ever had a romantic evening where every little thing your partner said or did was totally endearing to you? These are all examples of the caudate nucleus happily being flooded with dopamine.

When we are first born, there is a developmental time period where there is absolutely no separation between us and anything else. In utero, we are in a state of bliss, connected to everything and everyone, with every need met, floating in timelessness. When we are born, our impulse is to keep that connection and bliss, and remain attached to everyone and everything. In the best scenarios of attentive, caring, and loving parents, we are given safety, sustenance, and love, and our sense of peace and connection is maintained. But even the best parent cannot keep up with the level of service that we had when we were in the womb. In the womb, every need was immediately met, in a bath of warm water. Outside of the womb, our demands and needs are not necessarily immediately met. Sometimes our needs are understood, but the timeline with which those needs are met is hardly immediate. Other times, our parents guess at what the needs actually are, uncertain as to what the infant is yearning for or wants. Still, other times, our parents, with all of their own problems and unmet needs from their own childhoods, are unwilling or unable to meet our needs. They may be sad, exhausted, distracted, afraid, and they fail to maintain the feelings of peace, security, and comfort.

We are then desperate to restore those lost feelings of security and peace, and then adopt coping strategies to have our needs met—

perhaps by crying constantly to get attention; perhaps by withdrawing from our caretakers and creating our own inner world, perhaps by denying that we even have needs, or perhaps by reaching out for our caretakers and then withdrawing periodically when the feelings become too intense. As children, we did our best to adapt and restore those feelings of safety and security, but the world has already begun to feel unsafe.

For many infants, that feeling of bliss never existed. Research shows that if a pregnant woman feels humiliation, her fetus feels the same humiliation; so, whatever emotion is being pumped through the system of the mother, the infant is automatically feeling and floating in that same emotion. Likewise, research also shows that infants can feel the emotions of the mother in utero. In this way, there is also no separation. What that means is that if a woman is using drugs or alcohol during her pregnancy, or has extreme anxiety or depression, that is also the water that her child is growing in. So, instead of looking to return to feelings of bliss and safety, the infant has now been conditioned by a world that is unsafe, anxious, and dangerous.[6]

As you and I grow up and become socialized, we observe ways in which others are coping with the lack of safety or danger of the world. We see people repressing their own needs, or denying that they experience hurt or pain. We witness people controlling things or dominating other people. We watch as people adapt themselves to gain love and acceptance from their parents, teachers, authority figures, or peers. And in the interest of our own survival, we gradually begin to push down the parts of ourselves that we believe society, our families, friends, and the world find unlovable. If you spend time in a room of kindergarteners, the room is usually buzzing with full expression, tears, laughter, exuberance, and tenderness—the emotions run the gamut. But if you go into a high school, you will not see the same passion, self-expression, and exuberance for life. Instead, by the time kids arrive into high school, they are often depressed, anxious, rebellious, and feeling lousy about themselves.[7]

When we initially fall in love, and the dopamine is flooding the caudate nucleus, we believe that we have found that lost bliss of total acceptance, safety, and peace again. We feel totally understood, loved for who we are, and an insatiable need to be around our loved one all the time, like a drug. But then once a commitment is made, and once we get married or move in with each other, things start to disintegrate, and according to Harville Hendrix, "The veil of illusion falls away, and the qualities that were once endearing to us become annoying. It suddenly seems as if the person we fell in love with is gone, and instead there is a completely different person. We realize that this person is not going to be our salvation, and we are hurt. We become desperate to return to the state of bliss we had upon meeting our partner, and do everything possible to get them to love us through old coping strategies—we become needy and manipulative; we cry and strike out at them—anything to get them to love us the way that they initially did.[4]

Hendrix calls this your Imago partner, and defines it as "someone who is uniquely unqualified at the moment to give you the love you want." What I so love is that Hendrix uses the word, *uniquely*, meaning that this person is not unqualified in any average or random way; but rather, they are unqualified in the exact ways or areas where we specifically need them to be qualified. And according to Hendrix, this is exactly as it is supposed to occur, since our primitive brain has a "compelling, nonnegotiable drive to restore the feeling of aliveness and wholeness with which we came into the world." We look to repair the hurts from our childhood of having needs unmet, through finding a partner who will give us exactly what our caretakers failed to provide for us.[4]

So, if Dad left, either physically or emotionally, I may find a partner who leaves me or is completely emotionally unavailable. Or if I ended up feeling like I wasn't loved or valued by my mother, I may work incredibly hard to create my value to unconsciously prove I'm valuable. Or if Dad had a nervous breakdown, and I felt like I needed to be independent and handle everything myself, I may create an anxious partner who expects the same, or I may become the nervous one, wanting to be cared for. If I was raised by parents who took care of my every need, unconsciously I may think I am not capable, and find a partner who is going to do the same, giving me the idea that I am not capable. There are endless variations and love stories to match the variations.

We then set out to find partners that will give us what our caretakers did not. So, if Dad worked all of the time and was never available for concentrated intimacy and connection, we are consciously looking for someone who seems emotionally available. If Mom was cold and withdrawn, we look for someone who is super nurturing and a homebody. If Dad was smothering in his love, we may look for someone who gives us space. Or if Mom was not very confident, we may look for someone who is super confident and independent. And to be clear, this has little to do with the gender of our parent—we are looking for what both of our caretakers lacked, in one perfect package. Specifically, we are looking for whatever was our greatest need that was not met by our mother and father.

This is what is occurring consciously, but there is an unconscious need to find someone who has the same deficits in care and attention that hurt us in the first place, as a way to heal that original wounding. Our mind has an image of the perfect person, a synthesis of qualities formed in reaction to the way we were cared for as a child, as well as what was not given to us. The Imago is "the person who can make me whole again, a compilation of both the negative and positive traits of our caretakers." Additionally, our Imago carries the qualities that we believe are missing in ourselves—the parts that were repressed because we thought that they were unlovable or not okay. So, if we never express our anger, we may find a partner who has bouts of yelling and screaming in rage. If we are obsessed with order and neatness, our partner may leave trails of socks and laundry, and be a slob. If we unconsciously feel that we are not good enough, our partner may consistently express feelings of not being good enough. When our own repressed feelings—of anger, letting go, not being enough—are triggered through our partner, we react and then criticize that person for having too much anger, for being too lax with order, and for their feelings of inferiority. There is much written about the Imago, and I am appreciative to Harville and Gay Hendrix for their work in making this complex psychological concept accessible to people.[4]

At the Couples Retreat, when I ask couples, who moved in with each other or got married, if they felt like they were tricked and then wanted to run screaming away, hands go up. When I ask people if they felt like the person they fell in love with changed once they got married or made a commitment to each other, hands go up. And when I ask couples if they see that their partner carries aspects that they do not readily express, hands go up. At times, it seems more like a root canal than actually creating a deep and loving partnership. But conflict is supposed to happen as a way to call attention to the areas where both partners are meant to grow. Hendrix points out that "romantic love is supposed to end. It is the glue that initially bonds two incompatible people together so that they will do what needs to be done to heal themselves, and in the process, heal the rifts in nature, of which we are an integral part."[4]

Some people do everything in their power to avoid conflict; they separate or divorce, thinking that if they get rid of that particular partner and replace them with another, their problems will be solved. What ends up occurring is that the areas where that person was unwilling to grow, or whatever they were unwilling to face, then continues to show up again and again, no matter how many partners they eject. Again, remember the studies: There is a higher percentage of divorces the second time around, and an even higher percentage— 73%—the third time around. It's like we cannot escape ourselves! Whatever it is that is so intolerable in our partner, we end up with again—and again.

Yesterday, I was on the phone with Lionel, who called me in crisis. He and his wife, Lilly, have been participating in an intense period of discovery and growth. When they entered the process, their marriage was struggling. Lilly had suffered some health problems and was primarily bedridden, while Lionel cared for her and their two children. Initially, through work, Lilly got her health back, changing her diet to eliminate allergens, and dropping a considerable amount of weight. She began to feel beautiful and alive again. Lilly and Lionel both spend lots of time with others in community service projects and in support of their goals. Lilly fell in love with another man at her office, and since she believed that she and Lionel had pretty much decided their marriage was over, proceeded in a romantic relationship with him. Who did Lilly choose to fall in love with? You would think that since she had complained that Lionel was too passionate, impulsive, and spontaneous, she would find someone who was a little more cautious, steady, and analytical. No. Lilly chose someone a lot like Lionel. In fact, Lionel even said it himself: The man Lilly had chosen had the exact same qualities and characteristics that Lilly had complained about. But in these initial stages of dopamine flooding, Lilly couldn't see any of that. All that she could see was that this man was having her feel completely loved, accepted, and safe again...what had dissolved through the disagreements and freezing of her marriage with Lionel.

Romantic love ends. It takes real work to have some flame of it lit inside. Hollywood gives us repeated images of people swept up in a constant state of bliss. When couples make love in the movies, it is usually so passionate that everything else is swept away—desks are cleared, tabletops swept clean, with dishes breaking, beds toppled. In reality, there are children yelling in the other room, dinner to be made, and making love is fitting it in quickly between a million other things. In the movies, disagreements are resolved with laughter and heartfelt apologies. In reality, there are sometimes days or weeks of chilly silence or minimal talking, or blow ups, with partners saying horrible things to each other that are held forever in their minds. Real love that is sustainable and deeply aware bears little resemblance to what

Hollywood has given us. In *Pretty Woman*,[8] the successful businessman runs away with the prostitute. In *Titanic*,[9] the working-class bloke gets the high-society babe, and in *Say Anything*,[10] the misfit ends up with the valedictorian. All of them have the great beginnings of what could be a conscious relationship, where they have attracted both the positive and negative aspects of their caregivers, and parts of their lost selves in the chosen partner, but the credits roll, and we are left to believe that the romance lasts.

In a conscious relationship, we get to reclaim aspects of ourselves that were repressed, at the same time that we are giving our partner what they need, no matter how challenging it is (within reason), or how much it seems like it is against the grain of our personality or who we have understood ourselves to be—then we heal ourselves, and the other person in the process. In giving your partner what it is that they need, they feel that unconditional love and responsiveness. In other words, we get to stretch ourselves to meet their needs, being willing to access the parts of us that are currently unavailable or currently not accessed. Carl Jung said, "The meeting of two personalities is like the contact of two chemical substances: If there is any reaction, both are transformed." It isn't always easy, but in this way, we have an opportunity to discover beautiful aspects of ourselves and of our partner that are currently lying buried, waiting to be mined.

The scarlet macaw protests when they are not being attended to—the more their pain, struggle, and loneliness goes unrecognized and unacknowledged, the more aggressive they become. To one extent or another, that is each of us in a relationship when ignored or unseen. Maybe they can eat what is toxic to other animals and birds, in part because of the power of their bonds, as much as the power of the clay.

SECRET #5 TO HOT PARTNERING: PAY ATTENTION TO YOUR PARTNER, AND CARE FOR THEM BEYOND YOUR OWN COMFORT.

BIRD'S EYE VIEW: GENE & LYNNE

My husband, Gene, was born and raised in Southern California, and is third-generation Mexican-American. His great-grandfather trooped across the border with two of his siblings and his grandfather then established a name for himself in the olive and palm tree business, becoming an established figure that would pal around with the likes of James Cagney, at the time when Mexicans were not allowed to sit on the lower level of the movie houses. My husband was born in 1971, to a couple who were both just 24 years old, and who already had four other children. They prided themselves on not speaking Spanish in their home, so that the kids would have no trace of accent and be fully American. Gene was notably different from his siblings, where his two other brothers were solid figures in the peewee league; and into high school, Gene recalls, with tears in his eyes, the two years he played football, and the regret of feeling that he had to attempt to live up to his family's expectations. He felt truly seen when someone in his first-grade class told him that the dragon he drew was amazing. He is an artist at heart, prone to melancholy, deeply spiritual, and adept at seeing and living in worlds that are not the one that most people inhabit. He has felt misunderstood by most people, including his family. He is brooding, gentle, and most often kind—sometimes when he shouldn't be.

As expected, I am pretty much the opposite. The same year that my husband was born, my father and his wife kidnapped my brother and two sisters and me, taking us from Deerfield, Illinois to an Indian reservation in Northern Wisconsin. After my birth, my mother had a series of health problems, both physical and mental. She fell in a deep depression when my father had left her pregnant and about to give birth to her fourth child. For much of my first seven years, my mother was in and out of hospitals, enduring surgeries and wrestling to keep the family afloat without a career and a husband, but firmly with depression at her side. Often, that left my siblings and me with grandparents but at times very alone; and my second-oldest sister was attempting to juggle the demands of being a child and a mother as well. My father remarried when I was four, to a woman who had recently divorced and had four children of her own. Prior to the kidnapping day, he had taken my brother and sisters and I on visitations, and made periodic appearances in our lives. One night, he got a call from a concerned policeman, informing him that his children were going to be placed in foster care unless he came to get them. He and my stepmother flew down to get us. There had been a storm, with the trees blowing and scratching the window, and frightened, my older sister had called the police to make sure it wasn't a break in. After numerous calls to the house, the officer realized that we were often neglected and needed consistent care.

When I got to the Indian reservation in Northern Wisconsin, where I had my new home, I was now the youngest of eight children. I got lost in the shuffle, feeling as though I was an afterthought most of the time. My stepmother and I were like oil and water. I'm sure she felt confused as to how to mother me, and then rejected when she would reach for me. I wouldn't want to hug her, because I missed my mother. As a result, I became the scapegoat.

To compensate for feelings of worthlessness and feeling not very believed in, I worked hard to make myself incredibly valuable in my career and to other people. It was my way of trying to prove that I was valuable and, maybe someday, get my stepmother's approval or validation. That never came, but by then, I didn't need it from her, and I understood that she gave all she had to give to me, and I had hit wounds from her own childhood. The truth is that we were more alike than either of us ever admitted to each other. I became fiercely independent, not needing anyone.

My husband unconsciously devised another strategy. He pushed back against being what he was expected to be, and got comfortable with not being understood and fitting in. Instead, he built an active fantasy life, creating worlds inside of himself and in his dream that fed his art.

He thrived on affection and validation. So, he set up being an artist, where he would face constant rejection, questioning his talent and his worth, validating that he wasn't amounting to much when it didn't translate financially, and deeply caring about his value being acknowledged by others. And he chose me to consistently push for him to perform and make money, giving him the idea that he isn't valuable when he doesn't.

We have the same core wound. The way in which we both express that wound and protect it may appear to be opposite, but it is the same. What is required of me then is that I reach towards him, nurture, and show affection—even when I want to retreat into my work and my own world. In turn, he gets to step up and provide for our family, not to prove his worth or value, but because it matters to him. He gets to show me that I can count on him being there for me, in ways I felt like I could never count on my family. And I get to show him that he is accepted and loved for who he is, not for what he does. We get to stretch ourselves to heal the other's core wounds. It's not always comfortable or easy, but when we do it well, both of us are growing. Elizabeth Gilbert says it this way:

"This is what intimacy does to us over time. That's what a long marriage can do: It causes us to inherit and trade each other's stories."[11]

When you begin to see that you chose your partner as much for what drives you crazy about them as what you appreciate, even more so, you have unlocked the key to staying in it for the long haul. Now, dig in deeper to your own work, discovering a type of invincibility in your love. In Chapter Six, I'm delighted to say that you will learn some very real ways to heal your partner's core wounds, and authentically hear each other. I know I can't be the only one who feels like my husband and I are speaking in different languages at times. If you feel something similar, then Chapter Six will provide some very real solutions.

THE BIRDS

1. The Scarlet Macaw protests loudly when not given attention and time. What has your partner been protesting? Lack of sex? Lack of acknowledgement? Lack of support?

2. What have you been protesting? Where do you feel like you are not being seen or attended to?

3. The Scarlet Macaw can eat what is toxic to other animals and birds. What is toxic right now in your life? What would feel more tolerable if your partner were providing you with what you needed?

THE BEES

This exercise is an adaptation from an exercise in "Getting the Love You Want" workbook, by Harville Hendrix and Helen LaKelly Hunt. If you find it valuable and would like to explore the Imago further, pick up that workbook.

1. Before completing these questions, please read this entire paragraph, and then give yourself some quiet space alone to be in contemplation. Turn off the lights, lie down, put on soft music, and just let your mind think of everything pertaining to your early caregivers. Then, after a period of at least ten minutes of contemplation time, take out your journal and complete the following.

    Bring to mind your childhood home. Think of everything exactly as it was when you were a child—each room of the home, your backyard. What are the smells and sounds of your home? Perhaps you remember the feel of couch cushions, or the carpet from when you played on the floor. Envision it through the eyes of a child. Think of your mother and father and other important caregivers. What are the positive traits of your mother, the traits that you admire? What are the positive traits of your father? What are the negative traits of your mother? What are your father's negative traits? Is there anyone else who influenced you powerfully as a child? What were that person's negative and positive traits? What did you get angry about? See your early caregivers with a newfound clarity and wisdom.

2. List both the POSITIVE and NEGATIVE traits of all of your early caregivers, using simple adjectives to describe them, like: powerful, loving, nurturing, funny, etc.

3. Think of POSITIVE experiences and behaviors that occurred with your early caregivers, and then write the feelings that you experienced with each of those experiences or behaviors (loved, safe, happy, appreciated, valued, etc.). Do the same with the NEGATIVE experiences and behaviors. What were the feelings associated with each of those experiences (angry, sad, hurt, helpless, etc.)?

4. What is it that you needed that you did not get from your caregivers? (value, attention, love, nurturing, affection, etc.)

5. Now look at the POSITIVE and NEGATIVE traits. Circle those that your partner also shares (or are the total opposite; for example, quiet/internal instead of loud/charismatic, or calm/logical instead of angry/emotional).

6. When your partner is enacting the NEGATIVE traits, you may respond exactly as you responded with your early caregivers when they failed to give you what you lacked. When you respond to that lack, your partner continues with more of the negative behaviors, and you feel more and more like you are not getting what it is you need.

7. Allow it to sink in. This is the tip of the iceberg with the Imago. You chose the perfect partner to heal you, and in healing your partner, you also experience your own healing.

TAKE FLIGHT

6. Share what you have written in your journal with your partner. Listen to be in discovery of your partner. Remember you have no need to argue or defend anything. This is your partner's work that they are doing from their family of origin. You are simply the space to allow them to finally heal those wounds. Listen compassionately, and see if you can uncover what a "perfect" fit your partner actually is.

Sometimes it may not be readily apparent how your partner carries the traits of your mother or father. If that is the case, look for exact opposites. For example, if my mother and father were hippies, where there was little structure in my childhood, I may have a partner who is meticulous and exacting in details, liking things to be in a certain order. At times, we will gravitate towards what seems to be the exact opposite but is actually motivated from a similar place within. To further clarify, if my father was an alcoholic, and I yearned to escape, at sixteen years old, I may marry an alcoholic, because the chaos and life with addiction has become comfortable to me. Or I may marry the preacher's son, who never allows a drop of alcohol to enter the home. Either way, my reaction to growing up in an alcoholic household is determining the choice. Allow yourself to be present with why you chose the partner that you did, and what is necessary for healing for both of you.

2. Choose a Partner A, and a Partner B.

   Partner A, tell Partner B the story of how you met, taking at least five full minutes. What were your first impressions of your partner? What was it about your partner that had him/her stand out? How did you begin dating?

   Partner B, listen without interrupting. Notice how your partner may remember different details. Did you realize that is why your partner was attracted to you? What did you know of this story, and what didn't you know? How does this story differ from your version?

   Switch partners. Now, Partner B, tell your version of the same story, not "correcting" your partner, but rather telling how you experienced your partner, what stood out, and moved you.

   Partner A, how do your stories differ? How does your partner see it or you differently? Did you realize that was why your partner was attracted to you?

CHAPTER SIX

Till Death Do Us Part

"Oysters don't produce pearls because they want to make something beautiful. Pearls are the byproduct of an attempt to reduce their irritation (a grain of sand). Like the action of the oyster in response to the sand, self-soothing turns marriage's irritants into useful and productive relationship gems."
– David Schnarch[1]

In other words, expect to have irritants in your relationship. That's me being Captain Obvious. But David Schnarch takes it farther than most of us can imagine: Those irritants become the treasures of your relationship. Does that seem crazy from where you are sitting right now? It's not. In fact, most couples who have been married for decades will tell you something similar, just not in those words. Unfortunately, too many relationships break up before those gems are transformed. No question, it requires alchemy, and that process must come from within. But if you want to have a relationship where you mine the gems, and a love story that lasts for a lifetime, then that is what must occur. The Canada Goose is just the bird to teach us about lifelong love.

After all, hunters believe the Canada Goose to be the smartest of all birds. Human beings have quite a lot to learn from the Canada Goose, and we would probably be happier if we did. Let's start with the vocal variety: This honker has at least ten distinctive calls, and the male and female have very different voices. Anyone who has lived on the migration path of the Canada Goose can attest to the fact that they use their voices well.

The Canada Goose can travel up to 1000 kilometers a day while migrating, meaning that they could travel around the entire world in just 40 days.[2] Much has been written about their famous V-shaped formation, including the fact that it is more energetically efficient, with the air created by the front birds, giving lift to the birds behind them. They are said to take turns in the lead, giving each other breaks when needed at the back of the formation.

Instead of going extinct, they have managed to thrive WITH human beings, and have grown from less than 500,000 in the late 1980s, to over 5 million today. There is no doubt about it; these birds are in it for the long haul—in terms of distance that they can travel, and in beating the odds of extinction.[3]

But now for the real amazement: They are in it for the long haul in relationships. They are entirely monogamous throughout their relatively long lives. In the words of bird lady, Sharon Sorenson:

"Monogamous birds, Canada Geese remain loyal, even in injury, until death.

If a hunter's shot wounds a Canada Goose and brings the bird down, its mate drops from the flock to attend, and stays behind until the wound heals, or the mate dies—tender but heart-wrenching to watch.

I am certain, in spite of my being accused of carrying too much human emotional baggage, that these two gorgeous creatures feel a caring, if not a loving bond, for one another. Nothing will convince me otherwise.[4]

Let's start there. In *The Year of the Greylag Goose,* Dr. Konrad Lorenz, who devoted his life to studying geese, made it clear that in his entire time of studying geese, he only witnessed three times when a pair split up after breeding and raising their young. In two of the three instances, it was because the gander had previously lost his first great love. Lorenz observed and was moved by the fact that geese have a "human capacity" for grief. Like human beings who are enduring grief, geese become more vulnerable to accidents when grieving, flying into high-tension cables, or falling prey to predators because of reduced mental alertness.[5]

There are heart-wrenching articles describing pair bonds so strong that if one goose is shot down by a hunter, the partner will circle back and ignore the sound of shooting to return and die with its mate. And in *The Pig Who Sang to the Moon,* Jeffrey Moussaieff wrote about a goose who had broken a wing during the fall migration. As the other geese flew south, her gander traveled with her by air and by foot. Unable to fly, the goose was walking south, and he would periodically fly, calling to her with his wildest piercing cry, urging her to take flight. When she didn't fly, he would double back and walk with her. He did this until she was killed by carrion eagles. Only then did he continue his journey alone. [6]

Geese grieve. And they are great models for us as human beings that love doesn't end, and that grief is a process. So it is when we end relationships, divorce, or if our partner dies. Grief is one of the most challenging things to understand since it is unique to every person. It is a lonely journey that must be traveled alone, and that each person experiences in radically distinct ways. This book is not about grieving the loss of a partner or remarrying, although there are many good books on the subject. But since we all grieve in many ways, it is important to touch on.

We my grieve the loss of a career, the loss of a dream, the loss of a child, or even the loss of a partner. If you are in an intimate partnership with a partner who is grieving, it can be lonely and confusing. You want to support your partner and be there for them, but you may not know what your partner needs. At the same time, you may simply want them to return back to "themselves." There is no timeline for grief, and many people believe that grieving a partner or child doesn't ever end; we simply proceed with our heart slightly broken, like the goose who eventually moves on but is always in mourning. Needless to say, it's important that the person grieving get support, join a grief group, or engage in counseling. Likewise, it is important for the other partner to get support while they patiently hold space for the other partner's process.

If you are in relationship with a person who lost a partner, The Beatles probably said it well:

"Though I know I'll never lose affection,
For people and things that went before,
I know I'll often stop and think about them,
In my life, I'll love you more."[7]

In other words, you will need to be okay in sharing your partner—especially if that partnership or marriage was beautiful for them. That person has made room in their heart for another, and you must do the same. There will always be a "third" in the relationship. That doesn't mean that you are in competition, or that your partner doesn't love you. It means that your partner has made room in their heart to love two people concurrently, since love doesn't end. Just as you wouldn't want your partner to stop loving you after you die, they still love the other person. But that doesn't mean that they do not love you.

It does mean that you get to make peace with another person being a part of your relationship, and be secure enough to know that your partner loves you. When they share memories, or have a look of sadness wash over them, or tears, it doesn't mean that they do not want to be with you or are not happy with you. It means they are missing their other love, and need you to understand that loss. Love means sharing our partner with our children, the world, and sometimes a past partner. It also means being there for them in their grief, and sharing their love for a lost partner. That is love.

Throughout this book, I have discussed the fact that we all have wounding from our childhood, not because our parents were horrible or did or did not do deliberate things to hurt us. No matter how perfect the parent, we all made up interpretations that did not serve us. Each of us constructed beliefs about ourselves, other people, and the world around us that are not necessarily true. But then we begin to interact with those beliefs like they are absolutely true, and we generate evidence to substantiate our viewpoint, and maintain our paradigm and comfort zone.

You are probably more acutely aware of your own wounding than you are of your partner's wounding, but it is important that you bring your wound totally to the surface to understand all of the ways this impacts you in your relationship today. This is the heart of having compassion for your partner. The poet, Rumi, says it quite well when he writes:

"Be truthful now.
See yourself as you plainly are.
You've got a hidden wound,
And this is no time for posing.

When inward tenderness
Finds that secret hurt,
The pain itself will crack the rock
And AH! Let the soul emerge."[8]

This is the heart of having patience, understanding, and a depth in your partnership. Most of the arguments that we have as couples have nothing to do with what we are arguing about. In the same week, I had two couples in therapy sessions—one couple with an argument about *haystacks*, a Seventh Day Adventist, favorite crowd-pleasing food, on tortilla chips, adding a meat-alternative or beans, cheese, and going from there.[9] Another couple, that same week, was in an argument over pancakes. Was it just a bad week for food? No. What we argue about seems like it is about the things around us or situations, but ultimately, most arguments come down to our core wound. In one case, the wife was angry because she feels like she isn't seen as valuable, with her opinions mattering. The husband was feeling unworthy, like he could never really contribute anything of value. They argued about the food as a cover for the real wound. So it is with most of us when we get into the *dance* of arguing that we do with our partner. Our wound is always near the surface, and we have brought our partner to us to support in healing that wound. Then, when your partner flies off the handle about the trash not being taken out, or if you are devastated that your partner didn't consult you about the restaurant you are going to, you can realize it has very little to do with what is actually being discussed. It is the core wound that we attempt to cover up but so desperately want our partner to see and heal. So this is the heart of the matter.

In *The Comfort of Strangers,* Ian McEwan says it this way:

"...they knew each other as much as they knew themselves, and their intimacy, rather like too many suitcases, was a matter of perpetual concern; together they moved slowly, clumsily, effecting lugubrious compromises, attending to delicate shifts of mood, repairing breaches. As individuals, they didn't easily take offense; but together they managed to offend each other in surprising, unexpected ways; then the offender—it had happened twice since their arrival—became irritated by the cloying susceptibilities of the other, and they would continue to explore the twisting alleyways and sudden squares in

silence, and with each step, the city would recede as they locked tighter into each other's presence."[10]

No one manages to hit our raw spots and ram their fingers into our wounds better than our partner. With everyone else, we may express infinite patience and radiate light, but with our partner, while the blood is once again oozing from the perpetually open wound, we are pushed to the edge. I've been there—that was the moment I spoke of in the preamble to this book, with me holding the angel in my hand as I decorated the Christmas tree, feeling horrified at the things that my husband and I were saying to each other.

In my first eight years, my genius mother (Mensa verified) was intent on teaching me much, meaning that there were constant corrections. Add to that, my father and stepmother and I felt like no matter what I did as a child, I would never matter or be good enough to get the attention and approval I craved. I now hold myself to impossible standards. At times, I have been a belligerent task master, demanding perfection in everything I do. I have internalized my stepmother, or some extreme version of her in my mind, and I can be incredibly hard on myself. I tend to replay mistakes over and over again, desperate for a chance to re-do the moment or redeem myself. I have learned to have compassion for myself, but this lesson is painfully slow at times. For years, I thought that if someone volunteered to help me with something, it meant they thought I couldn't do it, and I would get defensive. I heard the slightest criticism as reasons that I would never be good enough or lovable. Apologies to my first two long-term boyfriends in my twenties; I was clueless and blissfully not self-aware. In other words, I blamed them for everything. Let me be clear; I didn't walk around advertising what I am telling you. I looked like I was successful, competent, and put-together. That was the cover story I wanted everyone to believe.

What that means is that at times, I STILL hear suggestions or criticisms as though my husband were attacking me. He is not. It also means that I STILL project that I am invincible and can do anything, but then when I get sick, and he admonishes me for not giving myself more time off, I get angry, feeling as though he expects me to be Wonder Woman. And yes, it means that I STILL expect everything to be perfect, according to my standards, with him at times, which is exhausting for him. If I was unaware of those wounds and the way they creep to the surface, it would be a nightmare. If he was unaware of them, it would have quickly been a recipe for disaster. God, it's gotten much better, thanks to good loving, good work, and awareness, and maybe by the time my husband and I are complete in this lifetime, it will be relaxed to almost nil. And yes, gradually I am making progress on Gene's... but he already has enough of his life shown to the world—I'll keep the focus only on my wound at this moment.

Lauren Oliver, in a beautiful piece of fiction, based of course on the reality we all live, wrote:

"I wonder if this is how people always get close: They heal each other's wounds; they repair the broken skin."[11] Yes, if we are caring for each other, like Canada Geese, we stay with our partner through the wound. We do not divorce. We do not run. Because, ultimately, we are just running from our own wounds.

My mom and dad divorced. My mother never remarried. Both my stepmother and father stuck it out on their third try. Nope, it's no surprise that I am an advocate for sticking it out. That being said, no one is in charge of someone else's happiness. I am incredibly happy that my father and stepmother found love that gave them joy before they left this earth. I wouldn't be married unless my husband had divorced! And I also believe that there is a possibility inherent in every relationship, especially when we care enough to walk down the aisle and declare our commitment to the world. I'm not guessing the percentage, but I believe that many that split could have found the hidden gems if they worked at it.

BIRD'S EYE VIEW: TIM & CAROLE

When my cell phone rang, it was a call from a man from New York, who has been tortured because he cheated on his wife some years back and has realized that he has since been building walls, keeping everyone out. Tim described to me feeling shame, knowing he is not honest and thinking that he is a fraud. His question was whether or not he could tell his wife and not lose her, as well as whether or not the Couples Retreats could support.

I shared with Tim about the courage I have witnessed with couples who are willing to be fully revealed, including their mistakes, affairs, desires, and shame. In fact, he actually called as I was writing about infidelity in an earlier chapter.

Here's the thing: Tim wanted to use the Couples Retreat to reveal his affair. That was his way of manipulating the situation to control her response. I explained that Carole deserved her reaction, whatever it may be—not to have her reaction managed or finessed in any way. Using the Couples Retreat as a way to re-build and re-establish trust could be a powerful opening for the relationship, instead of Tim having a hidden agenda for getting his wife to the retreat. That is just another way that Tim would be hiding from her. I recommended the book, *After the Affair,* and the section, "Should I Reveal the Affair or Keep it Hidden?" This chapter powerfully makes a case for when to keep an affair concealed, as well as when you can reveal it. I can easily say that I have collected ample evidence to validate that "the truth will set you free," but I also know that the choice must come from within that person.

Tim learned as a kid that the only way he'd be cared for was if he manipulated for attention, often acting out in school and hiding it, until his parents found out and were outraged. Then he would need to find a way to manipulate them to bring them back round again. He was repeating the pattern with Carole. And when Carole expressed that she felt she was being pushed away, Tim felt the same shame he felt as a kid when he disappointed his parents.

Meanwhile, Carole felt like she had to be perfect to be loved. Her mother was a perfectionist, and her father left at an early age. Carole felt that, at some level, she couldn't trust men to be there for her, and unless she was perfect, she would not be loved. This was the pattern she was repeating with Tim. The more she tried to be perfect, the more rigid she got, becoming focused on little details instead of the big picture. Then Tim, feeling ignored, would look elsewhere for attention, unconsciously destroying his relationship and needing to hide himself.

As we spoke, Tim reminded me about the beautiful tradition in Japan, of Kintsugi, where damaged ceramic objects are repaired by filling cracks, chips, and missing pieces with gold. In other words, they highlight the scars that came through life experiences, and see the *imperfection* as making the object more beautiful. This is the practice of Wabi Sabi, loving ourselves, partners, and friends, even with the flaws we have, and especially with those flaws. When an honored guest comes to the home, they are given the privilege of drinking from the cup that has been repeatedly broken and repaired with gold, because it has the most *character*.[12] I added that too often, when the cup is broken in our society, we want to get another cup instead of realizing that the gold is only added where there are fissures. The deeper the break, the more gold.

SECRET #6 OF HOT MONOGAMY – TEND EACH OTHER'S WOUNDS.

To get clear on your wound, I would like you to give yourself permission to remember some of the things that you may not always like to remember or think about. I would like you to curl up somewhere where you feel a sense of comfort and peace, perhaps with a blanket over you, and soft music playing in the background. I am going to ask you to take moments while you are reading, to set down the book and allow yourself to fully delve into the images that you are creating in your own mind. I am asking that you allow memories to envelope you, so that you have a full experience of remembering what it felt like as a child in moments when you felt afraid, insecure, ashamed, hurt, or sad. If you set down the book for a while, whenever it feels right to pick it up again and continue reading the next paragraph, do so. If you want to set it down after reading each paragraph, allowing yourself to envision what I am asking you to envision, then do so. Follow whatever process works for you in actually remembering what you felt as a child.

Quite often, when I do experiential trainings, people will say that they have no memory of their childhood. The more that we insist that we have no memory of our childhood, the more that will be so. The unconscious mind is totally wise. Often, your unconscious will withhold memories until it is fully certain that you are in a place to handle the memory and deal with it. Other times, our unconscious gives us glimpses of memories, or flickers, like a movie briefly shown in fast motion. But many times, people discount these images or flashes, and continue to insist that there are no memories. The more that you ignore your unconscious, discounting or diminishing what it gives to you, the more it may retreat. Our unconscious communicates through symbols and images. As such, it may not always make sense to you, but if you sit with an image, the power of that symbol may come through. First, you get to tell your unconscious that you are ready to listen to whatever it has to give you, and that you may have been stubborn and pushed it away, but now you are ready for its wisdom. If you simply allow whatever is there to bubble forth, without pressuring yourself or berating yourself, saying, "I never remember; I can't remember," then there is a chance that images may come forth. It doesn't need to be entire memories told like a movie script. It may be a smell. It may be the flash of a visual, or remembering a feeling in your body. Trust whatever is there for you, and give yourself permission to explore the image, letting go of whether or not it is "true," but holding on to why this image would present to you in this moment. In other words, be patient with yourself in this process.

If you would like to listen to this meditation, please go to Birds & Bees Extras, at www.Lynneesheridan.com.

Okay, make yourself comfortable. Take a few deep breaths in and out, breathing in relaxation and breathing out tension. Allow yourself a minute or two to fully relax in this moment. Now, I want you to bring to mind your earliest childhood home that you can remember—perhaps it is the home you lived in when you were about five, six, or seven years old, or perhaps it is even earlier. I want you to see yourself as a child in that home, and envision that everything looks exactly as it did when you were a child. If you want to take a moment and close your eyes, please do so. Just see your childhood home and everything exactly as it was when you were a child.

Now I ask that you envision yourself in a particular room in your house, in a dark or disturbing moment. Maybe you are in the living room, and you are cowering in a corner of the couch. Maybe you are in your bedroom, sobbing into a wet pillowcase. Maybe you are in the kitchen, memorizing the pattern on the floor as your mother yells at you. Envision a dark moment from your childhood. Let me remind you that you are safe in this moment and nothing can hurt you. But in your mind's eye, go back to that moment.

First envision a moment with your mother. It is a moment when you do not feel safe, cared for, or loved. Maybe it is a moment when you feel you have disappointed her in some way. Maybe it is a moment when she is unfairly accusing you of something you did not do. Maybe it is a moment when she is yelling at you for not doing something, or she is angry. See yourself in that moment. Envision your mother, and think about what you notice. Do you notice the wallpaper on the wall? Do you remember the feeling of the couch on the back of your legs?

Do you remember smelling what was cooking for dinner, or hearing a television in the distance? What is present with the memory?

How do you remember feeling? Do you remember feeling small? Perhaps you were ashamed or embarrassed? Maybe you felt shut down? Did you feel angry? Did you feel smothered?

What do you notice about your mother from this moment? Is she controlling? Is she overdramatic? Is she belligerent? Is she a coward? Is she weak or needy? What do you see about your mother in that moment?

Now I want you to remember a moment with your father that was not bright or beautiful, but dark and frightening or hurtful. It is a moment that may make your skin crawl or suck the breath from you. It is a moment when you may not have felt safe, loved, or cared for. You may have felt endangered, hurt, angry, or sad.

Envision yourself in a particular room in your home. Maybe it is the garage, and your father is yelling at you for not filling up the car after you used it. Maybe you are in the living room, and you are being lectured on something you didn't do that you were supposed to do. Maybe it is in your bedroom, and you feel cornered or small. I want to remind you that you are safe in this moment, and nothing can hurt you. But in your mind, I ask that you go back to that moment.

Notice your father. What is the predominant experience of your father in this dark moment? Maybe he is spanking you for doing something wrong, and you feel humiliated and small, laid over his knee. Maybe it is when your report card came in, and he is disappointed in you and saying that he isn't really sure that you will amount to much of anything. Maybe his footsteps are thundering down the hallway, and you are cowering because you know that he is always angry at something. What do you notice about that moment you are thinking of? Close your eyes if you want to really bring that moment clear.

What do you notice? Do you notice the color of the carpet and the feel of it on your toes? Do you notice the smell of your father's after-shave? Do you notice the temperature of the room or what season it is? What do you remember?

How do you feel in that moment? Do you feel small? Are you ashamed? Do you feel shut down? Do you feel smothered? Do you experience anger? In that moment, is your father a bully? Is he impatient? Is he demanding? Is your father the center of attention? Is he needy or wimpy? What do you see about your father in that moment? Remind yourself that you are safe in this moment.

Check in with yourself. Is there someone else who impacted you deeply as a child? Perhaps there is someone else who did something to hurt you; maybe they are in your home, and maybe they are not. I want you to envision some dark moment with that person. Take in all of the information from that moment. What did you feel? What were the negative qualities or characteristics of that other person? Did you feel fear? Sadness? Hurt? Loneliness? Just be present to what that child took on in that moment, and remind yourself that you are safe in this moment.

Now take a deep breath in, bringing yourself fully to the here and now. Gently bring yourself out of that space, and go right to your journal. I promise that by the end of Chapter 7, you will have a very practical tool to heal your partner and begin to put balm on the wounds.

THE BIRDS and THE BEES

1. Allow yourself to feel whatever you felt when you were with each of your caretakers in each of those dark moments. Were you afraid you wouldn't be cared for? That you would be neglected? Were you afraid that one of them would leave you? Were you afraid that the love of one of them would smother you? Were

you shamed or belittled by your mother or father? Were you made to feel guilty for something? Were you invisible to your mom or dad? Did you feel like you had no value? Maybe your fear is that you would be criticized, ostracized, or dominated by them? Maybe you thought they would realize you were defective and want to "send you back?" Perhaps you felt unloved? Maybe you were terrified of being separated from them? Perhaps you felt like you were being drained by your mother or father— depleted. Write down the deepest fear that you had with each of your caretakers. It may be a different fear for each of your caretakers.

2. Now describe your childhood wound as you understand it. Describe your deepest fear, in detail. Describe incidents from your childhood that caused those fears. What were other incidents from your childhood that reinforced that fear? And be sure to describe what occurs for you when your deepest fears are triggered. Make sure that you include your deepest unfulfilled desires. Describe how you felt when you didn't get what you wanted most as a child (love, attention, validation, etc.). Include any and all information to support your partner in understanding you and your wound. (Examples of fears: Were you afraid you wouldn't be cared for? Were you afraid you'd be neglected? Abandoned? Rejected? Smothered? Were you afraid you'd be shamed or belittled? Were you afraid you were invisible? Were you afraid you had no value? Were you afraid you'd get things wrong? Were you afraid you were unloved? Were you afraid they'd control you? Were you afraid they'd realize you were defective? Were you afraid of being depleted? Being separate from them? Being used by them?)

TAKE FLIGHT

1. Create a safe and supportive environment that is reverent and sacred, with candles, soft music, and space where you and your partner will not be interrupted. Let go of anything else from this day, and take some time to get fully present that this could be one of the most important things that you do with your partner for your relationship. The space is not casual; it is sacred, allowing your partner to fully reveal their deepest hurts

   When you are both truly present to your partner, the first partner, Partner A, is going to gently cradle Partner B in your lap, as though you are cradling a precious child in your lap. Make sure that you position your partner so that you can look into their eyes and remain connected and seeing them through this process, providing comfort and remaining intimate, with eye contact much of the time.

   Partner B is going to communicate your childhood wound. Set down your journal and speak from your heart, allowing all of the feelings to be brought forth in that moment. Partner A, you are simply listening, comforting your partner and validating how they felt, empathizing with how that must have felt. Ask questions empathetically to better support and know your partner. When Partner B is done speaking (allow at least ten minutes), Partner A, hold and rock your partner, like this is the last moment that you would ever have with each other. Take at least fifteen minutes just holding each other.

2. When you are ready, switch partners, with Partner B cradling Partner A, with eye contact and connection, empathetically listening, validating their feelings, and comforting Partner A (allow at least ten minutes again). Partner A, speak from your heart, and set aside any notes. Just communicate fully from your heart, with your partner. Then, Partner B, hold and rock your partner, realizing

the treasure that you have, and how that wound is often so near the surface.

CHAPTER SEVEN

Listen More Than You Talk

"The most basic of all human needs is the need to
understand and be understood.
The best way to understand people is to listen to them."
– Ralph Nichols[1]

When you think of the Mute Swan, it's likely that you think of *The Ugly Duckling,* the story by Hans Christian Anderson, of how an ugly duckling grew into a beautiful swan, admired and finally accepted.[2] From that work, and from simply watching them skim across the water with grace, swans are elegant representations of what it is to be beautiful. There is the famous ballet *Swan Lake,* with ballerinas delicately mirroring the floating and arching, as swans.[3] But there is more to the Mute Swan than beauty.

First, despite the name, they are not really mute; they have a variety of calls, and can even hiss like a snake when their territory or mate is threatened, and the sound of their wings in flight is like a humming or soft singing.

When courting, they gently touch their bills and breasts together until a romantic heart shape is formed, necks entwined. The female does most of the incubating of the eggs, but the male gives her breaks to go feed. Both parents take care of the young once the eggs hatch, and at times, you may see baby swans riding on their parents' backs. The young can fly by four or five months, but they remain with their parents through the first winter anyway.

Yes, they are monogamous and pair for life; however, they do "divorce," and when one mate dies, the other will find another partner. They are very territorial during breeding, and the male will actively attack other birds, dogs, and people to protect their mate. Swans are famous for being fiercely loyal to each other, and as a pair, will gang up on intruders, getting better year after year at protecting their nest and young.[4]

In other words, they are fiercely loyal. Loyalty is a matter of both principle and sentiment, according to its etymological roots, meaning that it shows up as allegiance in both principle and actions. This happens to be one of my strong suits: I am fiercely loyal. Some would say that I am insanely loyal. It definitely takes me awhile to give complete trust and be "all in" with someone, which is a not-so-hot trait of mine. But once that person has shown me, through their integrity, principles, and actions that they are sound, I am unabashedly go-to-the-ends-of-the-earth, defend-them-to-the-death loyal. Sometimes it has taken me years to realize that perhaps I should have questioned more at times. But that is the nature of loyalty.

Loyalty in a partnership means thinking about your partner in favorable ways. You are not focusing on what they have done wrong, or things that drive you crazy. You are actively focusing on what you love about them.

Loyalty means speaking favorably about your partner and giving them the benefit of the doubt. It means that if someone is bitching, moaning, and complaining about their partner, you don't join in and throw your own partner under the bus so that you can join misery's company. It doesn't mean that you complain about your partner to others, or make jokes at the expense of your partner. It means that your language shows your allegiance to your partner, even if you are presented with something that may seem questionable about your partner. You get to ask your partner directly about that thing, rather than take it from someone else. After all, you chose allegiance to your partner; that means even if there appears to be something that could shake that allegiance, you remain loyal, digging in with your partner rather than digging dirt with someone else.

Loyalty means acting consistent with your love and allegiance to your partner. It means going out of your way when you are tired. It means doing things you know they'd appreciate or enjoy, even if you don't (not pretending you enjoy it, but being with them while they enjoy it. I'm thinking of some movies my husband likes to watch, just as when he reads this sentence, he'll think of chick flicks he watches with me.).

No doubt, swans are loyal. They defend against intruders, share the parenting duties, return to the same territory year after year, and they are not quick to divorce.

So let's talk about why swans are said to divorce. The best answer right now applies to not only swans but barn owls and other traditionally monogamous birds. When a pair fails to produce any eggs, they often decide to give it a try elsewhere. But this isn't the first option; most pairs try repeatedly before they divorce.[5]

Human beings share a lot in common with swans. Do you know people who began talking about having children the minute they met their partner? They had always dreamed of a happy family, and now that there was a partner, that dream was becoming reality. But then children were not in the cards. Maybe you are experiencing this right now, or maybe you have good friends that are. For women, especially, the biological clock is always ticking, and there is a fear that if the window of opportunity is missed, it will be missed forever.

Maybe you and your partner have made making love into a scheduled time to hit ovulation, with about as much romance as basting a turkey. And often, with lesbian couples, the actual turkey baster comes in handy during these sessions. Then there is the waiting period, watching the clock, peeing on sticks, and praying. Then when the period comes, it seems like a final punctuation mark, ending hope until next month. Have you gone through this? I'm sure that all of us know couples caught in this cycle of hope, expectations, disappointment, loss, and grief. It can become all-encompassing and overwhelming.

Thankfully, I never had to endure that struggle. When I was a little girl, I used to tell my best friend, Julie Dobrinski, that I was going to be a stepmother or foster mother someday. I always had it in my mind that I wouldn't have children biologically, but I would definitely have children of my own. So, when I met my husband and he already had a son, Charlie, who was about one year old at that point, I thought it was absolutely perfect. Then, when Gene's ex-wife and her husband had their daughter, Caroline, a couple of years later, it was another joy that they named us to be the godparents. But that wasn't enough. We all decided that we didn't want to separate the kids over their lives for visitations at one house or the other. We then decided to raise both kids together, so that the kids could go back and forth between the houses. When they were younger, we all woke up together on Christmas morning, covered each other on vacations, and operated as a family. It's not perfect by any stretch of the imagination, but I feel incredibly blessed and grateful for our unique arrangement.

That being said, I can empathize with the struggle to have kids, and have witnessed it firsthand. My sister-in-law, Rosemary, and my brother, Jim, struggled to have children for years. If anyone should have been a mother, it is Rosemary. She is a homemaker extraordinaire, can fix just about anything in a house, and has huge amounts of love to give. I watched her and my brother go through attempt after attempt, with our family quietly sending love for every time it didn't work. That takes a toll on a relationship. They are not out of the woods yet, and the jury is still out on whether or not they will make it, and this is the story of many couples in our culture.

I am gently suggesting that when we meet our mate, we choose that person to be our family. This is challenging. Sometimes when we pick a partner, the choice is made on what they could be rather than what is in the moment. If she is studying to be a doctor, what a catch! If he is in line to take over his father's business, won't it be fantastic?! After all, princes and princesses are a catch because they are of royal lineage and are in line for the throne, or come with perks and privileges down the line. At times, our choice for a partner is chosen by what the future could be with that person, or by the past that we have shared together.

My husband, Gene, and his first wife, Lori, met in college and were best friends, as the story so often goes. At about eight years in, with the baby in their lap, they both simply looked at each other one day and said, "We don't want to be married to each other. We should have always just been best friends." Thankfully, they did marry, and we have Charlie, and even more thankfully, they divorced, so that they could find a partner that would support them, and they remain great friends. Gene and Lori still talk daily, and at times, she calls him when she is in crisis. I'm grateful that they share that connection. I'm sure you know stories of college or high school sweethearts, or people we partnered with because their families were best friends. There is nothing wrong with this, and many times it is successful. I am offering the possibility of choosing our partner by what is in the moment—not what could be or what has been. Maybe then there would be more patience for what did or did not unfold. Maybe then there would be a feeling that the partnership was enough, in and of itself. Maybe then there would be less disappointment of what was or was not realized.

If you are in the midst of building a family, having sex at regular intervals to hit ovulation just right, enjoy the journey. And when there is disappointment—because there always is disappointment about something—whether it is not getting pregnant, not getting a job, getting fired, or having family upsets, talk about it. It is beyond important that we don't just talk about what happened or didn't happen, but also talk about what we are feeling. It is challenging to express my own disappointment, hurt, and feelings that I am a failure or inadequate, but that is a real relationship. It is hard for my husband to open up about feeling like he is not enough or that he is disappointing himself, but when he does, we feel closer. We are sharing each other and knowing each other deeply, not just talking about things that we are doing or what is happening in that moment. There is an opportunity to listen beyond the words, to the music of his soul.

Let's look again at swans and their quiet courtship of bending necks and gently nudging each other. They do not honk or call, but simply glide across the surface of the water, side by side. I am using the Mute Swan to demonstrate that we have two ears and one mouth, and are meant to listen more than we speak.

As I am writing this chapter, I am present that this could be the Holy Grail of all possibilities for humanity. I am also present that the expression goes, "You teach what you most need to learn." I feel like I can spend a lifetime on listening and still be a novice with much room for growth. Ultimately, I am not paid for what I know or for being brilliant at presenting transformational distinctions; I am paid to listen to people, and I've found that the more acutely I listen to people, the more I earn my pay. I'll give you a tangible example of how poorly we listen as human beings. Most months, I facilitate a powerful workshop on living a life of transformation somewhere in the world. People come from all walks of life: CEOs, housewives, musicians, actors, authors, computer programmers, and just about every other profession you can think of is represented. A variety of ethnicities and cultures can be found, as well as ages and sexual orientation. There is a process on Friday night, where a game is played. It is a powerful game, ripe with opportunities for each participant to observe his or herself objectively, and how the choices that they are making, both conscious and unconscious, are impacting their lives. Prior to the designation of teams, and when I am outlining and explaining the game, I tell participants, AT LEAST six times, the purpose of the game and how to win it. I look each participant directly in the eye and say the same 20 words at least seven times, and then the game is played for a total of 30 minutes. At the end of the time period, I ask, "Who can tell me the exact words that I said about thirty-three minutes ago as to the purpose of the game and how to win?" Here is what happens most often: Initially, a few confidant people take the microphone and say a variety of things that they swore I said. Usually, how it plays out is that one after another, I tell them that it is not what I said. When the initial rush of confidence passes, people begin to think a little more deeply and start to question themselves. The hands that go up to answer the question are slower at this point. Many times, I will hear from up to twenty, and sometimes thirty, people, with no one saying the words that I said. Participants begin to realize that they have heard words other than the ones that I spoke, and that the words that they heard created a myriad of interpretations and experiences. I then bring up the point that if we did nothing else but see our listening, and how we often don't listen, or we hear only what we want to hear, it would be incredibly valuable. To put it mildly, when we are responding to what we believe someone is saying rather than what they are saying, there is a chance for massive miscommunication, misunderstandings, and unnecessary reactivity. I've noticed that Hollywood has a fascination with this scenario, with most chic flicks centered on a miscommunication that plays out for two hours. Often, when I go to the movies, and the audience is laughing, amused at how a simple communication could go so far off course, I am not laughing but find myself annoyed and wanting to get out of the theatre. I consistently get to witness, firsthand, the result of poor listening, and the pain that is created.

I'd like to start with listening from a couple of different vantage points. First, I want to start with listening to our own listening. What do I mean by that? Well, what do you listen for? Envision that you are talking to a girlfriend about her dreams and goals for her life. She tells you about traveling the world with a partner, being adventurous and at a hookah den in Marrakesh, and touring Tuscany on bicycles. When you ask her about what is stopping her, she says that she doesn't have the money, and that her family will not support her. She's afraid of traveling alone through Europe, and is worried about her safety. What do you hear? What do most people hear? Obstacles. Many people listen for obstacles, circumstances or reasons that something cannot happen or isn't possible. There are some listeners for possibility that would hear about her vision for her life, and that she didn't have the money or the support of her family, and was afraid, but they would focus instead on the possibility of their friend traveling the world.

What do you listen for in your partner? Do you listen to collect evidence of how your partner doesn't measure up to your expectations? Do you listen to be right about a belief you have about your partner? Do you listen for reasons as to why you shouldn't trust your partner? Do you listen to justify your own position in an argument?

Most of where we listen from has been in place since we were children. If you were in a home where a parent was a strong authoritarian, and there was always a *right* way to do everything, you might listen for people making you wrong, and then feel the need to defend yourself and be right. In other words, if that is your listening, you will hear right and wrong no matter what is coming out of the other person's mouth. Someone could be offering a helpful suggestion, but if you're listening through a filter of right and wrong, then you will hear that person making you wrong, and you will need to prove that you are right. In fact, you may be the one who ends up making others wrong.

If you were in a home where a parent did things for you, coddled you, and handled everything for you, then you may have received a subtle message that other people will do things for you, and that you are not capable of handling life on your own. You may begin to listen for reasons that you cannot do things or succeed. You may listen for people around you who you can depend on to handle things for you. And you may begin to listen for reasons that you cannot be self-sufficient or capable on your own. The other side of the coin is that you may attempt to prove how capable you are, and you may hear everything that is being said as someone questioning your capability; and as I shared earlier, you then may be on the defensive anytime someone offers assistance or support.

If you were in a home where you could not trust your parents or situations, you may then walk into any situation looking for reasons that you cannot trust people. In fact, out of your commitment to be right about your beliefs, you actually end up attracting situations and people to you, to then substantiate that framework. It's almost like we have a sign over our heads that reads: IF YOU ARE UNTRUSTWORTHY, THEN COME BE IN A RELATIONSHIP WITH ME. You then date that person, or initiate a relationship, they cheat, and you can once again affirm that people are untrustworthy. But you are the variable. There could be 98 trustworthy people in a room, and if you have a framework that people will screw you over, inevitably you will go for the two people who are not trustworthy, and then get to keep your belief in place—even if it is costing you dearly. At the same time, if you believe you can trust everyone, you may end up creating relationships that are trustworthy, or you may also end up generating relationships where people disappoint you by breaking your trust, and then you can yearn your whole life for the only people who you could trust: your parents. In other words, there is not one set way that our beliefs manifest. Sometimes our egos are very clever at disguising the pattern in our lives, so that we stumble into the same situations again and again, just with more and more interesting disguises to keep us from realizing that the person we are choosing is exactly the same.

I think a good place to start with listening is with a Korean parable, often quoted to illustrate an important quality of leadership. Yes, this is definitely an important quality of leadership, but more than that, it is a critical quality of listening and how closely leadership and listening are connected. This version of the story has been adapted throughout cultures and time.

The Sound of the Forest

Back in the third century A.D., King Ts'ao sent his son, Prince T'ai, to the temple to study under the great master, Pan Ku. Because Prince T'ai was to succeed his father as king, Pan Ku was to teach the boy the basics of being a good ruler. When the prince arrived at the temple, the master sent him alone to the Ming-Li forest. After one year, the prince was to return to the temple to describe the sound of the forest. When Prince T'ai returned, Pan Ku asked the boy to describe all that he could hear. "Master," replied the prince, "I could hear the cuckoos sing, the leaves rustle, the hummingbirds hum, the crickets chirp, the grass blow, the bees buzz, and the wind whisper and holler." When the prince had finished, the master shook his head and told him to go back to the forest to listen to what more he could hear. Had he not discerned every sound already? What more could there possibly be in listening? The prince was perplexed by his master's request, but being a devout disciple committed to growth, he surrendered. My God! What a boring assignment for a vibrant young prince!

Days and nights passed, with the prince on the forest floor. No exciting dates, balls, or battling of dragons. The dharma of this prince was to sit alone in the forest, listening with every ounce of who he was. Was the prince really listening? Was he caught up in his fantasies of pleasing his master? Was he reliving days past, when he was considered a "catch" and could oust any other prince in competition? Was he thinking of future days when he would recount what a stupendous listener he was? After all, he was the prince who listened to the forest for years on end. But the prince heard no sounds other than those he had already reported to his master, which he had heard in the first year of listening. (Does that sound familiar to those of you who have been married for years?)

One morning, which was not unlike the many other mornings he had endured in the forest, as the prince sat silently beneath the trees, he started to discern faint sounds unlike those he had ever heard before. The more acutely he listened, the clearer the sounds became, until he was shocked that he had missed hearing them for so long. All at once, the boy thought, "So this is what it feels to be enlightened!" His new awareness wrapped around him like a blanket from the cold. "These must be the sounds the master wished me to discern," he reflected.

When Prince T'ai returned to the temple, after welcoming him back, the master asked him what more he had heard. "Master," responded the prince reverently, "when I listened most closely, I could hear the unheard—the sound of flowers opening, the sound of the sun warming the earth, and the sound of the grass drinking the morning dew." The master nodded with approval. "To hear the unheard," remarked Pan Ku, "is a necessary discipline to be a good ruler. For only when a ruler has learned to listen closely to the people's hearts, hearing their feelings uncommunicated, pains unexpressed, and complaints not spoken of, can he hope to inspire confidence in his people, understand when something is wrong, and meet the true needs of his citizens. The demise of states comes when leaders listen only to superficial words and do not penetrate deeply into the souls of the people to hear their true opinions, feelings, and desires."[6]

This metaphor offers possibility for heads of state, heads of households, and every human being on our planet. I am quite certain that over the course of your lifetime, you have witnessed not only the demise of nations and rulers because of things unheard. As I write this book, there are battles raging in Syria, Lebanon, throughout the Middle East, and in the United States of America—because rulers didn't hear into the hearts of their people.

But what has been lost in your own relationships because of things unheard? What has been lost because we feel the need to get across our point of view or be right about our perspective? How often have you been engaged in an argument, waiting for your partner to complete what they are saying so that you can begin with the word, *but*. And even if you hear your partner and what they have said, and then you use the word, *but*, all that came before the "but" has been negated. You might as well have said, "All of that is well and good, but I am right, and what I am saying is the truth." The linguistic philosopher, Kathy Weingarten, defined *radical listening* as "authenticating—a way that is respectful, accepting, and welcoming; a way that searches for the unsaid as well as the said; the invisible as well as the visible." It is "helping a voice to be heard."[7] What could open up if you began to really listen to what your partner is saying from their perspective? What is possible in hearing what they are saying as well as what is unsaid?

What is lost when we hear something that isn't being said because of our own filters in listening? So, if I am afraid that I am incapable, and someone helps, I may bark back, "I've got it—do you think I'm stupid?!" If I don't feel worthy or good enough from some childhood wounding, and my partner asks, "Did you remember to buy the dog food?" then the response may be a sharp, "Yes, I bought the dog food—can't you trust that I am going to do things? I'm not a little kid." Or if we have a listening for needing to assert power, because we felt powerless as a child, then we may actually be keeping our partner small by handling everything—giving them a message that they are not capable, while we complain about how much there is for us to constantly handle. All of this, and more communication nightmares, are from not hearing into the heart of our partner, but instead, hearing from our own insecurities.

Yes, there is truth to what you are saying and feeling, and it is your truth. Likewise, there is truth to what your partner is saying, and it is their truth to be respected and heard just as much as yours deserves to be respected. Which truth is reality then? Or perhaps another way of looking at it is, which truth is NOT a possible reality?

I would like to offer a communication template to support you and your partner in hearing each other in disagreements and upsets, so that you are genuinely hearing what is usually not heard or held. The acronym for this communication template is I PAAVER, as in, I am the paver of the road to an intimate, connected, passionate relationship (yes, I added an A). First, let me be clear that while this tool is incredibly supportive, it is not THE ANSWER. Like any tool, this one can be used to create a masterpiece, or it can be used to wreak destruction, depending on whose hands it is in, and that person's intention. What I will say is that couples who have utilized this tool have created massive value in doing so. After the first Couples Retreat that I did, a couple, Tamara and Nancy, shared that they had typed it up on 3x5 index cards, laminated the cards, and had those cards in their glove compartments of their car, in the kitchen, living room— anywhere handy for when a disagreement or upset occurred. Through their contribution, every participant at retreats since then have received at least two laminated, 3x5 cards with this template, to start their collection. Here is the template, ready for you to make into your own set of 3x5 chances to avoid arguments where no one hears each other:

I   Partner A communicates an I message: I feel _____, when you _____.

P Partner B then **Paraphrases** and clarifies, saying what Partner A said, in their own words, then asking a question to better understand their partner.

A Partner A then makes **Adjustments** to the communication.

A Partner A **Acknowledges** feeling heard.

V Partner B then **Validates** the communication

E Partner B then **Empathizes** with Partner A's feelings.

R Partner A makes a **Request**, which Partner B can accept, decline, or negotiate.

First let me be clear that Partner B does the heavy lifting in this communication. If you are Partner B, you cannot argue, defend, or add in your justifications and explanations. What you are doing is authentically giving your partner space to communicate, and hearing your partner. You are more interested in who they are and what they have to say than you are in your position and being right. And in giving space for your partner to be heard, you will quickly realize that whatever the argument is supposedly about, it really isn't about the content of what you are arguing about.

Also, most often, Partner A and Partner B will go between Partner B **Paraphrasing** and clarifying, and Partner A making **Adjustments,** so that they are really heard, again and again. It isn't just the words or content being communicated; it is the feelings, and that often takes a little bit of digging to bring to the surface.

So let's say Partner A is the one who has the upset and needs to communicate, and they are the sender of the communication. Partner B is the receiver of the communication. Their job is not to engage or defend or argue, but to receive the communication and understand their partner better.

Partner begins with an **"I"** message that is as specific as possible. For example:

"I feel burdened and alone in this when you leave your socks on the floor, like it's up to me to pick them up."

"I feel uncared about when you turn up the TV when I ask to talk."

"I feel rejected when you say you don't want to have sex with me."

"I feel hurt when you look at your Smartphone during dinner instead of paying attention to me."

"I feel angry when you raise your eyebrows and say, 'Really, you're going to do the chore later today?"—like you don't believe in me."

The more specific the complaint, the more information your partner has—it could be your partner's tone of voice, the pitch, the tempo, a gesture, a look. Being specific will give your partner clear information. It is not valid to say, "I feel angry when you are an asshole." There is no complaint with that statement, or specific upset, but rather a contempt and criticism of the person, which is universal in nature. A statement like that will only elicit an attack back.

Once Partner A has communicated a specific complaint or upset, then Partner B, you **Paraphrase**, using your own words to repeat what Partner A has said. A word of warning: It supports if you use the EXACT SAME FEELING WORDS that your partner used, rather than using your own words to describe your partner's emotions. After all, they are the expert on their emotions, not you. If your partner said he or she felt unimportant, then in paraphrasing, you say that she was pissed, she will probably indeed get pissed, because she feels unheard. If your partner says "hurt," then use the word *hurt* in your paraphrasing to understand. When you have paraphrased, Partner B, then ask questions to clarify how your partner is feeling, to understand them more and have a clearer understanding of the situation or pattern. This is by far the most challenging step of I PAAVER for most couples. It is challenging to ask an open question without inserting our interpretation or point of view. Quite often, questions are not really questions but leading statements that give the person little room to clarify, but instead cause our partner to be defensive. Some examples of questions that clarify are:

- Can you tell me more about that (best fallback option if you can't think of anything else in that moment)?
- Can you help me understand more about how I do that?
- Can you give me some examples of how I do that?
- Are there other ways I make you feel _____?
- What do you make up as to why I am doing that?

Generally, it is a good idea to avoid "why" questions, which asks the person to defend their point of view, or gives your partner the idea that it isn't okay for them to be feeling whatever they are feeling. "Why" questions generally are answered by someone's preconceived reality or cognitions, and also take them out of the experience or feelings in the moment, which is really the part that you are looking to understand. Also, closed questions, where the only possible answer is yes or no, do not support your partner in opening up, and do not support you in understanding your partner better. Likewise, leading questions, where you are leading your partner to one specific response, feel manipulative and will only have your partner become angrier. For example, "Don't you understand now how you should have done it?" isn't going to open much possibility, and treats your partner like a child who needs to be fed answers rather than come up with them on their own.

Once Partner B asks the question to better understand, Partner A then makes **Adjustments** to the communication, saying more until they feel understood by their partner. For example, you may say, "I hear you saying that you are afraid that you are not lovable in some way, and that you will be ultimately abandoned by people that you love. Did I get what you said and how you are feeling? Is there anything more that you want to add?" Partner B is not responding with any point of view, making the feelings wrong, or attempting to analyze their partner in any way. Partner A may make **Adjustments**, and then Partner B goes back to **Paraphrasing** and clarifying until Partner A says something like:

EXACTLY.
YEP, THAT'S HOW I AM FEELING.
YES, THAT'S IT; I REALLY FEEL HEARD.
YES. THAT IS EXACTLY WHAT I HAVE BEEN TRYING TO SAY TO YOU.

Phrases like those above indicate that Partner A finally feels heard and seen. There is a moment in the movie, *Avatar,* where the Na'vi people say "I see you" to indicate that they are seeing your entire soul and who you *are* in the larger context of the world.[8] "I hear you" is equally powerful. If you did not feel completely and accurately heard when your partner paraphrased your communication, then help clarify their understanding of what you said until they do accurately understand. Again, this process may continue with Partner A adding more comments and feelings, until they feel truly heard and understood by Partner B. YOU MAY GO BACK AND FORTH ON THIS STEP REPEATEDLY. Generally, when there is a release of emotion from your partner— "YES, YES, that's it," or a tearful recognition—then it is time to move to the next step.

Partner B, once Partner A indicates that they feel totally heard and understood, then you **Validate** the message by saying something like:

"I can see how you felt that way, and I really get how much pain this is causing you."

"I can imagine how much that is annoying to you."

"I can hear how you have been hearing my comments and how hurtful they've been."

"I understand that when I leave the socks on the floor and make no moves to pick them up, it seems like I expect that from you; that's bound to get annoying."

"I understand that when I turn over and don't want sex with you, you feel rejected and like there is something wrong with you."

You are validating your partner's point of view, not agreeing with them or saying that how they see it is THE TRUTH. You are seeing from their vantage point, and understanding their view from their corner of the world, wherever that corner may be.

Partner B, once you have validated your partner's message, then you **Empathize** with your partner's feelings. For example:

"I can imagine how terrifying that is for you."

"I don't like to feel rejected either, and I imagine that my turning away from you consistently has really affected your self-esteem. I am so sorry."

"It's like you've been in a relationship with a child that you need to manage, and I imagine that isn't very fun or freeing for you."

"All of your upset makes sense now. I am so sorry that you've been carrying these feelings and hurting like this."

There is an old expression from Native Americans: "Don't judge until you have walked a mile in someone else's moccasins."[9] That is empathy. Empathy is not pity or sympathy, which tend to be condescending or from an elevated position. Empathy is putting yourself in the other person's position, seeing from their point of view, and understanding their feelings and what it is to be them.

Before we add the R, you may want to practice a simplified version, to get the feel of actually communicating to hear each other rather than communicating to get your point across. Too often, our intent in a relationship is to get our way or have our partner adapt to fill our needs. Sometimes in adding the R to I PAAVER, the focus becomes getting your partner to give you something, rather than having the focus be understanding and knowing your partner better. Again, my strong recommendation is to work through I PAAVE a few times until you feel that your focus is clearly on deepening your love and intimacy with your partner—then add the Request.

In adding the **Request**, Partner A, it is time to get very specific. You are not going to talk about what you don't want from your partner, or complain any more. You are making a specific request as to how you would like their behavior to change. So, if your partner is always late, you may request that they call at least ½ hour prior to the appointed time to let you know if they are running late, allowing you to choose whether or not to wait for them. You may request that they be ready 15 minutes before any appointed time that is set. Make requests as specific and concrete as possible. For example:

"I request that you initiate love-making at least once per week."

"I request that you go to the grocery store at least once per month."

"I request that you take the kids to school at least one day per week."

"I request that you set aside ten minutes in your day for us to catch up with each other."

"I request that you make dinner at least once per week."

These are examples of tangible and specific behavior change requests.

Partner B, these are requests, and it is important that you hear them as such, rather than demands. It is important that you hear how important they are to your partner, and how much pain, anguish, hurt, or upset your partner is feeling. Then, you have the gift of choice: choosing whether or not you intend on stretching yourself to meet the requests of your partner. Partner A, your partner is not obligated to grant your request. You are not entitled to them meeting your needs. If your partner chooses to grant a request, it is a tremendous gift that is requiring stretching and discomfort. The request may seem simple to you, but it often goes to the heart of a challenge for your partner. No matter what your partner chooses, it gets to be respected. Any stretching your partner gives to you, Partner A, is to be appreciated as a generous gift. Partner B, if you are granting a request, you can convey how challenging it will be for you to do so, and what belief it challenges within yourself.

Partner B, If you are not choosing to grant the request, you want to make sure that you are not withholding as a way to punish your partner or still be right about your perspective. If you are denying your partner's request, ask yourself what your purpose is in denying it. If this were the last day on earth, would you deny it? Are you attempting to teach your partner a "lesson?" Are you withholding as leverage for an idea of power? Do you not trust yourself to actually keep the request? In other words, are you not granting a request because of a limited belief about you or your partner or the situation? Understand why you are granting or not granting a request. Challenge yourself to stretch beyond where you are comfortable and what you believe you are capable or incapable of doing.

Partner B, you also have the option of negotiating with Partner A, with both partners understanding how important it is to both, and any concessions that can be made. Negotiating is not from the standpoint of getting your partner to give something that they do not want to give, because in the long run, this would be hurtful to both partners. Negotiating is looking for a way that both partner's feelings can be respected and given value, with concessions made.

Partner A, whether Partner B grants your request, negotiates, or denies your request, you then paraphrase what you heard, and appreciate whatever they have given you or whatever their feelings are.

I want to also make it clear that at the Passionate Partnering, the Level II Couples Retreat, participants have confided that when they use I PAAVER in an argument, it works; but sometimes they don't want to use it. They know that it works, have seen the value, but still want to end up arguing and fighting to be right. All of us, at one time or another, have been so angry that we simply want to get angry. If someone offers a solution, we don't want it. If someone wants to cut our expression of upset short, we will go out of our way to get even more upset. If you are past the point of no return, and simply want to be right and be angry, then absolutely don't use I PAAVER— acknowledge with your partner that you are too angry and just want to be right. Then walk away. Go shoot basketballs at a hoop until you are sweating. Go for a run or a brisk walk until you cannot sing a song because you are well winded. Go hit a tennis ball against the garage door with a racket, enjoying that smacking sound with every hit. Go dance in your room with headphones on, until all of the energy is out. Anger is a very powerful drug, and it has a way of taking over our bodies. In the groundbreaking movie, *What the Bleep do We Know?* Marlee Matlin plays Amanda, who is assigned to photograph a wedding that is occurring in the same church where she married her husband years earlier—but their marriage ended with his cheating. The movie paints a vivid image of how emotions like anger, shame, and inferiority bombard every cell in our bodies. And the more we feel those emotions, the more that the receptors at each cell are trained to latch on to the epinephrine and norepinephrine of those emotions. They become less and less adept at allowing in other nurturing emotions. Likewise, neuro pathways are being burned so that the moment those emotions are felt again, a whole web of connections are made within our minds, setting into motion certain emotions at a faster and faster rate.[10]

Are we all going to feel anger? Yes. And many of us were not given positive messages in our homes as children about expressing that anger. Whether the message was to shove it all inside and never express it, or it was to explode it onto others, causing damage, or to do it in a controlled and repressed manner, we all received messages about how and when it was okay to express anger. So if you are too angry to use I PAAVER, then don't; but then go release the anger in a healthy, physical way to get it out of your body. In the early days of therapy, therapists taught people to hit a pillow when they were angry, but then they realized that they were actually teaching people to hit whenever they were angry, and that this sometimes manifested in a person hitting their partner, or even hitting children—not so hot. Again, if you have anger to the point where you have ever hit a partner or a child, realize that your anger is not about your relationship, but rather a personal problem that you need to handle through therapy, anger management classes, or other internal work. Essentially, one of the simplest charts at the Couples Retreats is also one of my favorites:

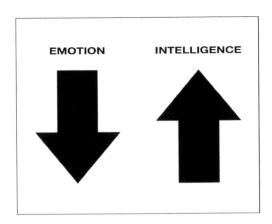

I first saw this simple and powerful chart at a Peak Potentials training, *Secrets of a Millionaire Mind.*[11]

Suffice it to say that when our emotions escalate, we cannot offer intelligent responses or arguments, no matter how much of a brilliant orator we believe that we are. A smarter response is to take a breather, get the energy out, and then come back when your anger has subsided, and use I PAAVER. It doesn't count if you go get the energy out by hitting a tennis ball against the garage door, while thinking the entire time about arguments to make your partner wrong. The time apart and getting the energy out is meant to have you letting go of your arguments and perspective, ready to hear your partner, rather than ready to fire off a new set of arguments as to why you are right, which you have thought of over the last hour while running through your neighborhood.

SECRET #7 OF HOT MONOGAMY – BE LOYAL AND LISTEN.

Really listen. Listen deeper to the words. Listen with your entire being. Here is a brief story before you practice I PAAVER and listening. I have hearing aids. I got them when I began training what is known as the Basic Training, the Intro to Discovery, Vision, Discovery—it has many names in many places, and it is the core work for a human being to dive into their own transformation. I had trained leadership for years and worked with people in their transformational journey, but when I began training Basic, I began hearing the source of many wounds, and it was unbearable (and still is) at times to listen to what humanity does. I think a part of me didn't want to hear all of it. It was too much to take in. After an intensive trainer with my mentor, Gabriel Nossovitch, for a year, I was ready for my first solo training. And right around that time, I got hearing aids. I think they are a blessing. I now have to give each person extra attention. I get to listen extra hard and notice things I wouldn't have noticed. I no longer take the simple act of hearing for granted, and that has me being a better listener, noticing cadence, intonation, pitch, volume or lack thereof, body language, and energy. I listen with my entire being. I am encouraging you to begin to listen to those you love, with that level of attention and care. Listen as though you need to be clear on what exactly they are saying, and the depth of it. Let go of you—your point of view, your interpretation, your agenda.

There is no time better than right now to put your new tool of I PAAVER into practice. Grab your journal and get to work; then find your partner to take flight together. When you are ready, you can head into Chapter 8 to discover how you can actually change how your partner is being. It's like magic, but it's going to require a little something from you too.

THE BIRDS

1. Swans gracefully share the load together, building the nest together, raising the young together, and are vehemently loyal, hissing and attacking when intruders threaten their mate or young. They "divorce" at times if they have not produced off-spring together, looking for another mate who they can build a family with.

    Have you been loyal to your partner beyond just sexuality? Do you build your partner up when around others, or make remarks that diminish them? Do you present a unified team with your children, if you have children, backing your partner?

    Did you choose your partner based on who they are in this moment, or who you were together in the past, or for what could be in the future? What would you need to let go of to be content with your partner for who they are in this moment, not what they could provide later?

If you have struggled to have children, do you communicate fully what the experience has been like for you, and the beliefs you have about yourself and your partner and your feelings? With other disappointments or challenges, do you communicate fully with your partner, really listening to what your partner is experiencing and feeling?

THE BEES

1. Think of one or two behaviors that your partner does that most annoy you. Do you get annoyed because your partner is always late to things? Do you feel rejected because your partner never wants to have sex with you? Do you get pissed off because your partner spends too much money? What are the things that you end up complaining and arguing about? Write two or three down in your journal.

2. Reflect on how you listen to your partner. Do you listen to be right about a past interpretation of this person? Do you listen for things to be annoyed about, policing their actions? Do you listen for what they can give you? Do you listen, waiting for a chance to speak? Do you listen, being right that you have nothing to contribute, turning over your voice and power to this person? Do you listen with an agenda in mind? Do you listen for the possibility that your partner is? Do you listen, looking for ways to support your partner? Do you listen for ways to validate how amazing your partner is? Do you listen from a blank canvas, in discovery about who this person is on this day? Do you listen to love and understand your partner more? Write two or three pages about what you notice about your listening of your partner.

3. It also may be valuable for you to write two or three pages about how you listen yourself, and the thoughts and feelings that you have about you. Do you listen to yourself from the perspective of

being critical and judgmental? Do you listen as a taskmaster, wanting more and more out of yourself? Do you listen to your thoughts from the perspective of them being good or bad or right or wrong? Do you think of yourself as dishonest, and doubt whether or not you will do what you say? Do you believe that you are incapable? How do you listen to yourself? Reflect through writing, and make notes on how that may be affecting your relationships.

TAKE FLIGHT

1. Using your journal as a place to begin, let's practice with an upset you want to communicate with your partner. Set your journal aside while you communicate—it does not establish intimacy to read from a piece of paper rather than speak directly with your partner. Besides, I am confident that you can remember the things that you consistently complain about.

   One partner is Partner A, who will be the *sender* in the following simplified version of I PAAVER, without the R, and with no requests being made. Partner B, you are the *receiver*, practicing hearing your partner and asking questions to better understand and love your partner.

   SENDER: COMMUNICATE (I feel ___ when you ____.)
   RECEIVER: PARAPHRASE AND ASK FOR CLARIFICATION.
   SENDER: MAKE ADJUSTMENTS UNTIL RECEIVER IS CLEAR IN PARAPHRASING.
   SENDER: ACKNOWLEDGE FEELING HEARD.
   RECEIVER: VALIDATE YOUR PARTNER'S MESSAGE.
   RECEIVER: EMPATHIZE WITH SENDER'S FEELINGS

2. Switch partners so that you both have an experience of being Partner B, whose job is more challenging, not defending or arguing their point of view, or subtly manipulating to get across their opinion.

3. Now, Partner A, go all the way through I PAAVER, being aware as you are making your request with your partner that it is not more complaining, but rather specifically what it is that you do want. Remind yourself that they are not obligated to grant your request, and you do not get to throw a fit, sulk, or attempt to coerce them into accepting. If it is granted, it is of their own free will, with you appreciating what a challenge it is for your partner.

4. Switch partners, keeping in mind that any accepting of requests are gifts given out of the spirit of love and intimacy, and should be valued as such. A simple *thanks* is not enough. Really paraphrase what you see it is taking from your partner to grant this request, and appreciate their love for you that they would grant it.

5. Practice using I PAAVER anytime that things get heated or there is an upset. Use the template as a way to keep the communication clean, and ensure that both partners are fully heard.

CHAPTER EIGHT

Be Whatever You Need to Be

"We but mirror the world. All the tendencies present in the outer world are to be found in the world of our body. If we could change ourselves, the tendencies in the world would also change.
As a man changes his own nature, so does the attitude of the world change towards him. This is the divine mystery supreme. A wonderful thing it is and the source of our happiness. We need not wait to see what others do."
– Mahatma Gandhi

That's the quote that is often paraphrased down to "Be the change you want to see in the world," which according to experts, Gandhi never actually said. Gandhi was once asked what his secret was, and he replied, "I try to make myself a zero." What he meant is that he was doing what he was doing not for his own gratification, but because every thought was love for others. You can create change in others when you are willing to do whatever is necessary to change from within.[1]

That is the lesson of the Mockingbird, who will do whatever it takes to get his mate. The male Mockingbird can mimic other birds, squirrels, home alarms, bells, sirens, washing machines, alarm clocks, lawn mowers, rusty gates, crickets, and other noises with unbelievable skill. Native Americans thought that they were ridiculing the other animals. The Algonquians called it "400 tongues," while the Biloxi Indians believed it "mocked one's words." The Choctaws called it the bird "that speaks a foreign tongue," and a Hopi myth says the Mockingbird gave the tribe the gift of language. Parrots, in captivity, can be taught to mimic, but the Northern Mockingbird is a master of imitation. But why?

It's the Mockingbird's way of lighting some candles, turning on Sinatra, putting on cologne and having some champagne on ice. Unrestrained singing by the males has shown to support in the production of testosterone and the resetting the females' reproductive system. When the male Mockingbird is singing during the breeding season, it entices the female. The message he is giving the female is that he has survived long enough in our world to pick up many tunes, and has an established territory. Thomas Jefferson is said to have kept one as a pet, and poet, Walt Whitman, wrote of a Mockingbird near his home, which Whitman believed sang all of the time because it lost its mate. That is pretty accurate, given that Mockingbirds have a relentless focus on breeding, at least four or five times per year. Most Mockingbirds master at least 180 new songs a month, in hope to attract a mate. That is about 400 songs per mating season, and they never stop adding to their playlist; they just keep adding songs. Once a female enters the male's territory, he will begin a recital of his repertoire, attempting to catch her attention and woo her.[2]

Mockingbird pairs usually split up for the fall and winter, establishing a separate smaller territory around a food source. The males continue to sing to show that they can hold a territory even during challenging conditions or times. This is resiliency. This is partnership based on total trust of the other, and endless learning to keep your partner.

Mockingbirds can recognize intruders and human beings in their territory, and even disguises have not fooled the Mockingbird. In other words, when they know you, they know you. Annie Dillard wrote, "The mockingbird's invention is limitless. He strews newness about as casually as a god."[3] Oh, to strew about newness for our partner! Instead, we end up strewing about our ideas from this morning, last year, or ten years ago. We become boring.

Here is the key: The Mockingbird is not really mocking anyone; rather, he is doing WHATEVER HE NEEDS TO DO to attract and keep his mate. He isn't learning just one song to keep her attention, because he is certain he doesn't want her to wander, and he wants her to sing with him the rest of their days.

When someone asks you about your partner, how do you describe him or her?   Do you choose to point out their limitations or what drives you crazy? Do you over-emphasize the *good,* and privately think of all the *bad?* In other words, how do you view your partner? Do you relate to an idea about your partner that was put into place years ago? Who have you decided that your partner actually is? That is a lot of questions that ultimately strike to the heart of how you see your partner and view them on a day-to-day basis.

When some people are asked to talk about their partner, they often begin by talking about their partner's career or work. In other words, they are identifying their partner as what it is that person does for a living. Some people talk about where their partner is from, or even talk about their partner's family, as if that somehow defines the person that they are with. Other people describe their partner by listing a diatribe about the annoyances or grievances they have about that person. How a person describes their partner can tell a lot about what it is that they value, or who that person has become for them.

In *Conversations with God,* Neale Donald Walsch writes:

"What you are invited to do is create your Self anew in this moment. Whatever you believe about your Self, and however long you have thought it, it is not who you are. You are invited to separate your Self from your former ideas about you, a remarkable percentage of which are foundationed in other people's ideas about you. Your life lived is your declaration. Every act is an act of self-definition."[4]

For many people, this is a revolutionary idea. Whoever you have been, it is not who you are in this moment. You are not your past, your history, your mistakes, or foibles. Nor are you your successes, your diplomas, accomplishments, or credits. Who are we then?

The philosopher, Soren Kierkegaard, spoke about Knights of Infinite Resignation (sounds appropriate for some couples), who have given up on love in the finite world as a philosophical act of self-recovery. In giving up the finite definitions given by the world, it allows them the possibility for self-definition rather than world definition. I am not proposing giving up on love in this world as a means to reconcile ourselves spiritually—but he has a point. Kierkegaard goes on to talk about a LEAP that is made: a moment of passion when one moves from one sphere of existence to another, by suddenly putting behind one's old self. This leap is performed by virtue of the absurd (an empty, meaningless world, where I give everything meaning). In other words, relinquishing what is in the finite world, for what is in the infinite. And sometimes in doing so, both the finite and infinite are gained.[5] In non-philosophy speak, letting go of our attachments to what people are thinking about us, rejection, needs of approval, and fear of pain, loss, and other mental preoccupations, we have the freedom to declare who we are and what is meaningful to us.

Before moving back to your partner, think about who you are and how you define yourself. Often, one choice begets another, and we stumble blindly through life, realizing that we were defined by something other than us. Take, for example, a daughter in an alcoholic household, who over-performs and is a *good girl* as a way to get positive reinforcement from her parents, and cut down on the constant arguments or yelling. That daughter may easily move into being a compliant wife, who defines herself by being a *good wife*, without complaints, doing all of the duties that she defines as a *good wife*. She may not speak out when her boundaries are infringed upon. She may not stand up for what she believes, for fear that others would see anger as being bad, or the behavior not that of a *good girl*.

Another example may be a boy who is looked over constantly by his father, not given recognition or praise, but another sibling is always held up as the model child. That boy may then grow into a man who is the valedictorian in his high school class. He then may go on to become a triple major in college, go on to medical school, and graduate with a host of special degrees and awards. He may choose the perfect trophy wife that he deems is ideal to be on the arm of a successful doctor, and drive flashy cars, always picking up the tab for his friends at restaurants, and using the Platinum American Express to do so.

Perhaps the only way that another boy receives attention is that he acts out. Everyone in his family is too busy to respond to him, and only do so when he is causing trouble at school or misbehaving. This boy then may become a man who is arrested at twenty years old for possession of drugs with intent to sell. He serves prison time and firmly solidifies his identity as a rule-breaking rebel. When he gets out, he attempts to get a normal job and settle down, but unfortunately, he is given little recognition or approval for stocking shelves at Vons or Ralphs. He then reverts back to selling drugs, or hits his girlfriend, breaks parole, and lands back in jail. By age 40, he is a *career criminal*, or possibly has managed to get himself killed by his desire for negative attention.

Maybe there is a girl who is told as a child that she is "shy." It may originate in a moment in the grocery store when she is hiding behind her mother's legs. When Mom's friend asks about the behavior, Mom says, "She's just shy." Maybe that isn't the answer at all. She may have been hiding and playing like she was in a jungle, and her mother's legs were tree stumps. She may have been pretending that she was a midget in the land of giants. There could be any number of explanations. But when the girl hears the explanation coming out of an adult's mouth, who has had all of the answers up until now, she then begins to believe it is true. After multiple times of being labeled as shy, the child actually becomes shy and embraces it as a descriptor for her. In college, she is too shy to approach any man or go on dates. In old movies, she would have ended up as the town librarian; but maybe now she would be a computer programmer, or home health aide, perhaps living out a lonely existence and never striking out on adventure because she believes fully that she is shy, and has collected a lifetime of evidence to substantiate that belief.

What I believe that Kierkegaard and Neale Donald Walsch are saying is that you have the ability to create your Self anew, no matter how you have defined yourself in the past. You are what Deepak Chopra describes as "pure consciousness," and *"pure consciousness is pure potentiality."*[6]

As such, you can access any aspect of that consciousness and call it your own. You can declare your Self anew in this moment, and then begin to live into that new declaration. No, it isn't as simple as declaring that you are a millionaire and then focusing on the Law of Attraction.[7]

You cannot begin to charge your credit cards to obscene amounts, believing that since you have declared it and are focusing on abundance and wealth, it will simply come. Years ago, when many people saw the movie, *The Secret,* [8] they thought that the universe was like a pinball machine, and if they thought positive thoughts, said affirmations that were self-affirming, and put their point of attention on what it is that they wanted, as though they already had it, they would achieve it. Then when many people took those steps and actions and still did not receive the wealth/relationship/money/peace or whatever it was that they were looking to attract, they became frustrated and resigned. I remember *Saturday Night Live* doing a series of sketches about Jack Handey, with the idea that if he said affirmations about himself, he would be popular, loved, and happy.[9]

I am grateful for the movie, *The Secret,* and for the number of people who saw the movie and were opened up to the ideas of transformation and quantum physics as the science of transformation. At the same time, an important distinction was not clarified in *The Secret,* not because it was not known to the creators of the film, but because the film was an introductory and not meant to be the definitive word.

Essentially, the missing piece is that I cannot simply declare that I am powerful, loving, honest, creative, or however you are committed to having your partner and the world experience you. You can affirm that you are all of those ways of being, or that you have all of those qualities or characteristics within you, but our conscious mind is around 10% of who we are; meaning that there is a vast amount of us that are unconscious, unknown to us, and operating under the water line. In other words, my conscious mind can want to go towards the future, and like the tip of an iceberg above the water, that is just a small amount of what is occurring. Under the water line are patterns that have emerged in my life, revealing myself to me. Under those patterns are beliefs that I have made up about myself, the world around me, others, and life. And under those beliefs are experiences where we generated the belief in the first place. This has nothing to do with whether or not we had a happy or unhappy childhood; it has to do with limited interpretations that you may have made up in the process of growing up. You can have the best parents in the world, and still make up negative interpretations to explain events. When we are children, we view our parents as God-like. They have all of the answers to impossible questions, provide food, shelter, and safety, and we cannot think of them as fallible as children. So, when Mom loses her temper, or Dad flies off the handle about something, we do not have a framework to think, "Boy, she's really losing it today."

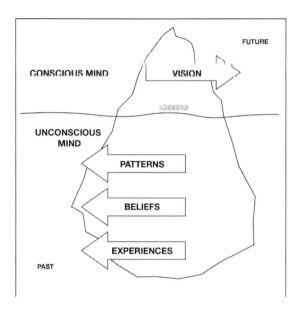

As children, we are in preconventional thinking, and do not have the capacity for logic and analysis. In defining developmental processes as human beings, psychologists have long observed that in young children, there is little capacity for analysis of situations and ordering the sequence of events.

Therefore, whenever something is not going according to plans, if Mom or Dad have a strong reaction or upset, the child then interprets that upset as being about them. The child may make up a belief that doesn't empower them or is a negative self-identifier. If there are multiple children in the same situation, each child may make up a different belief as a possible explanation, and begin to establish their own paradigm. As I wrote earlier in the book, I am the youngest of eight children, and we are all quite aware of the fact that we grew up in very different families, because our understanding of what was occurring, and our filters to understand and process what was occurring, were quite different. If you have siblings, I am sure that you have had the experience of recounting a family holiday, only to be met with, "No, it happened like this."

So it is that we make up our understanding of our identities and ourselves, through coping strategies, ways in which we were acknowledged or seen by others, what we were punished and rewarded for, and beliefs we made up to explain what was occurring. Then, all too often, that adopted identity defines our lives, and we generate experiences that manage to keep that identity solidly in place.

But many people learn that they do not need to hold interpretations of themselves, and continue to collect evidence to substantiate its validity. I am inviting you to learn to declare yourself into being, and then live into your declaration. If you say that you are powerful, creative, loving, and honest, you then get to take actions consistent with being that person. Now, here's the kicker: If you attempt to take actions consistent with your declaration, but you are still not being that person and generating the results of that kind of person, then there is something in the way. There is something going on under the water line, something unconscious to you that is generating what is occurring.

Internally, you may not believe my new declaration. If that is the case, then you are going to fall short in living into it. You may have a lifetime of memories within your body, which contradict being that person, and those memories are being held at a cellular level, with neural pathways so burned in your brain that it is challenging to burn a new path—like using a machete to clear an overgrown trail, while there is an eight-lane superhighway just to the left that goes automatically to your beliefs. Maybe there are other beliefs that are tied up into that same thinking and negative feelings, but those beliefs are not yet conscious.

The work then becomes in aligning your arrows so that your conscious mind is aligned with your unconscious mind, aligned with your feelings, aligned with your beliefs, aligned at a cellular level within you. The quickest way to begin to uncover what is unreconciled is to begin to look at patterns in your own life, and the beliefs that generated that pattern, as well as the experiences that planted the seed for those beliefs to grow. If you are committed to accomplishing your goals and showing up a certain way, then get very interested in lowering the water line to reveal where there are incongruences between what you are saying and how you are showing up.

Now let's turn to your partner and remember the Mockingbird. Did you think I forgot the little guy in all of my musings of Kierkegaard? Perhaps you are already seeing that who you think you are may not actually be who you really are. If a large percentage of how you show up, and who you think you are, has come from the past or other people's ideas about you, then the same is true for how you think about your partner. You are one of the main people who has decided who he or she actually is. There is a powerful distinction in transformation: Other people's possibilities exist only in our own conversation. Your partner will show up exactly how you expect them to show up.

There are countless examples of this, but one of the first and most memorable examples came in the wake of Dr. Martin Luther King's death, with a 1960's sociology experiment on racism, called "Blue Eyes, Brown Eyes." In the documentary, *The Eye of the Storm*, Jane Elliot told her students that all of the students with brown eyes were inferior or less than those with blue eyes. The students with blue eyes got special rewards and acknowledgement, while those with brown eyes were treated as inferior, scolded, and punished. Within a short amount of time, students with brown eyes were performing under their grade level and abilities, even if they had been star pupils prior to the experiment. Among those with blue eyes, grades improved, and even those children who were not performing up to par were now excelling. She then switched it and told the students that it was really the ones with brown eyes who were superior, and the ones with blue eyes inferior, and the results were soon the same.[10] The experiment is heartbreaking to watch, and there have since been countless studies that indicate that discrimination and racism are internalized, and soon the child is performing to meet expectations. If teachers are told that certain children are *gifted*, then that teacher begins collecting evidence to substantiate that perspective, even if the students were labeled as *failing*, by another teacher. So, if I am seeing someone as incapable or stubborn, it is highly likely they will live into my expectation. If I am seeing them as controlling or a person with anger problems, then they will live into that. If I see my partner as loving and supportive, then they will live into that interpretation.

Again, I don't doubt that any of us could list quite a bit of evidence to validate our interpretation of our spouse, whatever that interpretation is. The longer that we've been together, the more evidence we have to substantiate our point of view. If you see your partner in a certain framework, I don't doubt that you can give me countless examples to show me that you are right in your interpretation. But that doesn't mean it is reality. Maybe it is how that person has shown up in the past, but it is not who he or she innately is.

Picture this: The great musician, Yoyo Ma, went down into the subway, dressed in blue jeans and a t-shirt, and began to play. People hurried past him, many not even looking at him, and most not even bothering to stop and hear his music. This is a man who plays at the finest concert halls around the world, with people paying close to $200 a ticket for the privilege of hearing him and seeing him play. But when he was in the subway, playing like any other street musician, people literally couldn't even hear the gift that he had. They saw a street musician or a homeless person playing for money.[11]

Where are you seeing your partner as the "homeless person?" And what would be the cost to Yoyo Ma if he went down into that subway day after day without people looking at him, recognizing him, or seeing him as a possibility? It would wear anyone down. It is what we do with many people in our society, but are you viewing your partner a certain way? You can think that it really is your partner and that they really do show up; however, you believe that they do, but from the context of responsibility, you get to interpret that your partner is a reflection of how you are being. Again, I am not talking about domestic violence, rape, and extreme examples. However, if you are remaining in the situation when someone treats you horribly, you may ask yourself what your beliefs are about yourself that you think that is what you deserve.

I am asking you to look at the little things you complain about when talking about your partner. Ask yourself what the "payoff" is that you are getting by holding your partner in that light. In other words, what secret gain are you getting out of viewing your partner the way that you do? For example, if you see your partner as unmotivated and not carrying their weight in the partnership, then you may get to feel superior to mask your own feelings of inferiority. If you see your partner as controlling and angry, then you may get to be a victim, using them as your excuse. Perhaps you get to be right that anger is *bad*, and be the *good guy* in the relationship. If you view your partner as not warm or acknowledging, then you may get to be right that no one will ever recognize you, just like your parents did not recognize or value you. Be in an inquiry as to what your secret gain is that you are getting by holding your partner in the frame in which you have had them.

Recently, someone I love went through a nasty divorce. They were married close to twenty years, and a lot went into their deciding to call it quits. But the moment they moved towards divorce, he began telling everyone who would listen how horrible she was, all of her character defects, her "mental illness," and the ways she withheld sex. He was complaining that she was making his life a living hell, and that she was talking negatively about him, accusing him of the worst things imaginable, and had always criticized members of his own family. This is insanity to me, and it was to everyone he cornered to bend their ear. Do people expect family members, who went on holidays with the spouse, to suddenly say, "Yep, I never liked her anyway!" Or, "I told you he was an ass!" That would mean that for twenty years, those friends and family members had been pretending to like their choice for a mate but really did not. Also, why would you marry the person if they were so horrible? In reality, they loved and got hurt badly, and now want to avoid any responsibility; they want to hurt the other person instead of acknowledging the pain and the ways in which they contributed to the demise of the marriage.

I'll give another example. Often, when I am in a transformational workshop, I'll see family members on the final day of the training. They are eager to find out about how their family member or friend is changing, and they will approach me saying something like, "You have my dad in there; he's so stubborn, isn't he?" Or something to that effect. I often am shocked with their interpretation, and I will say something like, "Your dad is a honey; he's so sweet." They'll then give me a look of shock and confusion, saying, "My dad??!!" In other words, I don't have the same interpretation or understanding of that person's father, and out of that, there is space for him to show up differently. That person may have been seeing their father that way so that they could continue to be a victim of him, not showing up and being responsible in their life. That person may see their father in that way to stay protected from opening their heart. There could be any number of reasons—you will know yours when it strikes a chord of recognition.

Another example would be Helen Keller. Annie Sullivan saw Helen Keller as intelligent and able to learn. She didn't think that her grunts were a sign of stupidity. Out of being repeatedly perceived as someone who could learn and communicate, that is exactly what occurred. Helen Keller went on to be a powerful public speaker, impacting the lives of others, and clear that limits that exist are often those put on us by other people, which we can unshackle at any moment.

What if you spent moments every day thinking about how incredible your partner was? What if every time your thoughts travelled to your partner, you thought of how much you loved that person and how grateful you were for them? What would occur when you saw them at the end of the day? What would be the experience?

Let me dip into quantum physics and say it from another scientific perspective. William Braud examined the power of human intention and how those intentions manifested what is seen in the external world. In other words, Braud wanted to test our interconnectedness and see if he could achieve certain outcomes. He discovered that there is a constant exchange of information between all living beings that did provide that "by the act of observation and intention, we have the ability to extend a kind of super-radiance to the world." He clarified that this super-radiance existed not only in the physical realm but in the imaginal world and the world of thought. In other words, our intention could be used as an "extraordinary potent healing force...to establish a greater 'order' in another person... [acting] as a healing conduit."[12]

Bernard Grad took Braud's findings further and discovered that, "water treated by the healer had minor shifts in its molecular structure, and decreased hydrogen bonding between the molecules, similar to what happens when water is exposed to magnets." Grad's findings were later confirmed by a number of scientists in repeated experiments.[14] In a related study, biologist, Caroll Nash, confirmed that "people could influence the growth rate of bacteria just by willing it so."[15]

Even if there were not ample scientific studies confirming the power of our thoughts and intention, why wouldn't any of us want to send loving thoughts to our partner? Even if there were no scientific validations of our interconnectedness, why wouldn't we want to affirm that connection with the people closest to us, with regularity? The opportunity becomes shifting how I view my partner, when they are present and when they are not present—becoming their biggest fan and strongest supporter.

When we first meet our partners, often we cannot get enough of them. I remember my husband and me talking on the phone for eight hours, with little empty spaces, in the first days of our relationship. We couldn't talk enough, and wanted to be around each other as much as possible. How many married couples in a restaurant sit in silence with little left to say to their partners? Not that silence is bad, but the insatiable curiosity about the other person has waned. Now there is a known entity. I have heard most of the stories from my husband's childhood, and he has heard most of mine. I'm sure you know your partner's worries, fears, and desires. You are probably relating to your partner as though you know who he or she is, and that they are the same on this day as all of the other days before.

Do you wake up in the morning, leave for work, and say, "Love you," as you head out the door, without really feeling love in that exact moment? Are you on autopilot at times with your partner? I'd hazard to say that most of us are, a lot of the time—me included! Unless I jolt myself back awake. In other words, my idea of love from yesterday is not what exists in this moment. It is a concept, and I am the one who needs to bring it alive. Think about it: Who you are and who your partner is, is distinct from any other moment in history. Even the cells and molecules that make your body, are distinct from the cells and molecules that made up your body one week ago.

But more than that, how you view the world and yourself on this day may be very distinct from yesterday. How you are feeling about yourself, your life, and future may be very distinct on this day than any other day before. What you know on this day may be very different than on any other day—perhaps you learned something at a deeper level, or have a new understanding of existence. Also, the world is quite different in this moment on this day than it has ever been in any other moment before. If you allow yourself to experience love, versus having an idea or concept of love, then you have the space to be in your life in a distinct way. Instead of your ideas or concepts moving you from one interaction or moment to the next, allow yourself to be fully present in the moment, feeling what there is to feel in this moment, and creating love with your partner now, for who they are in the *now*. What would be possible if you saw your partner fully in this moment, and fully let go of your preconceived notions of who you think that they are? What would be possible if you did the same with yourself? And what if you cultivated a selective memory, cultivating the instances that your partner shined brilliantly instead of holding on to the moments that they disappointed or hurt you? Perhaps there would be space for them to shine brighter than you have ever experienced.

The Mockingbird? Let's be clear; the Mockingbird would learn whatever song he needed in order to get his mate's attention. He'd learn whatever song he needed to keep the attention, adding new tunes to the repertoire to keep her interested. The Mockingbird was never mocking the other animals of the forest or mocking his mate; he was doing whatever he needed to do to keep her interested. His focus was on getting and keeping the most amazing mate he could possibly find, and he knew he needed to change his own tune to do so. In other words, it's in your lap. If you alter how you are showing up, your partner will alter how they are showing up. And if you see your partner as loving, powerful, and amazing, you will willingly change your tune to keep them content, instead of focusing on that person being the one who changes for you. In *Mans Search for Meaning,* Victor Frankl wrote, "Every human being has the freedom to change at any moment."[16] Will you? Do you love your partner enough to reinvent yourself?

SECRET #8 TO HOT PARTNERING: GO TO EXTREME LENGTHS TO REINVENT YOURSELF FOR YOUR PARTNER.

Let go of focusing on changing them. Work on yourself, and they will shift—Gandhi in a Mockingbird!

It's that time again...time to put what you are learning into practice rather than just keeping it as a concept rattling around your mind. Grab your journal, do your work, and then set a juicy date with your partner to share with each other. Generally, quiet romantic restaurants work nicely, and they will think it's adorable that you have your journals out and are talking to each other instead of looking at your cell phones.

In Chapter Nine, you'll have a chance to challenge the idea of what you know about your partner and what they know about you. And you'll learn a sure-fire trick to boosting intimacy and love.

THE BIRDS

The Mockingbird learns up to 400 new songs in a mating season, to catch and keep their mate's attention, always adding more tunes to their playlist. The male Mockingbird will learn and do whatever he needs in order to keep his partner. He isn't expecting her to change.

1. Are you willing to learn new tunes to keep your partner interested? Give some examples of what new learning you have done for your partner lately, and how you have put it into practice.

2. Are you willing to work on changing aspects of your own character rather than focusing on what your partner has to change?

3. What qualities or characteristics have you complained about in your partner? Give an example of what you have been working on changing in yourself, and how you are practicing showing your partner this change.

4. How do you exhibit those same qualities and characteristics?

THE BEES

1. Write down your current interpretations of yourself—whatever you have identified as *you* up until now. Where did you get that idea of *you*? When was it formulated? If you did not identify with any preconceived ideas or interpretations of yourself, how would you like to show up in the world? What qualities and characteristics would people use to describe you (powerful, passionate, creative, honest, with integrity, free, joyful, loving, vulnerable, authentic, etc.)? In choosing your top three qualities or ways of being in the world, what kind of actions does that person take? How does that person engage in their day? What are the feelings that are congruent with those characteristics?

2. Write down your current interpretations of your partner— whatever you have identified as that person up until now. Where did you get that idea of that person? How have you formulated your understanding of that person? What would be possible in your relationship if you were to let go of negative interpretations or characterizations? How would you like to think about your partner? What qualities do they possess that you would like to acknowledge and begin to see more (love, caring, supporting, motivated, encouraging, devoted, loyal)? If you are noticing that you are holding on to limited interpretations of your partner, ask yourself why you would be doing so. What are you being right about? What is the "payoff" that you are getting by seeing your partner as limited?

3. Spend at least a few minutes throughout your day thinking of your partner in the way that you formulated above, sending loving energy and thoughts to them throughout their day.

4. Notice your thoughts and feelings about yourself as you go through your days. Are those thoughts and feelings consistent with the person that you have declared yourself to be? If there are incongruences, what are the beliefs or feelings that are incongruent, and where do you believe they are coming from?

TAKE FLIGHT

1. Take turns sharing your work from your journal, revealing how you want your partner to view you and how you are committed to seeing your partner. Commit to giving each other feedback when you are noticing that you are being congruent with the ways of being that you have declared, and taking actions that are consistent with that person. Also commit to giving each other feedback if your experience is that your partner is not accessing those characteristics. Frame your feedback as, "My experience of you is...," being direct, honest, and sharing, with an intention to serve and support your partner. This is not meant for you to be right and hold onto the past, but rather a chance for you to genuinely support each other in how you show up to each other.

2. What first attracted you to your partner? Be mindful of the qualities that were present in the beginning of your relationship, and remind yourself that they are still present. Better yet, remind each other.

3. Taking turns, share one of your happiest memories with your partner. What was special about that memory? Not so much the actions of what was occurring, but rather focus on how your partner was being. Listen to what your partner finds endearing or

special about you, and remind yourself to continue to focus on what is endearing or special about your partner, because it is available in every moment, not just in certain places or on special occasions.

4. Taking turns, share what you admire most about your partner. Describe a situation where you were inspired or in a challenging time for both of you, and how your partner responded or behaved that supported you through the challenge. What is a strength that you recognize your partner brings when the chips are down?

CHAPTER NINE

Will Your Partner Become an Albatross Around Your Neck?

You guessed it; we are going to take some lessons from the Albatross. Oh, the poor Albatross, condemned to be a source of woe ever since Samuel Taylor Coleridge wrote *The Rime of the Ancient Mariner* (1798).[1] In English, to refer to someone or something as an Albatross, indicates that you see them as an annoying burden to you.[2] According to Phrases.org, a site that traces the origin of phrases, this British phrase comes from Coleridge's poem in which a sailor shoots a friendly Albatross and then is forced to wear its carcass around his neck as punishment.

In the *Ancient Mariner,* an Albatross begins to follow a ship, which in seafaring culture was often viewed as a sign of good luck. In this case, the mariner was driven south by an unexpected storm into Antarctic waters. The Albatross appears and begins to lead them out of the ice jam, and even though the entire crew praises the bird, the mariner shoots the Albatross. The crew is outraged, believing the bird had brought the south wind to get them out of the jam. However, when the weather begins to become warmer and the mist disappears, the sailors change their minds as they journey into unchartered waters. They again blame the mariner for their struggle and torment, and in anger, force the mariner to wear the dead Albatross around his neck, maybe to illustrate the burden he must suffer from killing it, or as a symbol of regret.

> Ah! Well a-day! What evil looks
> Had I from old and young!
> Instead of the cross, the Albatross
> About my neck was hung.

Soon, the ship encounters a death ship, much like the ghostly vessel of *Pirates of the Caribbean: Dead Men Tell No Tales*.[3] In the *Ancient Mariner*, "Death" and a ghostly woman play dice for the souls of the crew and mariner. The woman wins the soul of the mariner, and it is clear that his fate is far worse than death for killing the Albatross. He is cursed to witness his entire crew killed before his eyes, until, in agony, he finally begins to notice the beauty of the sea creatures and his surroundings. Only then does his now ghostly crew begin to rise to carry him home, and the albatross falls from his neck. The mariner returns home, repeating his lesson for all who will heed the warning:

> He prayeth best, who loveth best
> All things both great and small;
> For the dear God who loveth us,
> He made and loveth all.

And so, if we are schooled well by Coleridge, we would be wise to pay attention to the Albatross, and love him well. There is much to learn from the Albatross. Let's start with the obvious, as it relates to the ancient mariner within each one of us: Love your partner well, or you may end up carrying them around like an Albatross.

Have you ever had your partner refer to something you said three or four years ago? Or bring up an offense you committed ten years ago? Please notice that I did not ask if you were the one who resurrects conversations from the grave. Somehow, it is often easier to see when it is "over there." What we are doing when we resurrect old grievances is keeping our partner in a "fixed" perspective. In holding on to that old hurt or pain, we do not allow any space for things to be different. In *Man's Search for Meaning*, Victor Frankl wrote, "Every human being has the freedom to change at any instant."[4]

Do we have the freedom to change if we are being held in some interpretation from the past? Yes, because we do not need to agree to be held in that limited perspective. I'll tell on myself here. Often, people are shocked that I will remember things that they said ten or fifteen years ago. I will remember a key moment, or something from their childhood perhaps, because it is as though that moment is burned into my memory, since it formed a key part of who that person became. It's impressive. Even I find it dazzling when I work with tens of thousands of people. And it is also a nightmare for my partner. At times, I will refer to things that he said ten years ago. Yep, I am not only walking around with the Albatross around my neck, I have gilded it, put on a safety clasp, and it is often my ego's prized piece of jewelry.

I am getting better at letting go. Still, it doesn't come easy for me. In Robert Pirsig's *Zen and the Art of Motorcycle Maintenance,* he describes "the old South Indian Monkey Trap,"[5] where a trap is set of "a hollowed-out coconut, chained to a stake. The coconut has some rice inside (or peanuts, or bananas, depending on the origin of the story), which can be grabbed through a small hole." The monkey's hand fits through the hole, but when he clenches the food and makes a full fist, he cannot pull his hand back out. The monkey becomes trapped, but in actuality, there is no real trap. If he let go of the food, the monkey could easily pull out his hand, yet he doesn't. The monkey remains trapped by an idea that if he has a chance to get rice, he should hold on tight to that rice. That idea now has him trapped. The economist, John Maynard Keynes, pointed out that "the difficulty lies not in the new ideas but in escaping from the old ones, which ramify for those brought up as most of us have been, into every corner of our minds."[6]

Sometimes it's easier to let go of things if they are worn out, tired, or no longer working for us. But when we have gotten rewards or goodies for something, it is far tougher to release our grip. Instead of peanuts in the jungle, the nuts may be honey roasted, and we become even more reluctant to release our grip. In other words, if I have been arrogant in my relationships, but that arrogance has benefitted me in business, with people imagining extreme confidence in decisions, then even if my marriage disintegrates because of that arrogance, I'll be reluctant to let it go. After all, I believe that my arrogance has garnered rewards, money, and clients in my work. It isn't the truth, but internally we believe that if we let go, we'll lose what we have. And human beings hold on tight.

We get to let go. Let go of being right, as we covered earlier. Let go of our interpretations of who we believe our partner to be. Let go of grudges, grievances, pain, and hurt. Let go of ideas about ourselves and what we believe that we deserve.

Because we don't just have old ideas and pains that we are carrying about our partner, we have a hoard of ideas we carry about ourselves. For example, a person may believe, at their core, that they are unlovable or don't deserve good things. As we've been working on in past chapters, these are not conscious beliefs but the core of us, established in childhood.

An extreme example of not letting go is apparent in domestic violence cases. It's easy for many people to question why someone would stay in an abusive relationship. "On average, a woman will leave an abusive relationship seven times before she leaves for good, according to the National Domestic Violence Hotline."[7] And on average, a woman is assaulted 35 times before she first calls the police.[8] The question that most people ask is, why? Why doesn't she leave? Why does she stay, especially when her life is increasingly at risk? There are multiple factors at play in this extreme example of not letting go of that Albatross around the neck.

First, sometimes people have big judgment when they ask those questions. They simply don't understand why the person cannot walk away and let go of the relationship. I say "person" because often people erroneously believe that women are the ones who are abused. In fact, nearly three in ten women, or 29% of women, and one in ten men, 10%, in the U.S., have experienced rape, physical violence, and/or stalking by a partner, and have reported an impact on their level of functioning because of the trauma.[9] And these are only the ones that reported it!

If the person felt that they could walk away, then they would. But often, the natural functioning of our brain actually prevents that from happening. There are few critical chemical processes that occur in our brains to increase and contribute to someone's "addiction" to their abuser. Oxytocin, which is known as the cuddle chemical, and encourages bonding, has a double punch for women. In men, vasopressin signals relationship distress, while oxytocin is responsible for that function in women. However—and this is a BIG however—because oxytocin is highly responsive to our social environment, in women it is released when there is a stressor – the threat of the partner leaving or upset, as well as when there is connection, often causing a double bind with the woman connecting the cycle of violence to love. Psychological or physical stressors prompt the release of oxytocin.

If there are high levels of oxytocin, a neuropeptide, it can have two distinct meanings: It can serve to calm our anxiety, and it can also serve to heighten it. So heightened levels of oxytocin work to calm and reduce stress, working with receptors in the amygdala to take things down a notch. BUT high levels of oxytocin also signal social distress, working with the receptors in the lateral septum. So, for those of you who completely tuned out when I began using words like oxytocin and receptors, what does this really mean in practical terms?

When we bond deeply, the brain doesn't want to let go of the relationship easily. The chemical, oxytocin, is one of the reasons the person is pushing so powerfully towards "reuniting" when the abuser returns. That person has an undeniable drive to reconnect and keep the connection with the abuser.

Add on to that the fact that endogenous opioids, which are responsible for our pleasure and pain responses and withdrawal and dependence, are also coming into play. Those chemicals are storming the brain, causing an intense need for relief of any kind. There is a drive to do anything to end the pain and loss, pushing that person to actually pursue the person who left—the one who actually hurt them.

Then add in a corticotrophin-releasing factor, which occurs when there is withdrawal, and initiates a stress response and dopamine, which is signaling a craving, frantic seeking, and desperate wanting. With that flood occurring in the brain, it is incredibly difficult for the person to manage their emotions and make rational decisions. If from the outside looking in, it appears that the person is addicted to their abuser, then that is actually what is occurring from a brain standpoint.

When human beings fall in love and are deeply connected with someone new, the neurochemistry of the reward system kicks in to deepen and establish a bond. But when abuse is occurring, the brain is forming that same attachment that anyone would have towards a person that they love, with one important difference: For someone in an abusive relationship, the person they love is also the one who is endangering them. That love is not safe to them, and it is not nurturing, caring, and sustaining. So if the abuser is behaving in a negative way, oxytocin and the other brain cocktail of chemicals responds in the same way that someone in a *normal* relationship would not experience, increasing the bond.[10]

As a result of that neurochemical storm, two processes occur in the brain automatically, as though there is a superhighway with only one on-ramp to the freeway: the *trauma bond* and *cognitive dissonance*. Both of these functions ignore proper reasoning, and actually block the person from risking freedom.

When a person experiences trauma at the hands of someone that they love, the flood of chemicals becomes significantly dysregulated, triggering intense craving, an increased value of the abuser, and intense hyper-focus on the relationship, and resolving whatever the conflict was so that the person can be reunited. The brain then moves to self-deception and rationalizations to alleviate the cognitive dissonance, which looks like making excuses for the abuser or minimizing the abuser's violent behaviors. This is the only way for the person to "make sense" of what has occurred, and why someone who loved them would hurt them.

Other thought patterns that are put into play through the chemical storm within the brain are thoughts that things will eventually change. Thoughts like, "My love will change him," "he just hasn't been loved enough by the right person," "I know I can be difficult and drive him/her to behave like this, but we'll work through it," often cycle through to make sense of what doesn't make sense.

Also, many people who are in abusive relationships grew up in abusive households or have only been in abusive relationships. If you watched Dad hit Mom, and you saw uncles and aunts replaying the same pattern, and then the same occurred with your first love, you would probably think it was normal that violence was a part of a relationship. In other words, people who have been abused do not always recognize that abuse has no part of a healthy relationship.

Then there is very real fear in leaving the abusive relationship. Statistics show that approximately 75% of women who are killed by their batterers are murdered when they attempt to leave, or after they have left an abusive relationship.[11] For people to cavalierly tell someone who is being abused that they have nothing to fear, isn't responsible. In fact, many people return to abusive relationships because their lives are being threatened.

If you, or someone you love, is in an abusive relationship, help is required: to protect, to heal the brain functions, and to safely begin again. Sometimes people believe that abuse occurs only in certain cultures, or at lower socio-economic levels or with a lower education. ALL OF THESE BELIEFS ARE FALSE. Domestic violence occurs among the rich and poor, across every culture, and with those who have many degrees lining the walls, as well as those who stopped their formal education in grade school. Domestic violence does not discriminate; therefore, we also do not get to discriminate. You can contact 1-800-799-7233, or TTY 1-800-787-3224. And please know that if you are in the United States without legal documentation, as of this writing, your immigration status will not be compromised. Please contact a domestic violence shelter for legal advice, where you can safely have a conversation about your options. Thankfully, there are now laws to protect those who are being abused, without challenging immigration status, so that there is not additional fear associated with getting help.

For those of us gratefully not in abusive relationships, the same brain chemistry is coming into play, as are cognitive dissonance, self-deception, and denial. We just take out those tools at different times to justify our choices or keep us stuck in the same repetitive pattern. All of us have to know when to let go. When do we let go of a person? When do we let go of a limited idea about ourselves, like "I don't deserve good things," or "I'm not good enough to get someone else?" When is the statute of limitations to bringing up some past argument, statement, or upset? Do you keep using it as a battering rod against the person that you love?

Holding on to misery, resentment, and anger only punishes ourselves. It is like drinking poison and expecting the other person to die. And why would we want to poison our partner or our relationship?

Thankfully, I'll admit that I'm in recovery from the unhealthy habit of bringing the past into the current situation or moment. Maybe it's a part of the aging process as much as it is concentrated effort, but I have definitely made headway on this in the last five years. The result is that my husband has space to be a different person in this moment. And we are a helluva lot happier, and do a better job of getting through disagreements, when the entire kitchen sink isn't brought into play again and again.

There is power in choosing, moment to moment, to let go of the past and be present in the next moment. Many of us love experiencing being with a total stranger who doesn't know a thing about us. We then can define ourselves to that person, as opposed to being with someone who sees us as *one way*. I've often heard people and felt myself that it is easier to open possibility, and encourage someone to take action on something uncomfortable that will grow them, if they are a *stranger*. Family and close friends tend to relate to us as who they have known us to be over time, rather than seeing us in a new and credible light. When we choose to see our partners in that moment in time, without carrying forward an idea of them from before, we give space for something new to emerge, from them and from us. Again, this doesn't apply to people who are struggling with domestic abuse, since addiction is in play and, as we have discussed, there are differences occurring in the brain.

How do we say "I'm sorry," let go, and then move on? In the book, *Why Won't You Apologize? Healing Big Betrayals and Little Hurts*, Harriet Lerner clarifies that there are nine essential ingredients to an authentic apology, and if an apology is not authentic, it does not heal, and in fact may do harm.[12] First, a true apology does not use the word, *but*. When someone says, "I love you, but you are so frustrating," the "but" takes away everything that precedes it, and fills it in with something else. When you blow it with your partner, apologize without the word "but" taking away the real intent.

Second, a true apology keeps the focus on your actions and not on the other person's response. You are apologizing for what you did, rather than putting the focus on how the other person responded. In other words, you do not get to blame them for how they responded to your actions, but rather keep your eye on the ball and own up to whatever you did or did not do. Not "I'm sorry you got so upset," but instead, "I'm sorry I didn't ask if you wanted something when I got myself a drink at the coffee shop."

Third, according to Lerner, a good apology includes an offer of reparation or restitution that fits the situation. If there is a way to repair the offense, do so. If you sent out an email to the entire family, acknowledging each person's contribution to a family gathering, but left off your partner, you can resend the email, acknowledging your omission in addition to simply apologizing. There are times when there is not a way to make a reparation or restitution, but to the best of our ability, we can attempt to do so. And if we are at a failure of how to make it right, we can ask our partner for input on how to do so.

Fourth, a true apology does not overdo. Have you ever had someone apologize to you, and it became so overblown with repeated "I'm sorrys" that you were the one who ended up comforting the other person and minimizing what had occurred? That is pretty slick manipulation. In other words, the person does something to hurt you, then apologizes in a way that has you apologizing that they are in such distress. Simply apologize, and be specific about what it is you are apologizing for.

Fifth, a true apology doesn't get caught up in who's more to blame or who started it. From my work with couples over the past two decades, this is a big one. In other words, the message is "If you hadn't reacted the way that you did, I wouldn't have to do X." Blaming your partner is not an apology. Not a real one anyway. And for those of us who have ventured into this no-man's land, it can only result in our partners becoming more upset or outraged.

Sixth, a true apology requires that you do your best to avoid a repeat performance. You can't keep apologizing for leaving your socks on the floor, and then continue doing it (yes, that one was aimed directly at my husband, and he will undoubtedly recognize it). You cannot continue to say "I'm sorry," and continue to do it, because it will erode your partner's trust in you. If you were really sorry, you'd act differently.

Seventh, a true apology should not serve to silence the other person. If there is a condition like, "We will never speak of this again," or "If you bring this up again…," then it isn't an apology. A real apology opens up communication and both people understanding each other; it does not shut it down.

Eighth, a true apology should not be offered to make you feel better if it risks making the other person feel worse. The goal is to serve the other person, not to have it be about the other person making you feel better, and tempering your own feelings of guilt. This is dicey territory. The ego likes to get involved in whether or not it would make the other person feel worse. In other words, if I did not take a job offer because it meant more time away from the family, even though it was a higher income, and I failed to tell my partner about this, my ego may justify that my partner would only feel worse if they knew about it, since they are very worried about finances in the home. That is not an open, transparent relationship, and will always cost in the end. This may mean not telling your brother that on Mom's deathbed, she acknowledged that she favored you over your brother, and you are sorry about that. Or not telling your partner that you are sorry that you didn't marry someone with more of a sex drive. That is an apology disguised as a left hook to the jaw, and will not be well received.

Finally, ninth, a true apology does not ask the other person to do anything, including to forgive. If you are wanting to get something back from the other person, it is about you, not about being responsible and owning up to your choices, actions, and feelings. The intent is for you to repair damage you did—to their heart and soul—not for you to feel better about it.

In *Why Won't You Apologize? Healing Big Betrayals and Little Hurts*, Harriet Lerner clarifies that choosing to apologize puts the relationship ahead of your ego. Instead of collecting evidence to validate your case, you are willing to see through the eyes of the other person, and understand what occurred for them.

So, where is the Albatross in all of this? There is so much to say about letting go that I lost the big lucky sea bird in there somewhere. Let me tell you a few amazing facts about the Albatross. These amazing birds have the longest wingspan of any bird—up to 11 feet! They use the power of that expanse to ride ocean winds and sometimes glide for hours, without needing to flap their wings or resting. It's a good reminder for all of us that we can make things easier at times, gliding on the wind instead of flapping our wings. Where can you let go and glide instead of being a flurry of activity with your partner? Running to see movies, going out to dinner, taking a bike ride—often, couples are in a constant state of activity instead of simply connecting and being present with each other.

The astounding Albatross, which has been known to live as long as 50 years, is rarely seen on land except for when they gather to breed, in large colonies, on remote islands. When they mate, they produce a single egg, and in that egg, their future resides; therefore, they take turns caring for it. Young Albatrosses may fly within three to ten months, but they do not fly the coop. They leave the land behind after five to ten years, usually around eight, when they reach sexual maturity.[13] According to John Klavitter, U.S. Fish and Wildlife Service biologist at Midway Atoll, "If they do lose their mate, they will go through a mourning period of a year or two. After that, they will do a courtship dance to try to find another mate."[14]

Midway Atoll Wildlife Refuge is home to the majority of the Laysan Albatross population, and is also home to Wisdom, an albatross in her 60s, who is the oldest known U.S. bird to give birth. Since adult Albatrosses mate for life, it is unknown as to whether she had this chick with her original partner or if she has outlived her original partner.[15]

Let's use the Albatross to talk about a couple of more appropriately huge points as they relate to partnership, one being attachment.

In the animal kingdom, it is remarkable that the Albatross doesn't leave the nest or its parents for nearly ten years. Both parents are caring for the young Albatross, feeding the young one and making sure that their off-spring is big and strong enough to take care of themselves on their own. And the young birds do not leave early to mate, knowing that they need to be stronger or more solid inside of themselves prior to venturing into the world. Human beings urgently need to take a feather from the Albatross. This is an example of solid attachment to each other.[16]

Two psychologists, John Bowlby and Mary Ainsworth, founded the modern attachment theory by studying the relationship between children and their caregivers. Mary Ainsworth, a student of Bowlby, developed an experiment with toddlers, called the Strange Situation. An example and powerful demonstration of this experiment can be found online, with a short clip at https://www.youtube.com/watch?v=PnFKaaOSPmk offering a vivid example.[17]

In the Strange Situation, "a researcher invites a mother and child into an unfamiliar room. After a few minutes, the mother leaves the child alone with the researcher, who tries to comfort if needed. Three minutes later, the mother comes back. The separation and reunion are repeated once more." When the mother walks out, the majority of toddlers are upset, rocking, crying, and throwing toys. But upon the mother's return, some children are more resilient. They quickly can calm themselves down and then reconnect easily with their mother upon return. They seem confident that their mother is there and will be there if needed. Less resilient children are anxious and aggressive, or become detached or distant upon the mother's return. The children who can calm themselves down usually have warmer mothers who are more responsive to their needs than the moms of angry children, who are colder and more dismissive of needs. In other words, these two researchers began to track love in action, and code the patterns connected with healthy and unhealthy love.

If there is what is called a *secure attachment*, the child uses the caregiver as a secure base for exploration, protesting the caregiver's departure and seeking closeness upon the return, receiving comfort from the stranger but showing a clear preference for the caregiver. And the caregiver responds appropriately, promptly, and consistently to the child's needs.

If there is *dismissive-avoidant attachment*, the toddler shows little emotion during play, little or no distress when the caregiver leaves the room, and little or no visible response to the caregiver's return, even going so far as to ignore or turn away, with no effort to maintain contact or connection. The toddler treats the stranger remarkably similar to the caregiver. And on the part of the caregiver, they show little or no response to the distressed child, discouraging crying and encouraging independence. They may even say things like, "Come on, there's no need to cry," or "Don't be a baby," or "Big boys don't cry."

A toddler who is characterized as *ambivalent-resistant attachment style* is unable to use the caregiver as a secure base, seeking to remain close even before separation occurs. The child becomes distressed upon separation, showing anger and ambivalence. When the caregiver returns, the child is reluctant to warm to them or return to play, becoming preoccupied with the caregiver's availability, seeking contact but resisting angrily when touch or comfort is given. The toddler is not easily calmed by the stranger, and the caregiver in this case has been inconsistent, alternating between appropriate care and neglectful responses.

A child with *disorganized attachment style* may freeze or rock upon the caretaker's return. There are contradictory, disoriented behaviors, such as approaching but with the back turned. This is the result of a caregiver who has shown frightening behavior or has been in a state of fear themselves. The caregiver is often intrusive, withdrawn, or negative, and there is often role confusion, with the parent asking or expecting to be cared for by the child, perhaps saying things like, "Don't upset Mommy; it upsets Mommy when you cry." This is the attachment style that occurs with abuse and mistreatment.[18] In fact, 80% of maltreated infants are likely to be classified as disorganized, as opposed to about 12% of non-maltreated samples. Only about 15% of maltreated infants are likely to be classified as secure. Children with a disorganized pattern in infancy are likely to be classified as secure, and relationships with peers can often be characterized by a "fight or flight" pattern, alternating between aggression and withdrawal. And maltreated children are also more likely to become maltreating parents, passing on a disorganized attachment style, and that continuing into adult relationships. Disorganized attachment is likely to increase risks for psychopathology that cuts across conventional diagnostic categories and makes long-term relationships challenging.[19]

Early insecure attachment is a liability for a child as they move into adulthood, especially if the parental behaviors occur throughout the entire childhood. Adjustment of insecure children puts future relationships in jeopardy. Psychiatrist and psychoanalyst, John Bowlby, described attachment as an emotional bond that impacts behavior "from the cradle to the grave." How you bond with caregivers during early childhood impacts how you behave and bond in relationships and friendships throughout your life. It impacts how in touch you are with your emotions, and how willing you are to express those emotions, showing love to others on a conscious level. The belief system about child-caregiver interactions then, to a large degree, predicts how the child will interact with romantic partners, friends, colleagues, bosses, teachers, and mentors.

Examples of this impact were felt in the 1980s and 1990s, when a ban on abortion in Romania led to increases in the number of infants that were sent to orphanages. Their basic needs were met, being kept clean and fed, but they failed to develop healthy bonds and connections with caregivers. As a result of that attachment breakdown, they developed autistic-like behaviors, repetitively rocking and banging their heads. They failed to understand language, and even had a smaller head circumference.

It has been shown that because of this gap in secure attachment, often institutionalized children are cared for, but because they do not receive love, they develop weakened immune systems, and their physical abilities are diminished; they have challenges with learning, and problems with social interactions. They often fail to gain weight or achieve the height that they could, and they may have trouble sleeping, become autistic, or be on the autism spectrum, and/or develop depression.[20]

A meta-analysis of research shows that 40–50 percent of babies are insecurely attached because their early caregivers were either distracted, overbearing, dismissive, unreliable, absent, or threatening.[21] I personally believe that this number is significantly higher than is being reported right now. Ideally, a caregiver carries the infant in their arms, makes eye contact with the baby, and shows empathetic mirroring—in other words, giving verbal and non-verbal cues to indicate that they are present for their child's communication. When we validate the baby's feelings, we are communicating care and curiosity. And when we match our emotions and our tone of voice and facial expressions in a way that explores meaning, we are mirroring the child.[22] In fact, "when studying healthy parents who are instructed to play with their infant, this type of attunement, 'acting the same way at the same time,' only happens on average 13% at 3 months, 10% at 6 months, and 21% at 9 months (Tronick, 2007 p 155). Acting the same at the same time only happens ~15% of the time in normal infant-mother interactions." And then the author says, "So don't worry if you are not doing this all the time!"[23] No one can maintain eye contact and connection all of the time; that's true. There is a normal percentage of time when the caregiver breaks contact to do something, and then also a percentage when the infant becomes overwhelmed with the emotion or connection, and breaks the gaze. These studies pre-date the increased role of social media and use of cell phones, as well as the distractions of today's world. I am certain that the percentage of breaks in establishing attachment are most often far higher now. It is tough finding a statistic or a study to document this downturn, and if you would like to share any that you know of with me, I'd appreciate and welcome it. Suffice it to say that with cell phones ringing, surfing the internet and social media, parental connection is often suffering, and so is the TRUE number of those who are securely attached.

This is where the care of both Albatross parents come into play. They spend an extraordinary amount of time, especially in fowl time, attending to their one egg. They only lay one egg, and all their time and attention goes towards building the strength of their chick, until they run less of a risk of being eaten alive in the wild—literally. It would be great if that concentrated attention was showered on our young prior to sexual maturity, dating, and marriage. Because if there was no *secure attachment* in childhood, it is highly unlikely that there will be in adulthood or in a romantic relationship. How can we expect to attach in a healthy way to the love of our lives, when most of us didn't have consistent examples of care, love, attention, and bonding in childhood?

For adults, four styles of attachment have been identified in adults that emerge from the childhood attachment styles: secure, anxious-preoccupied, dismissive-avoidant, and fearful-avoidant. With appreciation for the book, *Attached: The New Science of Adult Attachment and How It Can Help You Find—and Keep—Love,* Amir Levine and Rachel Heller do a good job of supporting readers in sifting out their ego, which often wants to claim *secure attachment,* because let's be clear; it sounds a lot better than *insecure.*[24] For the purpose of simplifying a lot of research, including that of Cindy Hazan and Philip Shaver, who first applied attachment theory to adult romantic relationships, I will use some of their concise clarifications:

- The attachment system set up from childhood in your brain, generates your desire for intimacy and how much closeness you want with your partner and with others.

- There is a *threat detection system* within you to detect when your level of intimacy is in danger of changing, and that system will try to get you to do something about that threat through *activation strategies.*

- *Activation strategies* are uncomfortable thoughts and feelings that have you "upset" at your partner.

- Once you are activated, you engage in *protest behavior* that is designed to diminish the threat and return to a safe and happy level of intimacy.

- There are threats where intimacy will lower from the ideal level, and there are those where intimacy will raise from your ideal level. People respond to those threats in two different ways: anxiety or avoidance. If your threat detection system is hypersensitive to losing intimacy, then you are high on the anxious scale. If your threat detection system is hypersensitive around too much intimacy, then you are high on the avoidant scale.

If you want to take a test to determine your attachment style, you can go to Psychology Today (https://www.psychologytoday.com/test/3265)to get a good idea. I say a "good idea," since in mental health questionnaires, it is an acknowledged challenge to have the *ego* not find ways to outsmart or manipulate the results. The following thoughts and actions, provided in *Attached,* offer some great hallmarks to support in identifying your attachment style:

Common Securely Attached Thoughts:

- My partner loves me (even if they are distant, angry, upset, etc.).
- If I'm upset, I want to reach for my partner.
- I can do my own thing, and my partner will support me.
- I can be there for my partner without needing to like the things they like, or do the things that they do.
- If my partner is upset, or says something harsh, I know they are hurting or upset, and I get to be a space for them to communicate.
- I don't need to take everything personally; what is going on for my partner may or may not have anything to do with me.
- I want to get closer to my partner.
- I know my partner will support my dreams, and I will support theirs.

We are not the same people, so sometimes we may unconsciously hurt each other, and we get to communicate the upset, then become closer through knowing where the other person gets hurt or is sensitive.

Common Securely Attached Emotions:

- Loved, cared for, joy, understanding, intimate, committed, free, alive, engaged, seen and heard, valued, cherished, treasured, appreciated, compassionate, passionate, trusting, giving, forgiving.

Common Securely Attached Actions:

- Reach towards partner when he/she is upset.
- Consistently asks for what he/she wants and needs.
- Goes after his/her own dreams and desires fully.
- Talks about what moves and inspires both partners.
- Wants to understand and know his/her partner fully, including when the partner is angry because of something triggered.
- Forgives easily when there is a misunderstanding.
- Understands that he/she is different from his/her partner, so they do not need to do or like the same activities, people, or things.
- Works to support his/her partner in their endeavors.
- Uses partner as a base of support in which to move to/from in the world.

Possible Attachment Principles at play for Secure Attachment Style are:

- Available.
- Does not interfere in what is not theirs to handle.
- Are encouraging of their partner.
- Communicates directly and effectively their emotions.
- Does not play games to have their partner try to guess at what they feel, or jump through hoops to reach them.
- Does not view themselves as responsible for their partner's well-being..
- Focus on the problem at hand, rather than carry the past (Albatross) forward.
- Does not make generalizations in their partner's character, in arguments.
- Attends to their partner's upsets before they escalate.

This explains why, in general, securely attached adults tend to have positive views of themselves, their partners, and their relationships. They feel comfortable with a balance of intimacy and independence, balancing the two.

People feel less anxious when close to their partners because that person can provide support, comfort, assistance, and information during difficult situations. Attachment influences both the perception of support from others as well as the tendency to seek support from others. Those with *secure attachment* seek more support from their relationship partners, and they actually GET MORE SUPPORT, while people with other attachment styles seek less support, and get less support from their relationship partners.[25] People with *secure attachment* styles may trust their partners to provide support because their partners have reliably offered support in the past. Likewise, those with *insecure attachment* styles often do not have a history of responsiveness from their partners, so they are less likely to receive support or ask for it. When we feel a secure attachment, comfortable with closeness and confident in depending on our loved ones, we are better at seeking support, and better at giving it. When we feel safely connected to our partners, we more easily roll with the hurts that they inevitably inflict, and are less likely to be hostile when we are angry with them. The more we can reach out to our partners for support, the more independent we can be.

Common Anxious-Preoccupied Thoughts:

- Mind reading: That's it; I know she's/he's leaving me.
- I'll never find anyone else.
- I knew that this was too good to last.
- All-or-nothing thinking: I've ruined everything; there's nothing I can do to fix the situation.
- She/he can't treat me this way! I'll show him/her!
- I knew something would go wrong: nothing ever works out right for me.

- She/he had better coming crawling back to beg my forgiveness; otherwise she/he can forget about me forever.
- Maybe if I look drop-dead gorgeous or act seductive, things will work out.
- She/he is so amazing; why would she/he want to be with me anyway?
- Remembering all the good things your partner ever did and said, calming down immediately after an argument.
- Remembering only the bad things your partner has ever done in an argument.

Common Anxious -Preoccupied Emotions:

- Sad, angry, fearful, resentful, frustrated, depressed, hopeless, despairing, jealous, hostile, vengeful, guilty, self-loathing, restless, uneasy, humiliated, hate-filled, uncertain, agitated, rejected, unloved, lonely, misunderstood, unappreciated.

Common Anxious -Preoccupied Actions:

- Act out.
- Attempt to re-establish contact *at any cost.*
- Pick a fight.
- Wait for them to make the first reconciliation move.
- Threaten to leave (but don't).
- Act hostile—roll your eyes, look disdainful.
- Try to make him/her feel jealous.
- Act busy or unapproachable.
- Withdraw—stop talking to your partner or turn away from him/her physically.
- Act manipulatively.

Possible Attachment Principles at Play for Anxious-Preoccupied Style:

- Protest behavior—any behavior that's intended to reconnect.
- Activation strategies—any thought, feeling, or behavior that will result in an *increased desire* to reconnect, even if it appears to be lashing out at the partner.
- Putting your partner on a pedestal.
- Feeling small and inferior in comparison to your partner.
- Seeing/remembering only the best in your partner after a fight (and forgetting the negative side).
- Mistaking an activated attachment system for love.
- Living in the danger zone: constantly being afraid of losing attachment.
- Living on an emotional roller coaster—getting addicted to the highs and lows.

People who are *anxious-preoccupied* want to be completely emotionally intimate with others, but often find that others are reluctant to get as close as they would like. They want close relationships but worry that they are not as valued in the relationship. They seek high levels of intimacy, approval, and responsiveness from their partners, which appears as clinginess. People who are *anxious-preoccupied* in their attachment style tend to have a less positive view about themselves. They often doubt themselves, their worth, and their value, and attribute their partner's lack of responsiveness to some negative attribute about themselves. These people also seem to exhibit high levels of emotional expressiveness, worry, and impulsiveness in their relationships.

Common Dismissive-Avoidant Thoughts:

- All-or-nothing thinking: I knew she/he wasn't right for me; this proves it!
- Overgeneralizing: I knew I wasn't made to be in a close relationship.
- She's/he's taking over my life; I can't take it.
- Now I have to do everything his/her way; the price is too high.
- I need to get out of here; I feel suffocated.
- If she/he was "the one," this kind of thing wouldn't happen.
- When I was with (phantom X), this wouldn't have happened.
- Malicious intent: She's/he's really out to annoy me; it's so obvious.
- She/he just wants to tie me down; this isn't true love.
- Fantasize about having sex with other people.
- I'll be better off on my own.
- Ugh, she's/he's so needy! It's pathetic!

Common Dismissive-Avoidant Emotions:

- Withdrawn, frustrated, angry, pressured, unappreciated, arrogant, disdain, misunderstood, resentful, hostile, aloof, empty, deceived, tense, hate-filled, self-righteous, contemptuous, despairing, scornful, restless, distrustful.

Common Dismissive-Avoidant Actions:

- Act out.
- Get up and leave.
- Belittle your partner.
- Act hostile; look disdainful.
- Make critical remarks.
- Withdraw mentally or physically.
- Minimize physical contact.

- Keep emotional sharing to a minimum.
- Stop listening to your partner. Ignore him/her.

Possible Attachment Principles at Play for Dismissive-Avoidant Style:

- Deactivating strategies—any thought, feeling, or behavior that will result in a *decreased desire* to reconnect.
- Mistaking self-reliance for independence.
- Inflating your own importance and self-esteem while putting your partner down.
- Seeing only the negative in your partner, and ignoring the positive.
- Assuming malicious intent in your partner's actions.
- Disregarding your partner's emotional cues.
- Yearning for the phantom ex.
- Fantasizing about being alone, or fantasizing about "the one."
- Repressing loving feelings and emotions.

People with *dismissive-avoidant* style of attachment often seem to be very comfortable with their independence, putting less emphasis on having close emotional relationships. They prefer to have someone dependent on them, rather than depend on another person, and have a high need for independence. To others, this high need for independence often seems to others like attempts to completely avoid attachment completely. These people view themselves as self-sufficient and invulnerable to feelings associated with being closely attached and connected to others. They may deny needing close relationships, spending the majority of their time at work, and may even view close relationships as relatively unimportant in the scheme of things. They may unconsciously see "needing someone" as a weakness. Not surprisingly, they seek less intimacy with their relationship partners, who they view slightly less positively than they view themselves. People who have dismissive-avoidant attachment style tend to suppress and hide their feelings, and tend to deal with rejection by distancing themselves from the sources of rejection.

Common Fearful Anxious-Avoidant Thoughts:

- I knew I'd mess this up.
- I want to be close to you, but as we get closer, I feel like I need to leave.
- I have no clue how to do relationships.
- If I open up, you'll reject me.
- I just don't think you are the *right one* for me.
- I can't trust that if I actually commit, you will make me happy
- There is something wrong with me at my core, and if you discovered it, you would leave me.
- You will betray me in the end.
- I can't explain myself, and you'll never understand me.
- I'm more invested in this than you are.
- Withdraw mentally or physically.

Common Fearful Anxious-Avoidant Emotions:

- Lonely, needy, flawed, broken, misunderstood, mistrusting, fearful, anxious, protective, unacceptable, not good enough, unworthy, suspicious, hesitant, angry, depressed, disgusted, shame, tortured, hollow, performing, hard work, inhibited.

Common Fearful Anxious-Avoidant Actions:

- When relationship gets close, leave.
- Withdraw mentally or physically.
- Lash out when partner begins to connect.
- Overwork or *perform* to gain approval.
- Withhold communication.
- Protect and wall off.
- I can't explain myself, and you'll never understand me.

- Take a long time getting into relationship but then get dependent when they do.
- Avoids conflict.
- Hesitant and reserved with expression of feelings.
- Have hard time breaking off relationship for fear that they will not find another partner.

Possible Attachment Principles at play for Fearful Anxious-Avoidant Style:

- Feel lonely with a deep desire to connect, but they fear that the other person will reject them once they are allowed to be close.
- *False Self* was developed in childhood to appear competent and well-adjusted, but believe they are hollow inside.
- Pushing away partner, the more that person begins to understand them.
- Feels he/she must remain protected or the partner will betray or reject them.
- Hide any authentic or true feelings because they will not be accepted.
- Do not expect others to love or care for you.

People who have *fearful anxious-avoidant* attachment style want to have close and intimate relationships, but also feel unworthy of that relationship. They fear that if people discovered who they really are, they will be rejected outright. They do not trust others to care for them, and believe that they will ultimately be rejected or betrayed. They therefore tend to deal with rejection by distancing themselves from the sources of rejection. They worry that they will be hurt if they allow themselves to become too close or attached to others. They want to have emotionally close relationships but also are afraid that they will not have it turn out. They feel unworthy, riddled with self-doubt, while also doubting the true intentions of their partners. These partners may have a pattern of taking a long time to get into a relationship, then becoming dependent once in a relationship, and then when the partner comes closer and wants commitment, they tend to leave the relationship. They suppress and hide their feelings from their partners, and often appear quite competent to the outside world, learning to create a *false self* in order to be loved and accepted.

Okay, all of this information is great, but how do we become like the Albatross? How do we alter our attachment styles? How do we have a secure *attachment* style in our partnerships. A researcher in the early 1990s actually discovered something called mirror cells—amazing little cells within our brain that actually explain how we seem to read each other's minds, and also support in our feeling empathy.[26] We are all born with a basic configuration of mirror cells, but the development of the mirror neurons depends on the interaction we have with other people through mirroring, and successful mirroring actually has our bodies naturally produce opioids and a sense of well-being.

The good news is that, like the Albatross, we can move towards *secure attachment* in our relationship, even if we are not securely attached now.[27] Research indicates that adult attachment style can be changed through systematic interventions. But there is a big difference between a brief change in a controlled setting and long-term change. John Bowlby made it clear that "the development of an attachment orientation in childhood is based on many encounters and interactions with caregivers, which gradually create a mental network of relatively stable expectations and concerns. Thus, it may take many episodes of security priming to affect attachment style."[28]

Relational psychologists and therapists have been leading the way towards attachment breakthroughs in working with children on the autism spectrum. They have discovered that when children with autism or Asperger's interact repeatedly with a person who *keeps the relational loop open,* new neuropathways are actually burned, with many of these children being mainstreamed into the school system.

What does it mean to *keep the relational loop open?* It means communicating without arguing or debating. It also means not answering questions but engaging in Socratic dialogue—in other words, asking a question back to the other person. However, a key component of keeping the relational loop open, is asking the question *with emotion* present. The longer that the questioning can occur back and forth, the more that pathways are being opened.[29]

Research shows that a thought without intense emotion or feeling has no significant power to effectively engage neural pathways. Our minds do not give meaning, value, or power to thoughts without emotion. But if there is intense emotion, the more neurons are activated, making an experience a solidified habit. Emotions and feelings are often described by neuro researchers as acting "as the glue that binds you to experiences. They are the juice, the energy, behind your thoughts that give power to your memories, goals, hopes, and dreams."[30] After all, *emotion* comes from Latin, *emovere*, "to move." We speak of being moved when we experience deep love or connection. It makes sense that emotions support in moving us towards a more secure attachment. It also doesn't seem to matter what the positive emotion expressed is. For example, the emotion may be joy, laughter, playfulness, empathy, understanding, vulnerability, or love.

Some of the research coming out of brain plasticity and the burning of new neuropathways in children who are on the autism spectrum, provides interesting information for all of us. Asperger children, who do relational therapy with the use of Socratic questioning, are being mainstreamed into classrooms after one or two years of bi-weekly therapy. What happens? This questioning with emotion present is shown to improve social and emotional abilities, support in the expression of viewpoints, and support in recognizing the distinction between a personal viewpoint and a conflict of ideas. The use of questions with emotions has shown to support people with:

- Expressing their viewpoints
- Developing language skills
- Increasing ability to interact with others
- Increasing cooperation with others
- Managing difficulties and sorting through complicated emotions.

These are all hallmarks of *secure attachment*, and the effects are shown to be lasting.[31]

An important part of secure attachment in a relationship is using the eyes of those we love to reflect back a sense of ourselves. If you can continue to support your partner through questions, combining emotions and interest, then you are actually burning new neuropathways, and there is strong evidence that we can alter our partner's attachment style.

An important part of attachment is that we use the eyes of those we love to reflect back a sense of ourselves. That means that we can continue to support our partners in growing their capacity for intimacy, burning new neuropathways. What that takes is asking questions, with interest and emotion. In doing that, we are responding to our partner's need for assurance and, quite probably, altering their attachment style over time.

It would be great if your partner consistently told you that they needed assurance, but let's be realistic, that sometimes isn't the case. Often, instead of saying that we need assurance, we initiate the *dance*, reacting rather than realizing that a button got pushed from an earlier wound in our lives. To become securely attached, we need to work on hearing the wound underneath the lashing out, and respond with emotion, eye contact, and interest and exploration.

Keep in mind that you cannot use logic to calm a two-year-old who is throwing food at you from their highchair. It doesn't matter if you explain that the child is making a mess, or why you needed to take away the crackers. It is the same for your partner. When they throw a bomb at you, lash out or zap a zinger your way, it is the equivalent of a two-year-old throwing the food to get your attention. They are protesting a lack of attachment. Instead of responding by throwing a bomb back or using logic, what is needed is deep connection: eye contact, using empathy or love, asking questions to better understand your partner and what they are experiencing in that moment, a hug, holding the pain or sadness—just as we would with a child, to have that child know they are secure and that their feelings are important.

If you notice that you are having challenges with emotional reactivity, consistently lashing out at your partner and then feeling badly later, then I am encouraging you to get a coach or therapist to do deeper work on letting go and self-soothing, which many of us never learned as a child. Likewise, mindfulness is an important practice to learn to support in emotional reactivity, and you can find more information from mindfulness expert, Dan Siegel, or the UCLA Mindfulness Awareness Research Center.[32]

The Albatross works at attachment. It isn't easy to foster attachment over the course of years on remote islands in the middle of the seas, but this talisman of sailors does it. This bird teaches us that sometimes there is tremendous power in apologizing, to create space for our partner to let go of the hurt that they are carrying, and to move forward.

SECRET #9 TO HOT PARTNERING: LET GO TO BE HAPPY.

Hold onto your partner, working consciously on secure attachment, and then let go of the stuff you get to let go of to be happy. The Albatross offers a powerful lesson in letting go instead of carrying pain, shame, resentment, and hurt around forever—not always easy lessons, but they are beyond important to create intimacy.

THE BIRDS

1. In your journal, write down things that you have been holding onto about your partner. What is your interpretation of them that may be limiting? What is your payoff in holding onto that interpretation? What have you not forgiven your partner for? What has occurred that has put mistrust or distance between you and your partner, which you have refused to let go of?

2. What haven't you apologized for? In the past, when you have apologized to your partner, what element of the apology has been missing from Harriet Lerner's work? What have you held back from your partner? Why do you believe you have held those things back?

3. What do you think your attachment style is? What do you believe is your partner's attachment style? How has this impacted intimacy and connection in your relationship? When your partner throws a bomb or lashes out, how can you support yourself in remembering that they are protesting a lack of attachment?

THE BEES

1. Write down what qualities you get to bring forth during your next disagreement or upset that will impact your partner positively.

2. Do you ask your partner open-ended questions, and respond with eye contact and emotion? Is most of your conversation handling logistics instead of genuine connection?

3. What is your own tolerance level for connection and intimacy? Do you find yourself squirming, using distractions or humor, or wanting to change the topic when things get deep and your partner looks into your eyes? Why? What do you experience that is uncomfortable?

4. What did you learn about intimacy and deep connection from your parents or family or origin?

TAKE FLIGHT

1. The Sanskrit word, *Tantra*, is related to the concept of weaving strands of our nature into a unified whole, expanding ourselves. Sometimes in the West, Tantra is seen as only relating to sex, where it is really an approach of not rejecting the body but embracing the body on the road to enlightenment. In this homework, you are practicing the Tantric posture named yab-yum, to support in the burning of new neural pathways. Most couples emphasize the YUM of this position. To do yab-yum, one person sits with legs crossed, and the other sits in their lap. If you are not quite as limber as the figures above, or Gumby, one person

can sit with their back against a wall or a support pillow, legs open and extended. The other person sits on the ground between the legs, with their own legs wrapped over the legs of the person leaning on the wall. You can also sit on a pillow within the legs. If you want, you can wrap your arms around your partner to give them back support.

Put on some beautiful music. In the yab-yum position, form eye contact for at least ten minutes without speaking. Feel your partner through your breath. See if you can experience your connection to your partner through every one of your chakras. Look deeper than your partner's eyes or facial features—gaze behind the eyes into your partner's soul. Look predominantly in your partner's left eye (the receiving eye), but you can look in both. You are relaxed. You can blink if you feel like it. Stay with gazing if you get distracted. Notice whatever feelings come up for you (fear, embarrassment, love). Keep breathing. Notice your body's reactions (lips tightening, squinting, coughing, shifting).

2. One partner, take at least 20 minutes to share about how you experienced today or this week. What are you feeling, or is there anything coming up for you in your relationship? The other partner works on keeping the relationship loop open with emotion, asking questions to explore more about how their partner feels, what they are thinking, and what realizations they are having. Switch partners. Keep eye contact and yab-yum while you are communicating. See if you can work on keeping the relationship loop open (open-ended questions with eye contact and emotion present) for quite some time—coming to no answers or conclusions but sustaining inquiry.

3. Take at least ten minutes to acknowledge your partner. Tell your partner what you most appreciate about them—what you value. When your partner is speaking to you and acknowledging you, you may acknowledge by saying thank you or questioning to

explore more about what your partner is saying (with emotion). You are not to negate or debate what they are saying. Let in their acknowledgement.

CHAPTER TEN

Be Lovebirds

*"It is not time or opportunity that is to determine intimacy
—it is disposition alone. Seven years would be insufficient
to make some people acquainted with each other, and seven days
are more than enough for others."*
– Jane Austen[1]

"The opposite of loneliness is not togetherness; it's intimacy."
– Richard Bach[2]

What better symbol for love than the Lovebird? These sweet little birds mate for life and are in a state of courtship throughout much of their 15-year lifespan. If a mate dies or gets separated from the flock, its partner demonstrates a type of erratic behavior that ornithologists have said is like a kind of depression. In other words, they protest being alone, and pine for their companion's return. And just like in Walt Disney's *Lady and the Tramp,* these birds re-establish their bond by feeding each other.[3] And many agree that we have these dainty birds to thank for Valentine's Day. Geoffrey Chaucer's poem, "Parliament of Foules," is often cited as the first reference of St. Valentine's Day as a celebration of romantic love. This poem features two birds who exhibit all of the markings of human love; in other words, Lovebirds.[4]

We're going to look to our Lovebirds first, for lessons in intimacy. After all, it is incredibly intimate to feed your partner. It is intimate and romantic to be in a state of courtship over our entire lives, and to pine away for our partner when we are not with them.

The word *intimacy* comes from Latin, meaning *profoundly within* or *within-est.* In other words, there is no deeper place than that. In recent days, the word *intimate* has been collapsed with being sexual, which is ironic because our culture has moved dramatically away from intimacy being an active part of sexual expression. In the younger generation, in the United States of America, "hooking up" has become common, and often the people choosing to have sex know little about each other, including names. Many young people think that they are in relationship with a person if they have been chatting with that person on the internet. In fact, you may have read stories about young boys and girls who had been chatting with older men online, thinking that the person they were talking to was around their age—then going to meet that person and discovering that they were much older, with the results being sexual assault or molestation—all because there was a false sense of intimacy in talking to someone over the computer.

Large communities have been created online—Facebook, Instagram, Snapshot, and others—with the goal being to connect with "friends." But how deep are the interactions? Often, when younger people participate in the work of transformation, they are challenged to reach out and intimately talk with someone that they love. When encouraged to reach out, heal a relationship, or speak with someone that they care about, many pull out their phones and start texting. Think about it: How intimate is chatting through an email or a text? There is no human-to-human contact. There are no eyes to look into, no body gestures to read, no intonations, no changes in pitch, tempo, or pacing. Perhaps you have had the experience with email where someone read what you wrote in another way than what it was meant, and there was a miscommunication. But for our younger generation, these forms of communicating have become the way that they establish relationships, intimacy, and community. Don't get me wrong; I am not an Internet basher or someone that wishes we were back in the days of the longhand letter (my handwriting alone would have had me grossly misunderstood). The web has opened up our world, allowed the creation of connections, and opened up the possibility for relationships around the world. But it is not a substitute for being with another person, with or without words. And it is not the main path to intimacy. Again, there are exceptions to every rule— there are those who are putting in a tremendous amount of effort to create intimacy through mass interaction. I think of the Dove campaign, to have young girls accept their bodies as they are, and embrace their own inner beauty, with pictures of courageous women of all shapes, sizes, and colors, posing in their underwear.[5] There are people sharing deep stories of sadness, looking to support others going through the same struggles, and there are blogs that are almost too personal. A *New Yorker* travel writer, Peter Hessler, observes:

"The American appetite for loneliness impressed me, and there was something about this solitude that freed conversation. One night at a bar, I met a man, and within five minutes he explained that he had just been released from prison. Another drinker told me that his wife had passed away, and he had recently suffered a heart attack, and now he hoped that he would die within the year. I learned that there's no reliable small talk in America; at any moment, a conversation can become personal."[6]

This is a rush to intimacy, used like duct tape to hold the edge of a wound together briefly, but rarely meant to be a permanent connection of either gaping side. The intimacy that I am speaking of is maintained not just for moments, but ongoing. Psychologists would agree that if someone wants to tell you every dark secret on the first date, it is a warning sign for a possible mental health issue. Likewise, if you have dated someone for seven years, and you were unaware that they were one of four children, it is also a sign of some concerns with attachment.

Also, ironically, sometimes a person says that they have an *intimate* relationship with another person, and many people immediately jump to thinking that the relationship is sexual. If you go on websites discussing intimacy, it is often intertwined with sexuality. Yes, the origins of the word date back beyond Biblical times, when to "know" someone was to also have had sex with that person.[7] But now, often, a person is not "known," even when they are having sex. In truth, intimacy may or may not have anything to do with sexual expression. But when intimacy is involved in sexuality, the experience is a deepening of connection, love, and passion.

We've all seen it: couples who gaze longingly across a room for each other. Intimacy is revealed in a wife ordering her husband's meal in a restaurant when he is in the restroom, then telling her husband what she ordered. In that moment, the husband smiles and feels known. That is intimacy. And intimacy is present when a husband knows simply to listen to his wife rather than interject something, or attempt to come up with a solution to some problem. He knows that she simply needs to talk it out to feel okay. Intimacy is his knowing that this is the gift his wife needs in that moment. Intimacy is what takes an already great partnership and makes it so amazing that words cannot possibly do it justice. Many partnerships revolve around activities, doing things together, and going places together. The relationship centers on what is occurring externally, rather than what is occurring internally or in the space in between two people. Intimate relationships cultivate the space inside each person, and the space in between the people.

So, how is intimacy created or generated? In a way, it can feel like attempting to name and quantify air—when it is present, it is often not the point of attention, but when it is absent, it is immediately noticeable. Intimacy is created through a multitude of factors.

First, let's start with feeling known by another person, or having a sense that they care enough about us to know us. It is that sense of being known that makes friendships so special. My best friend knows what I am thinking in just about any situation. She has known me so well over the years that she immediately knows what I will find funny, what will bother or annoy me, and what delights me. She could order my meals for me in a restaurant and do just fine (in fact, she has). She knows when to listen to my rants, without interrupting or taking me seriously. She could pick out a suit for me, arrange a trip—just about anything, because she knows me so well.

One time, about twenty years ago, we were travelling with a group of friends, spending a beautiful Christmas in a rural Virginia home. There were about six of us on the trip, and we decided that a fun aspect of the trip would be playing games. On one of the first nights, we played a game called Rapidoh,[8] where you need to use lumps of clay to shape hints for your partner to guess the objects, movies, activities, and other things selected from the deck of cards. My best friend, Lisa, and I formed one team against the other two teams. We were on a roll. At times, I would begin to shape a lump of clay, and while it was still a shapeless mass, she would guess what I was shaping. I did the same with her amorphous blobs. After three or four repetitions of this impressive show, another friend got quite upset and accused us of cheating. We questioned how we could possibly cheat, making it clear that our blobs were far from Michelangelo. She conceded and simply complained, "You shouldn't be on the same team—you know each other too well." She was talking about intimacy.

That level of intimacy has been work for me with my husband. Our knowing each other comes in different forms. For example, I am much better at knowing what he likes and dislikes, his pet peeves, and joys and pleasures for him. He sometimes doesn't do so hot when ordering for me in a restaurant, and says that it's because I'm "hard." He's right about that; I am—but my best friend often manages to know my current coffee obsession, or what food I am currently loving. On the other hand, Gene is gifted in knowing what I need in my soul even before I do, or even if I am negating it. He will tell me when I need a massage, or remind me that we should stop and eat rather than pushing a drive home after a training. He will give me space without interrupting when I am a tornado of activity. He does these things naturally. I often cannot read when he wants space and doesn't want to be bothered with yet another request from me to fix one of my electronics. When he is anxious or fearful and lashing out, I will sometimes get offended and lash back, instead of catching his clues and realizing that he is really afraid. It has taken me work to feel his anxiety before he tells me about it. This is true of all intimacy. It takes work knowing not just what is important to another person, but the ways in which they express fear, anger, sadness, upset, loss, or any other emotion.

What do you think determines how happy a wife is? Is it her husband listening to her? Is it money not being a worry? No. I'll let you know in a minute. Let's go to the husbands. What determines their satisfaction with their relationship? How many times they have sex each week? How much personal space they are given? No. It may be surprising to you that the single most determinant of husbands and wives feeling satisfaction with sex, romance, and passion in their relationship all comes back to one thing: the quality of the couple's friendship. According to research done by John Gottman in his famous (infamous?) love lab in Seattle, Washington, 70% of those surveyed say that a friendship is the single most important factor in their relationship.[9] Not anything else. Is that surprising to you? Gottman gives examples of couples who have been married for forty years, who have had sex once in that entire time, but both are incredibly satisfied in the relationship. He talks about other couples who have sex two or three times a day and are satisfied in the relationship. There are couples like Mary Matalin and James Carville, who share a love of politics but vehemently disagree on the best way for our nation to be governed, yet they clearly adore each other. In other words, we do not need to have the same viewpoints as our partner. We do not need to have the same sex drive or hobbies or anything else. What we get to do is develop a friendship with our partners, based on mutual respect and the genuine enjoyment of each other's company.

A lot of time when we are with friends, the time goes so quickly. It is as though there is total comfort and a genuine desire to soak up every moment of the person. That is what we get to foster and develop in our partnerships if we currently do not have it. Have you ever been shopping and saw something, instantly thought of a friend, and bought it for them? You knew that they would absolutely love it, and you wanted to get a little something to show them how well you know them. This is an example of intimacy in action.

How well versed are you in your partner? Do you know your partner's likes and dislikes? Do you know their little quirks, hopes, dreams, and fears? Are you present to the little ways that they express their fondness of you? Are you present to how they feel loved by you and when they do not feel love? Knowing your partner as a friend, and respecting who they are, what and how they choose, is a first major step to intimacy. I like to use the example of our partner being a foreign country. If you were going to Japan, you would probably want to buy a guidebook to Japan. You may want a basic translation book to be able to communicate. Perhaps you would want to learn some of the customs, so that you didn't inadvertently offend anyone, and so that you could express gratitude in a way that it was understood. You and your partner are foreign countries, even if you actually grew up in the same country. For those of you that grew up in different countries or have different cultural or ethnic backgrounds, you have naturally had to approach your partner with more of a curiosity than most of us do, learning about their culture, ethnicity, and traditions, what they identify with, and what they do not identify with.

I know a couple where the husband is from Syria and the wife is from Lebanon, and both immigrated to the United States when they were teenagers. To many Americans, both countries would be labeled the Middle East, and we would imagine great similarities. But to each of them, there are major differences as well, with Syria having greater restrictions on women, and Lebanon being the "Paris" of the Middle East, with free thinking but a war shaping much of her childhood. Both partners do not assume that they know what it was like for the other to grow up in that culture, and they are willing to have their partner explain it to them. And just because they both came to the United States when they were teens, it doesn't mean that their experience was the same. So it is that we get to approach our partner like they are a different country, and we want to become fluent in their "language and customs," and all the nuances that make that person who they are.

Another way to develop intimacy is through being together. This has nothing to do with the amount of time that you are together, but simply the act of coming and being together. Think about it; if we were sitting next to a stranger on an airplane, we may spend much of the flight engrossed in a book, working, sleeping, and not really being intimate with that person. But if the flight attendant got on the loudspeaker and announced that the plane lost an engine and was going down, the chances that you would immediately come together and create intimacy are incredibly high. My husband tells a story about his grandfather, Joe Morales, being on an airplane, coming back from Texas, in the 1960s. The plane needed to make an emergency landing, and there was concern that they might not make it. He and the man in the seat next to him began sharing about the loves of their lives, family, and what they had wanted to achieve in their lives. As the plane began going down, they clasped each other's hands and said prayers.

The story ends well with the plane landing safely. The man in the seat next to my husband's grandfather was James Cagney, and they remained lifelong friends until the day that James Cagney died. Intimacy had been created in about twenty minutes, and was present for a lifetime—such is the nature of intimacy. Sometimes people have a tendency to think that it takes a long time to build, but as Jane Austen noted, it can take just minutes. It is the quality of the connection, versus words that are being spoken or a quantity of time. Most of us have had experiences of meeting someone and experiencing an instant connection or desire to know them more. That connection was present because we were allowing it to be.

From the perspective of quantum physics, or as I like to think of it, the science of transformation, there is no separation between any of us. Where one body ends and another begins is actually only what our eyes can see. In actuality, everything is one giant swirling mass of energy, with the energy that makes up who I am, moving into the table, the chair, my dog—everything in constant motion and movement. There is no separation. For me, if I had one veil to strip away from humanity, it would be the veil of separation that prevents us from seeing that what I do to another, I am doing to myself. What affects one, affects the whole—all of humanity, the earth, the universe, and beyond. So really, we all already are very much in relationship with each other, whether or not we are choosing to acknowledge it. We all already have an innate knowing of another, if we allow it and choose to bring it forth. It wouldn't be weird for me to know that I was moving my little finger; after all, I am the one moving it, and it is a part of me. What would be the possibility if we viewed each other all part of the same whole, allowing ourselves to feel and be present to another, innately knowing them?

Enough from the larger perspective, but let's chunk it down now to bite-size pieces that are applicable in our daily lives. Often, when we spend time with our partners, much of the time is spent talking about our agenda, our philosophies, our point of view, our truth, or our sermonizing. True conversation is a dying art.

Thomas Moore wrote that "conversation is different from discussion or argument." He says that it is "less pointed and focused. In its early history, the word *converse* meant not only to talk, but to live and dwell, and was sometimes used to mean sexual intercourse."[10] As a therapist and coach, it is not uncommon for me to see a couple come into my office with little to say to each other. They are so angry that there is little conversation. It is no surprise when they say that they are not having sex.

According to Moore, conversation has no bottom line to it. There is no agenda on the part of one partner or another. There are no testimonies attempting to persuade the other partner, or being right about a position or point of view. There is no theorizing about philosophies or perspectives. Conversation finds a rhythm all its own. It grows and meanders at its own pace, stopping in interesting resting points. In conversation, the links between topics may not seem logical; in fact, they may be quite illogical. The transitions are not predictable. The topics do not need to be deep at all. Sometimes the best conversations have to do with ordinary moments, nature, observations, and experiences in the present moment.

Children are adept at the art of conversation. On a walk with our dogs some years ago, my husband and I were passing the schoolyard near our house, at recess. A boy, about ten years old, was at the fence watching us approach, and as we got closer, he blurted out, "My mom has a dog, but my dad doesn't like it when he drops us at her house." That was definitely a case of immediate intimacy but also an example of conversation—simply noticing what is occurring in the moment, and sharing. He quickly jumped to the size of his dog and the size of our dogs. Then he was talking about playing with his dog. And as suddenly as the conversation started, it ended with him noticing his friends and running to play. If you spend some time on the playground listening, you'll be amazed at how the conversation jumps from topic to topic, with everyone following along quite nicely. That is part of the magic of childhood.

If I am on my agenda with my husband, rattling off my list of things to get done, or planning out the future or giving him my philosophy on the internet or politics, or whatever it is, there is little space for intimacy. It is as though the information is being dumped by a dump truck on the receiver. There is no breathing space or room for actual spontaneous connections. So, in being together, it isn't simply spending time watching the television, or giving your philosophy of economic decline, or doing errands and bustling through the day. It is creating the space to be with each other and amble through conversation. If you begin to practice creating these spaces with each other, you will notice a marked increase in intimacy.

Intimacy is also born of trust. There is a fantastic book, *The Book of Qualities*, by J. Ruth Gendler, that I have had for years, which has deepened my understanding of different emotions. I feel like I have single-handedly done quite a bit of marketing for Gendler, since this is a little gem that sits on my shelf. In that book, the author has personified many of the emotions, qualities, and characteristics, both those considered *positive* and those considered *negative*. In the book, she says this about trust:

"Trust is the daughter of Truth. She has an objective memory, neither embellishing nor denying the past. She is an ideal confidant—gracious, candid, and discreet. Trust talks to people who need to hear her; she listens to those who need to be heard; she sits quietly with those who are skeptical of words. Her presence is subtle, simple, and undeniable.

Trust rarely buys round trip tickets because she is never sure how long she will be gone or when she will return. Trust is at home in the desert and the city, with dolphins and tigers, with outlaws, lovers, and saints. When Trust bought her house, she tore out all the internal walls, strengthened the foundation, and rebuilt the door. Trust is not fragile, but she has no need to advertise her strength. She has a gamblers respect for the interplay between luck and skill; she is the mother of Love."[11]

I love this. For me, this is saying that Trust does not remember through her filters, but sees things in the light of day for what really occurred. She doesn't deny, sugarcoat, or color things to fit her interpretation. She knows when to speak and when to listen, and knows that it isn't her words that will move someone, but her *beingness*. She trusts the magic of life unfolding, and is open to changing her plans, agenda, and mind as she sees fit. And Trust is not stupid or blind; when she built her home, she tore out her internal walls, knowing herself fully, and she rebuilt the door, having clear boundaries. Her power doesn't overpower; it is felt. And of course, Trust gives birth to Love, both important aspects of intimacy. If you are willing to open yourself to another, being wholly revealed and transparent, then you are trusting that person, and creating the space for love to grow.

Much of the time, at Couples Retreats, couples are afraid of their partner finding something out from their past. They are afraid that they would be unloved or abandoned if the truth was revealed. And so for years, they have attempted to hide whatever it is that they did. They hide their secret with a sense of shame. And the more that the person hides that secret, the more the message of shame is reinforced, affecting self-esteem, self-expression, and self-love. These could be affairs that the person has been hiding for years, like carrying a hundred-pound weight. It could be flirtations, secret desires, fears— something they have determined they must hide in order to be loved. In their mind, what they have done is unforgivable, a threat to their love and, therefore, must be hidden. Most therapists agree that secrets and lies destroy intimacy, trust, and eventually the relationship. Maybe the secret is that Dad is an alcoholic, and a kid never invites friends or talks about it—the relationship is beyond damaged. Maybe it is a friend who cheated with your wife—the relationship is compromised. And definitely, if a partner has cheated, there will be real work to do to make the way back to trust and intimacy.

About twelve years ago, I heard about a workshop called Radical Honesty, conducted by Dr. Brad Blanton, in the Shenandoah mountains.[12] What I heard about the workshop just about made me sick to my stomach with fear. I had heard that an aspect of the workshop was to stand up in front of all of the other participants, totally naked, and talk about your entire sexual history in great detail, talking about what you liked, didn't like, and everything in between. As if that wasn't enough, the entire thing was videotaped and then played back to the group the next day on big screen television, so that you could really see your mannerisms and expressions, and understand some of the messages being relayed. I was already a good six years into transformation, and thought that I knew a lot more than I really knew, but one thing was clear: I was terrified, and I knew that I didn't want fear to have any of my power—not for me and not for the people I cared about. I also couldn't stomach the thought of me getting up in front of rooms full of people, encouraging them to dive into their fears and know that they were not really real, while all the while I was terrified of my own body, carrying old shame and being invested in an image versus really being comfortable "in my own skin."

I enrolled immediately. It was probably the longest nine days of my life, with me counting down each day to that fateful moment. In the end, I was just another naked body. Watching myself on the big screen, relaying my sexual exploits and embarrassments, I actually had compassion and a sense of tenderness for all that I had carried for so long. I also had a freedom of releasing secrets that I had made mean so much about me. The secrets didn't define me. Yes, they were a part of who I had become, but they did not define who I was. I had used them to define and limit myself. I decided then and there that I wouldn't hold secrets again, and I certainly would never let my past or any of what I did or did not do define the future. At that same workshop, I had the opportunity to see how my judgments actually get in the way of learning and being in discovery (Radical Honesty). Dr. Blanton is one-of-a-kind, a cross between a radical revolutionary, a hippy, a genius, and lecherous fool. I immediately dismissed him, judging his use of recreational drugs, judging his past and how he chose to sleep with many of his students, and I felt an air of superiority in my assessments, always a warning bell for me to look inward. Through the course of the training, I learned many valuable lessons, including not to judge or dismiss anyone as a powerful messenger of truth. He has remained a friend, and is someone I respect to this day

When I think about secrets and lies, I also think of my relationship with my father. When I first went through transformational trainings, I really wanted my father to participate. I dreamed of a relationship where we could talk honestly about the past, without judgment, and have comfort in having real conversations. It took me seven years to enroll my father in participating. In the process, I saw that our relationship was more of a façade, discussing interesting topics but without real intimacy. During the course of the seven years, I rolled up my sleeves and fought for something real. I made it clear that I wanted to know the real deal, including things that were hurtful, things he was ashamed of, and where he thought he failed or missed the mark. I remember one conversation where I was crying, and he was crying, and he made it clear that if we were going to be completely honest, he wanted the same from me. Over the course of time, we talked about affairs that he had, a relationship where I cheated, his motivations, my own, and areas where we felt we had fallen short. He talked about his challenges as a husband and a father. Eventually, he participated in transformational trainings, and it was one of the greatest treasures of my life. There was nothing off-limits, and I felt like I fully understood my father for the first time in my life.

My father passed away two years ago, and when my brothers and sisters and I celebrated his life, I did not have an ounce of regret, anger, or upset. I felt nothing but gratitude for the years of very real conversations that we had. In the end, I had a father, not an "idea" of a father. That is intimacy and real relationships. INTO ME YOU SEE is another way I think of intimacy, allowing someone to see all of you, the joys, fears, doubts, and delights.

When I got my Master's in Counseling Psychology, and began seeing clients, it became clear that a lot of the cases we were discussing in supervision involved secrets of one kind or another. A call I took recently summarizes it pretty well. Tim was talking about how he realized that since he cheated on his wife in Las Vegas, he had not allowed himself to get close to anyone— not clients, not friends, and certainly not his wife. He said that it was like he realized inside what a fraud he was, and was disgusted by it. He also had begun not trusting himself in any relationships. We talked about how no one could be the one to tell him whether or not to reveal what had occurred to his wife, but that it was a decision that needed to come directly from him. When we hung up the phone, he was pretty clear that his wife deserved to know him instead of an image, and that she deserved the truth. He was still afraid, but something was greater than his fear: him wanting his honesty and integrity back to rebuild his marriage. The Kabbalist Rabbi, Yehuda Berg, writes, "There's no separation in a true relationship. No hiding. No holding shameful secrets. Real love is total confession. (It isn't always easy, but it is incredibly rewarding.)"[13]

Begin to get practiced at telling the truth, whatever that truth may be for you in the moment—the truth of what you are feeling, thinking, and experiencing. The act of sharing who you are in the present moment with another human being opens up possibility that is not based on the past or defining yourself or the other person from the framework of the past. Let go of secrets, and allow your partner to do the same, realizing that you are the chooser about how you respond. You can choose to be insecure about some romance in the past. If you do so, your insecurity is yours to work on and has nothing to do with your partner's past choices. You could choose to feel inadequate based on a past sexual experience that your partner had. If you do so, your inadequacy undoubtedly manifested in other ways in your life, and you have the opportunity of working on it in this moment, regardless of what your partner revealed. You could choose to define your partner based on their past. But I don't imagine that you want to be defined based on your past or experiences. If the behavior is ongoing, then you may have some different choices to make. If your partner has had, or is having, multiple affairs, then you have the choice of determining if the behavior and arrangement works for both partners. If it does, you can keep it. If you decide it does not, then you both will choose that. But do not remain in the marriage continuing to complain about it. You chose it.

In the act of revealing whatever is there, you could choose to be interested, to know your partner more. You could choose to know that you are creating something special with your partner from this moment forward; otherwise they wouldn't feel safe enough to even reveal the past. You can interpret it any way that you choose. Why not choose an empowering interpretation that forwards your commitment and growth? You can remind yourself that your partner is with you in this moment. They did not choose any of the other people from the past, no matter how great the flirtation, the body, or the attraction. They are choosing to be with you, and to develop real intimacy, friendship, respect, trust, and love with you, as exemplified by their willingness to be revealed and transparent. I invite you to choose to be grateful; grateful to really know the *real deal* instead of a façade or image.

So our Lovebirds are showing that intimacy is being transparent, honest, revealed, and open. Intimacy is making sure you are in courtship during your entire time with each other, and showing that love, whether it is feeding each other in a restaurant, or picking up your partner's favorite coffee order, or sitting through a movie that wouldn't be at the top of your list, but it's at the top of theirs.

Another lesson that we can learn from Lovebirds...for most species of Lovebirds, it is almost impossible to tell the male apart from the female. There are no different markings or differences in size. They are androgynous, and often there is no way to differentiate the male from the female unless there is a DNA test. Some people think that it is real love if they become their partner. In Asia, sometimes couples dress alike, with the same shirt or sweatshirt. It's their way of showing that they are a unit. As if we couldn't tell that they were together by the fact that they were holding hands!

But this is often the thought of what it is to be in a relationship. Sometimes there is a fantasy that the two will fuse together and become "one." When the movie, *Jerry McGuire,*[14] came out, there were a few iconic lines that made their way into the cultural conversation, and one was, "You complete me." When Tom Cruise speaks that line to Renee Zellweger, you could hear a collective whimper or collected "ahh" in the audience. It isn't only this movie by any stretch of the imagination. Disney starts us early with the prince rescuing the princess at the end of almost every movie. (Thank you, Disney, for allowing the princess in *Frozen*[15] to be the first who isn't rescued or married off by the end of the movie.) The message is clear: You need to have someone else to complete you.

Then there is most pop music. Think about the songs that we listen to….Chicago, "If you leave me now, you take away the biggest part of me."[16] Or U2, "I can't live with or without you."[17] Or Whitney Houston singing, "I have nothing, nothing, NOTHING without you."[18] The message we are consistently getting is that we need a partner to complete us, and that we are somehow not whole without one. If someone walked up to you and said, "I am fundamentally missing something. I am not whole, and I need you to give me what I am missing so that I am whole," you would run screaming away from that person. But somehow, there is an idea that we need something or someone outside of ourselves to be whole, happy, and complete. I know that this may sound like a contradiction; after all, you are reading a book on passionate partnerships. But fusing with a partner to become "one," and operating in perfect harmony, is a fantasy. It is like the synchronized swimmers, in perfect unison with their toes pointed, or figure skaters matching every stroke with each other in a routine. But that is what it is: a routine. It isn't life.

Differentiation is a psychological term that is beyond tricky for most of us to get, first as a concept, then moving it into an explanation that makes sense, and then, over the course of ten to thirty years, getting it. I personally don't think that most people differentiate from their own families of origin. And for those who do, it is like an incredibly slow motion version of a butterfly coming out of the cocoon. Murray Bowen, a psychologist known as one of the founders of family systems therapy, offered differentiation as a possibility for all of us as human beings.[19] It puts equal emphasis on being meaningfully connected to significant others, while expressing our own individual thoughts and beliefs, in that the individual moves from labeling different family members or categorizing them, and towards acceptance of family generational patterns. I'll give an example. Have you ever gone to your family of origin for a holiday dinner and felt like you became the "kid" again? Have you ever felt as though the moment you start saying what matters to you, a brother or sister or a parent jumps in with a different point of view, and you shut down? Have you gotten unwritten rules like, "We are Republicans, and any other viewpoint is not welcome," or the same for Democrats? Those are examples of where it may feel like you, as an individual, cannot have your own interests, desires, and beliefs as your family of origin.

Emotional fusion is the opposite of differentiation. It is a different kind of connection, more like an invisible force field holding people in place. When a person is undifferentiated, there is an overwhelming need for togetherness. It can feel like there is a neediness to be loved and accepted. Pseudo differentiation is when poorly differentiated people feel the pull of that force field of fusion. They may start increasing physical distance to make themselves feel better—like moving to Siberia, Hong Kong, or England instead of remaining in the United States, closer to their family of origin. And yes, I travel quite a bit to

Asia; it is also the same as moving from Taipei to Canada so that you can finally be you. In other words, I need to travel halfway around the world to be able to be myself. The other version of emotional fusion is the thinking that everyone needs to be together constantly. It is the idea of having dinner once a week with the parents, and everyone living within a ten mile radius. In other words, the unwritten rule is that "you can't leave."

When there is little differentiation, our identity is based on what is called a reflected sense of self, and it is just like it sounds: We need constant contact, validation, agreement, or disagreement, from our family members. We exist in relationship to our family. In emotionally fused families, there are set roles, or places. For example, in our example family, Dad needs to sit at the head of the table, and Mom on the other end. Joey is supposed to be the funny brother. Amanda is supposed to get straight A's and do well in school. Kris is supposed to be the problem child who is too internal, and we're concerned. These are all unwritten rules and roles without fluidity.

This shows up in relationship, with one person needing to remain fixed, or stay in their "role" without deviation. If a partner is seen as the patient one who does everything, then that is what is expected always. If the other partner is the fun, irresponsible one, they are expected to remain that way, even if it is not serving the relationship or either of them. They exist in their roles in relation to each other.

Another point about emotional fusion that relates to our Lovebirds: Jealousy is a form of emotional fusion. Essentially, jealousy shows an intolerance for being separated from those we love, and for the boundaries that they've set. Our Lovebirds are famously jealous. They get incredibly jealous during mating season, and can become quite aggressive. So, just as they are an emotional fusion fantasy, rather than differentiated, they also exemplify the insecurity of jealousy.

In well-differentiated families, seats can change at the dinner table without it being an issue, because Dad and Mom know who they are as individuals, not in relation to the family. And the other roles are fluid, with each individual themselves not in relation to the whole.

Differentiation is not about becoming separate from your partner or family of origin. It isn't about individuality, autonomy, or independence. And it is not about emotional distance from those that you love. It is about maintaining who you are, while you are close to the people around you. It involves the balance of connection and autonomy. Emotional fusion is connection without valuing individuality, and it ends up separating us from those we care about. In differentiation, you want to be yourself fully, while you are together and intimate with your partner. In other words, unlike our Lovebirds, you don't want to become a mirror image of your partner to keep the peace, losing your individual markings. Some people end up feeling trapped in a marriage because they feel like they have to give up who they are, what they love, and their freedom, to be in the relationship. Then they leave the relationship. Others feel like they need ten texts a day to check in, and constant reassurance that their partner is there, and they have no life or interests outside of the relationship. Both are emotional fusion.

In differentiation, you can maintain your sense of self even when, and especially when, you are close to others. Even if that person is incredibly close to you, you can agree with something, and feel as though you are not giving in, or disagree without feeling resentment or alienation. In other words, you can remain deeply connected, and disagree or have radically different perspectives.

Sometimes in undifferentiated families, a young adult will feel like they need to move across the country or world to minimize their parents' impact on them. Another hallmark of lack of differentiation is emotional cut-offs, when family members cut themselves off from each other emotionally rather than staying in touch. In other words, they cannot tolerate being around a family member with a radically different point of view or perspective. Often times, in an undifferentiated family, development will be choked off, with someone perpetually acting like a little boy or little girl. Another example is when family members feel like they need to use guilt to get others to do what they want rather than allow for free choice.

And there is a marked increase in this occurring in the United States of America, with recent political elections. There are a flood of articles showing that with the election of President Trump, many families are "in a cold war place."[20] There is a challenge in listening to each other and empathizing with different perspectives. This is another example of enmeshment, where there are unwritten rules that those we love think the way that we think, like what we like, and believe what we believe.

In *Passionate Marriage,* David Schnarch says that when we pick marriage partners, it is not uncommon to pick someone whose family tried the opposite way of dealing with emotional fusion—but who was no more successful.[21] Some people attempt to put physical distance to balance the pressure of being together. Other families turn inward and thwart the desire to go on their own individual way. My husband's family considers us living away from them, since we are about 15 miles away, while the rest of the family is within a couple of miles. My family? You guessed it....we are all over. For a while, one of my brothers lived in Hong Kong and the Philippines. We're all closer now—Virginia, California, Illinois, Arizona, and Oregon—but certainly farther than 15 miles.

Differentiation occurs by being able to be around someone important to you, instead of getting away from them. Highly differentiated people have deeply close relationships, choosing connection out of deep care or liking, without being pulled towards them compulsively or driven away from them.

In emotional fusion, sometimes couples remain together even though others can see their misery. They hang onto each other because their pseudo self is propped up through the relationship. A solid self knows what they want and need, whereas a pseudo self reacts only to those around it. In other words, it is the false sense that needs the validation and approval of others. I'm sure you know a couple, or it could be you, with one partner who looks like they encourage the other partner to be autonomous, but then suppresses it constantly on a daily basis. Like the wife who wants to start her own greeting card line and the husband who says it is a great idea, but then reminds her on a daily basis that she's the one who needs to handle the kids or pick up the dry cleaning; after all, they made a deal when they married that she'd take care of the home and hearth. For the husband, his false self or pseudo self is being propped up consistently. He is the one accomplishing what he wants, looks encouraging to his wife, and is functioning well according to the outside world.

In differentiation, you can maintain your sense of self, even when your partner is away or when you are not in a primary love relationship, because you exist with your own interests, desires, and beliefs, even without the "other." Differentiated people are aware of their impact on others, and take their partner's needs into account. It means having a core set of values and beliefs that you can change or alter without losing your identity. You can permit yourself to be influenced by others and choose to change a belief, but you cannot be manipulated and molded to satisfy your partner or anyone else. You can connect deeply with your partner, without fear of your partner's emotions overtaking you. Your feelings do not control or define your sense of self. David Schnarch says that "when you've reached a high level of differentiation, your view of conflict in relationship shifts dramatically. 'What I want for myself versus what I want for you, shifts to what I want for myself versus my wanting for you what you want for yourself.'"

Schnarch also says that because of generational boundaries and patterns across the generations, differentiation generally stays the same from one generation to the next. It only changes when a family member is motivated to rewrite the family legacy and differentiate him or herself. If you're like me, you may want to think that you are more differentiated than your partner, but nope. Research shows you'll choose a partner who is at about the same level of differentiation. If you're not at the same level, the relationship will usually end early.

Unlike the Lovebirds, you are setting yourself apart from your partner, while opening space for real togetherness and intimacy. It is about being distinctly you, while you get closer to each other. In intimacy, you are sharing the ways in which you are separate from each other, and consistently revealing new parts of yourself rather than caretaking the other person. Other validated intimacy means that you expect acceptance, validation, approval, recognition, or reciprocal disclosure from your partner. Quid pro quo. Self-validated intimacy is you maintaining your own identity and self-worth without expectation of acceptance, validation, recognition, or reciprocity from your partner. This is differentiation: the ability to maintain a clear sense of self even when loved ones are pressuring or demanding that you conform, think the same, make the same choices, or be the same.

And so our Lovebirds have taught us valuable lessons. Court your partner over your entire relationship. Actively work on intimacy and knowing your partner, keeping track of what they love, what moves them and delights them, and what they hate and don't want any part of. And don't attempt to be identical to your partner or emotionally fused. Jealousy is a waste of time and has nothing to do with your partner, and everything to do with you. Be your own individual while remaining intimately connected to your partner.

BONUS SECRET TO HOT PARTNERING: HAVE YOUR OWN DREAMS AND LIFE.

Have your own friends, interests, dreams, and desires, and let your partner have their own, enjoying when they are different from your own. It's not your partner's job to make you happy, fulfill you, or have your life turn out. It is your own. Take it on with gusto.

Isn't it about time to talk about some sex? After all, this is a book about hot partnering. And yes, Chapter 11 will take a deeper dive into connected, passionate sex, now that you have laid the groundwork for deep intimacy rather than just going through the motions. Your homework will be GREAT preparation to get in the mood, and will require you to use the tools learned throughout the book, including honesty, trust, and using I PAAVER. If you get triggered, take space, then return, reminding yourself that your partner loves you, and do the work.

THE BIRDS – JOURNAL EXERCISE

1. What are your fears about being totally intimate with your partner? What are your fears about being totally revealed and transparent? Where did that fear originate? In other words, in your childhood, did you reveal something and get in trouble? Did you see someone hold the truth against another person, being vindictive or vengeful? Were you taught to take care of someone else's feelings by withholding your truth? Write about your fears of being totally transparent, honest, and revealed with your partner.

2. What are you afraid that your partner will say? What have you already made up about what they have done or not done in their life and in the course of your relationship? How would you normally respond in hearing about past flirtations or liaisons? How do you want to respond? What would be created for your future if you were both completely willing to be expressed and honest? Take some time to write about your fears and what it is

that you want, with full self-expression between you and your partner.

3. Take some time to write whether or not you feel known by your partner. Do you feel like you know your partner deeply and intimately? Reflect and write.

4. Are you often on your own agenda, making a point, philosophizing, sermonizing, or driving discussions towards a point? What possibility opens up out of listening and practicing the art of conversation?

THE BEES – Working towards differentiation over the course of years...

1. Begin to tune into the voices in your head that are critical, attacking, or destructive. Start to name and identify these voices, and begin to reflect on the source of the negative thoughts. What are the experiences you had that led to that thinking? Who were the individuals that planted the thoughts within you? Be on alert that some of the voices may seem positive but keep you limited, in a rut, or small.

2. What are negative personality traits within you that you have incorporated from caregivers, parents, siblings, and other strong influences? Where do you see yourself acting exactly like your mother or father? Or doing the exact opposite? Have compassion for yourself in this process. Begin to let these traits go, first by simply noticing them, then working towards a choice more consistent with who you want to be. Remind yourself that you can change these traits.

3. How did you get through the pain or tough times of your childhood? What were the coping strategies you used to minimize

your distress (denial, avoidance, mistrust, busyness, rebellion, control, need for approval, external validation, playing it safe or mediocre, playing powerless in the face of circumstances, etc.)? These were ways that you protected yourself, but they are not serving you in your adult life. Begin to identify where these coping strategies have taken over your life, and begin to play with other ways of moving through distress or pain that are not damaging to you or others.

4. What do you value? What is important to you? If you had three or four main values, what are they (integrity, commitment, honesty, authenticity, generosity, giving, love, honor, passion, freedom, vulnerability, personal power, etc.)? What are some fundamental beliefs you have about yourself? The world? What does it mean to be a "good" person? Identify what is important to you. How are these distinct from those of your family? Culture? How do you live according to your ideals rather than the values of others? How do you bring meaning to your life in the long-run?

5. Practice being with those you love deeply, connecting, and hearing their opinions, values, and beliefs. Listen and know them better. Share your beliefs, opinions, and values without the need to convince anyone of anything, or to argue, or to give up what you think. If you should choose to shift a belief, it is out of your own choice rather than because you believe you will be alienated, not loved, or ridiculed.

TAKE FLIGHT

Remember to be gentle and loving with each other in this process. Use generous listening with your partner, without interrupting or adding any of your own commentary while your partner is speaking. Work on hearing and really seeing each other honestly. Create a beautiful space to complete this work with each other. If you choose to have candles, incense, or soft music playing while you share with each other, do so. Have it be your intention to hear your partner in a way you may have never heard them before. Take breathers if necessary, being patient with each partner and making sure that you are allowing space for really hearing each other. Use I PAAVER (Chapter Seven) if you get into any upset, and remind yourself that you cannot use I PAAVER until high emotion is released. If emotion gets high, take a "Time Out" to release the energy before you continue, giving each other the space for this as needed.

This exercise may be done in one evening, or spread across many—it is your choice as to how it will best serve you.

1. Take turns asking each other the following questions to explore how well you know your partner. If your partner doesn't get the answer correct (the entire answer, not just one part of the answer), tell them "No," and place a check mark next to that question, indicating that they did not get it correct. If they do get the answer correct, then place a plus sign (+) next to that question, indicating that they got it correct. Take turns going back and forth with the questions. Remember, only the partner that the question is about has the right to say whether or not the answer is correct; after all, the question is about them. And be clear: This is meant to be fun and a way to learn how much you know about each other, giving you a chance on the other side to deepen your knowing and intimacy with your partner. Do not use this exercise as a way to be right that your partner doesn't care or know you. You are utilizing this book, and your partner is participating so that you do grow closer and more intimate. Keep that present in playing this personalized version of the old 1960's television show, *The Dating Game.*[20]

2. Now spend time with each other, sharing each of your answers to all of the questions. This is a GREAT date night activity. Don't just read the question and share your answer. Tell the stories behind

each of the responses, and fully spend time and attention learning about your partner.

3. Take a walk with your partner, engaging in the art of conversation. Do not have a particular destination in mind for your walk. Do not walk with the purpose of getting exercise. Simply walk with each other for at least 30 minutes, longer if you choose. Have a soulful conversation with your partner while you walk. Remember, there does not have to be a deep or intense subject you are talking about. There are no points being made, no theories, no sermons, and no agendas; rather, it is an ambling sharing.

4. Tell each other of any affairs, near-affairs, necking, arousals, daydreams, or flirtations you have engaged in since you have known each other. Communicate about what qualities or characteristics you find yourself consistently drawn to, and what this reveals about you. Take breathers if necessary, and remind yourself that the purpose of this process is to be known and let go of the past, not to punish each other for the past and continue to engage like the past is a current reality. Take breathers if necessary. Use IPAAVER to support if challenges come up. If needed, take an hour or two, or follow up with a professional if additional support is needed.

5. Take turns. One partner speaks for 30 minutes, while the other is silent and listening without any responses. Tell your partner everything you resent them for, and everything you appreciate about them. After you have both taken turns and communicated everything, talk with each other about what you really heard the other person communicating, and what you felt as they spoke.

QUESTIONS FOR YOUR PERSONALIZED "DATING GAME"

(Adapted John Gottman, *The Seven Principles for Making a Marriage Work,* 1999, Three Rivers Press, New York, New York. p.52-54)

1. Name your partner's best friends.
2. Who has been irritating your partner lately?
3. Name one of your partner's long-term dreams.
4. Name at least three of your partner's favorite movies.
5. Name at least three of your partner's favorite songs.
6. What is your partner's favorite take-out food?
7. What is your partner's favorite "splurge" restaurant?
8. Name one accomplishment that your partner is most proud of.
9. What was your partner's most embarrassing moment in their life?
10. Name one time that your partner felt like they failed or didn't measure up.
11. Where did you and your partner go on your first date?
12. What is your anniversary date?
13. If your partner were an animal, which one would they choose to be?
14. What was your partner's favorite vacation?
15. What was your partner's least favorite vacation?
16. What medical condition runs in your partner's family?
17. What is a concern that your partner has about their health?
18. Name your partner's favorite to order in a restaurant.
19. What is your partner's favorite meal to order in an American restaurant?
20. What is your partner's order at the coffee shop? (If there are two or three different shops you go to, and the order changes, which at each shop?)
21. When your partner was a child, what did they want to be when they grew up?
22. What is your partner's favorite television show?
23. What is your partner's greatest fear?
24. Name three things on your partner's bucket list.

25. Name at least one gift that would delight your partner.
26. If your partner was buying a new car, which one would they choose (make/color/model)?
27. What is your partner's favorite perfume, cologne, or after-shave?
28. Name a smell that disgusts your partner.
29. Name a smell that your partner enjoys.
30. What is your partner's favorite time of day to make love?
31. What turns your partner on sexually?
32. What does your partner want when they are upset?
33. How does your partner feel loved by you (with gifts given, loving words, actions, etc.)?
34. If your partner were taking a vacation right now, where would they go?
35. What are your partner's most important principles in their life (honesty, love, authenticity, passion, integrity, giving, leadership, etc.)?
36. What are two or three of your partner's favorite books (can divide categories if you would like – nonfiction/fiction/reference, etc.)?
37. What is your partner sad about lately?
38. What is your partner most angered by lately?
39. What moves your partner?
40. What does your partner consider their greatest strength or quality?
41. What does your partner consider your *worst* quality or characteristic?
42. Name two people that your partner admires.
43. What is a quality that your partner has from his/her mother?
44. What is a characteristic that your partner has from his/her father?
45. What is a fantasy that you have?
46. Name a dream or nightmare that your partner has had in their life? (If one repeats, name that one.)
47. What was the name of one of your partner's favorite pets?
48. What physical feature is your partner insecure about?
49. If your partner had one week left to live, what would they do?
50. What is your partner's legacy? What is the mark they want to leave on the world?

CHAPTER ELEVEN

THE DANCE OF PASSION

*"My fault, my failure, is not in the passions I have,
but in my lack of control of them."*
– Allen Ginsberg[1]

*"Jason once told me that eye contact is the most intimacy two
people can have—forget sex— because the optic nerve is technically
an extension of the brain, and when two people look into each
other's eyes, it's brain-to-brain."*[2]
– Douglas Coupland

OK, I don't want to give the snuggly and studious looking Barn Owl a
reputation, but these little night creatures are a good representation
of passion. First, some of us would love to stay up all night and sleep

all day like the Barn Owl. And many of us would like to get the amount of action that they are getting.

When you look at the image of the Barn Owl, it may seem cuddly and wise, but I want to give you a few sobering facts that challenge that image. Let's start with the fact that Barn Owls swallow their prey whole—skin, bones, everything. And since that is quite a bit to pass through their digestive tract, twice a day they cough up pellets of their prey. Ever feel like swallowing your partner whole in an argument? Annihilating them?

The Barn Owl is like a ghost hunter, with wings that make no noise in flight, with excellent low-light vision to easily find their prey by sight. But the Barn Owl's ability to locate their prey solely by sound is the best of *any animal that has ever been tested.* They can catch mice in complete darkness in a lab, or when that mouse is hidden under vegetation or snow, by hearing them—like Ninjas.[3]

Yes, Barn Owls are usually monogamous and mate for life, although there are some reports of males having more than one mate. To snag their partner, the male Barn Owl will demonstrate amazing displays of flights, including the "moth flight," where he hovers in front of the female for several seconds with his feet dangling.[4]

Once the pair form, the male begins bringing the female prey, often far more than she can consume, and when the female reaches peak weight, the male then provides a ritual presentation of food, then copulation occurs at the nest. These little buggers can be quite active, laying between 2–18 eggs. And the pair has 2–3 clutches per year, but in some climates or in captivity, they can breed year-round. In fact, in years with plenty of food, clutches may overlap, with the female incubating a second set of eggs, and the male continuing to feed the recent little ones.[5] Even after the newly hatched birds are in the nest, the male continues to copulate with the female when he brings food.[6] The Barn Owl isn't particularly territorial, but if the nest is threatened, it will not hesitate to attack, including humans, using their serrated feet and talons directed on the intruder's face and eyes.

The Barn Owl seems like a good example for passion. After all, they have talons and won't hesitate to tear the eyes out of an intruder, and that passion is also directed in quite a bit of action in the nest. And they manage to find a way to have action even when they've got little ones in the nest with them! Something that parents with kids under the age of three undoubtedly envy. So let's get down to it.

What would a book on creating a "10" partnership with your beloved be if I didn't touch on the subject of sex (yes, double entendre)? This is obviously not the sole focus of this book, and there is ample material and books available that dwell exclusively on sexual expression, freedom, and techniques. But with the first ten chapters as foreplay, sex is bound to be pretty incredible, right? Because if you are really getting that your partner is perfect for you, understanding their deepest wounding, listening deeply to them and being totally revealed, then yes, sex is bound to be connected, present, and deeply connected—when you choose it to be.

But this chapter doesn't only focus on sex. You may be thinking, how did sex wind up with fighting? Most marriage and family therapists and psychologists can probably guess. When couples come into therapy and they are arguing, passionately enraged at what the other person is saying or vehemently disagreeing, there is energy that is present. And we only bring energy forth when we actually care. Fighting is a form of intimacy, because it shows caring for the other person and their position or point of view. If we didn't care, then there would be no energy for arguing. Conversely, when couples enter a therapist's office, and they sit apart from each other in a chilly silence with no energy to disagree, it is a warning sign that the relationship is in significant trouble, because they do not even have the energy or emotional connection to argue. So this final chapter explores two extremes of the expression of passion, the first through sexuality, and the second through fair fighting versus fighting that damages either partner or the relationship.

Before I write another word, I want to come clean. As exemplified in the previous chapter and my experience at Radical Honesty, the expression of sexuality has not always been easy or natural for me. It has been a major challenge of my lifetime, and me simply accepting that I have a body and get to fully inhabit that body, is likewise an opportunity that I have spent, and will spend, a lifetime learning. I can talk about intellectual topics, and I love delving into the mysteries of the universe. I dwell in big possibilities, and I love engaging in philosophical inquiry, psychological inquiry, and metaphysical explorations. I love full self-expression of feelings, and can cry at a Kleenex commercial. And when it comes to feeling my body, I am challenged. What is the politically correct verbiage? Inhabiting-body challenged? This manifests not only in sex but in a myriad of other ways. For example, when my kids were little, they would joke that I had superpowers because I could turn things over in a frying pan with my hands, and pull hot things out of the oven without oven mitts (not pans on broil, but hot). I have seen my son stare at me in horror with his mouth wide open because I had cut my arm in the kitchen, and blood was dripping down my arm and onto the floor, without me realizing it. I was talking and laughing away. I have broken bones and needed friends to tell me that it was sticking out and that I should probably go to the hospital. And in an extreme example, during a "rebirthing" process years ago, I stopped breathing for great length of time, happy as can be, but seriously unsettling the facilitator. You get the idea. Thankfully, about six years ago, I did intensive training on Conscious Breathing, and in addition to now doing powerful Breathwork trainings, I use the practice to actually inhabit my body, but it can still be a challenge.

Who's to say where this out-of-body comes from. I have had a lot of pretty amazing mystical experiences that give me the idea that having this body is an opportunity for me this time around. I once did a four-hour meditation, with the experience of flying with an angel in some universal realm (no LSD or anything), and feeling seriously saddened when I needed to go back into my body. From another perspective, when I was a child, I was sexually molested, either on a handful of occasions or multiple. As with most children in those situations, I have vivid memories of the wallpaper as it occurred. I remember the feel of the carpeting or the shaft of sunlight coming in through the window, but I do not remember much of what occurred or what I was feeling. It is a fabulous coping strategy that our minds create as a way to deal with things that we cannot process, or situations that threaten us in some way. So another hypothesis is that I dissociated out of my body in challenging situations, and it became as comfortable for me to be out of my body as to be in it.

Either way, I hold no resentment for what has occurred, and talked with the person who did the molesting, letting go of what occurred. I am actually grateful for the experience because it has allowed me to see what other people and therapists sometimes miss. It is as though I now have an antenna that can pick up signals unheard or unseen by many others. Because of that, I have been able to help others free themselves and let go of the past.

In my personal relationships, and the expression of sexuality, it has been a challenge, more for my partner than for me. I therefore don't intend to be hypocritical and talk about techniques, marathon lovemaking sessions, or losing yourself with abandon. I do want to focus on what this entire book has been about: creating intimacy, closeness, and connection in sexual expression, and being totally revealed. That is enough to challenge a lot of people who are quite comfortable with the actual act of fucking (yes, I said it), but not so comfortable with allowing someone to see into them. In his beautiful book, *Soul Mates,* Thomas Moore says that,

"Sex is exceedingly human—bodily, passionate, often satisfyingly improper. Some theories of humor suggest that sex often provides material for humor, precisely because it liberates us from the burden of propriety and the repression of passion. Sex also offers the rare gift of deeply felt, unreasoned joy, and laughter can sometimes be the expression of pure joy. On the other hand, perhaps because it is difficult to contain and mold into stable forms, sex can also bring with it considerable anxiety."[7]

Yes, Thomas Moore and I are actually intellectualizing a primal topic, but the point is still a good one, and the understatement of the century. If a comic goes into a sexual rift, there are nervous glances, muffled laughter, and the room is charged with anxiety. Thomas Moore goes on to say that sex can be the "means through which we allow the archetype of life to show itself, so that we live more fully and manifest ourselves more transparently."

To clarify, Carl Jung wrote about archetypes as a universal representation or expression of eternal myths and universal meaning:

"The fact is that archetypal images are so packed with meaning in themselves that people never think of asking what they really do mean...In reality, however, he has merely discovered that up till then he has never thought about his images at all. And when he starts thinking about them, he does so with the help of what he calls "reason"—which in point of fact is nothing more than the sum-total of all his prejudices and myopic views."[8]

Even in writing about archetypes, or speaking about them, our prejudices and views come through—whatever they may be. For example, no matter where you are born on our planet, or when you were born, if I say "mother," there is a representation and thoughts that go with that word. If I say "hermit," that brings to mind a different image; it is a symbol or representation that is universal. Marilyn Monroe actually became an archetype of a sex kitten. When Thomas Moore says that sex can be the means through which the archetype of life shows itself, I take it to mean that it is full expression of emotion:

joy, sadness, vulnerability, trust, passion, raunchiness, intimacy, tenderness, and any number of other feelings. It allows the full expression of body and bodily functions: with excretions, noises like quaffs, farts, even blood. It allows for full expression of thoughts: insecurities, exhibitionism, self-consciousness, other-consciousness, and on and on.

A lot of the time, books, radio, and television shows reduce sex to the medical or biological, with diagrams and discussions of different organs. In doing so, we are taking something so complex and layered, trying to reduce it in some way into something more manageable or safe. Maybe some of you remember Dr. Ruth? It was incredibly safe for an old lady to be talking in a technical way about sex. But sex, by virtue of definition, is not necessarily manageable or safe (not in the physical expression, but what is brought forth for both partners). Moore asserts that the entire "sphere of sex—emotion, body, fantasy, and relationship—fall within the domain of the soul."

What does that mean? Carl Jung distinguished between soul and spirit, and the realms of both as opportunities for us in life. Spirit can be thought of as the realm of the masculine—not male but imbued with masculine energy. Words that exemplify the experience of the masculine are: sun, accomplishment, results, time, doingness, checklists, thoughts, ambitions, and direction. Soul can be thought of as the realm of the feminine—again, not female but feminine. Words that exemplify the experience of the feminine are: moon, out of time, relationship, breathe, earth, sensate, mystical, unexplained. It's fun to think of countries or cities from the perspective of masculine and feminine, as a way to better experience the distinction—Italy: clearly feminine; United States of America: clearly masculine; Paris: feminine (just think of the Moulin Rouge and the ideals of truth and beauty); Zurich: masculine (after all, it is the city that is known for time).

Sex is of the soul and the realm of the soul. Thomas Moore points out that sexual fantasies and dreams are often signals of what is going on deep in the soul. It isn't that we want the sexual fantasy to actually occur in reality, but there is an *erotic magnetism* being pointed out. I got my master's degree at Pacifica Graduate Institute, with an emphasis on archetype, myth, dreams, and depth—all the realm and genius of Carl Jung. In that program, I felt that a whole different world was opening up when I began to look at my dreams in a different way, and to begin to respect the messages being given. When I was younger, I used to buy books on dream analysis and symbols. I used to want to reduce a dream to a concise explanation, and *de-code* it. With my exposure to the work of Carl Jung, James Hillman, and Marion Woodman, I began to see that much more is occurring when we are given dreams or fantasies through the unconscious mind.

For example, Thomas Moore describes having a dream of making love to his teacher, while he was in the seminary. Initially, he was confused by the dream, but after examining it more closely, and allowing the dream to unfold itself to him, he realized it was a signal of his deep love of education that was manifesting. He didn't want to be a priest after all, but rather a teacher, and the dream was communicating that message from his soul, through the symbol of his teacher.

Thomas Moore didn't want to make love with his teacher, or find that person sexually attractive, but his unconscious was using Eros, the god of love, to send a message pointing to something he did love: education and being the source of awakening for others.

The language of dreams and the soul is through the unconscious or fantasy. People often will take a dream and analyze it, reducing the symbols to a quick interpretation. This is one way to work with dreams, or one way to view a facet of a diamond. In depth psychology, the symbol itself is rich. For example, if you were to walk into a church and see the cross hanging in the front, that symbol has more than a simple definition. There are many feelings, thoughts, images, and connections that go with the symbol of the cross. So it is with our dreams and fantasies. I am inviting you to be in an inquiry as to the symbols of your dreams and fantasies. For example, if a woman has a fantasy of a brutal rape, it does not mean in any way, shape, or form that she wants that rape to occur. It may mean that she is feeling raped or attacked in another way. Maybe her femininity is under attack. Perhaps she wants to lose control or let go of holding on to appropriateness or the burdens of her day-to-day. If you are in inquiry about what the symbol represents, then you can bring that message into your bedroom. Not the actual fantasy, but the message or spirit behind the fantasy.

In sharing dreams and fantasies with your partner, you get to be fully revealed, and trust that your partner can hold what you are saying without simplifying it, thinking that you actually want it to occur. The original meaning of psychotherapy was the "tending of the soul."[9] So it is that you get to tend the soul of your partner. Often, our dreams and fantasies are the voice of the unconscious, prodding us along and pointing us to the next step for the growth and development of our souls, and inner yearning for growth or direction in life. When you begin to listen to the voice of the soul with your partner, your lives take on a different meaning and dimension, with total intimacy and support for the development of both partners.

Yes, if you choose to activate a fantasy or enact it, then great. It is being able to differentiate between desires of the soul, and ones that we want to bring alive through role and sex play. The full sharing of fantasies, dreams, and desires definitely opens up rich possibility of full expression when it comes to all expressions, including sexual.

Moore says, "A man and wife are in a sexual relationship all day long, every day: What happens in bed cannot be separated from what happens in life. It's no accident that the word intercourse means both physical lovemaking and intimate conversation." This brings us to the passionate expression of anger.

Some of us were raised in homes where we were taught that anger was bad. In those homes, anger is not expressed, but it has a way of seeping into the foundation and being breathed into every wall. There are tight silences, clipped remarks, heavy sighing and seething rage just below the surface. The medical community has now done ample research, connecting the suppression of emotions, like anger, with heart-disease and other illness, but still, for many people, anger is an emotion that is off-limits.

Other people were raised in homes where anger was modeled in a destructive way. There was raging, yelling, sometimes even hitting, punching, punching of walls, throwing of objects, name-calling, and other explosions. Studies now show that male toddlers who witness a father repeatedly beating their mother, will identify with the male, and are likely to perpetuate violence in their relationships. There are many studies showing that children who witness domestic violence are more likely to be affected by violence as adults, either as victims or perpetrators.[10]

This expression of anger has become pandemic in our culture, with fans at football and baseball games killing other fans out of rage. It is passed from one generation to the next, often without the cycle being broken.

But anger itself is not bad; it is even healthy. It is how that anger is expressed that makes all the difference. Harville Hendrix says that anger is "like a fire. If we contain fire appropriately and allow it to burn safely, it nourishes us, keeps us alive, and provides us with warmth and light. If we let it rage out of control, it damages or destroys us. If we suffocate it and stamp it out, eventually the cold and the dark will seep into our bones, and we become numb."[11] If fire is lit in a forest and rages out of control, there is destruction in its path, and the loss of life. Yet the firefighters light a fire line to actually stop the raging fire from jumping highways, swallowing homes, and doing more damage. Used powerfully, it can be a tremendous force for good. So it is with the expression of anger.

Children fully express anger, and when they do, it immediately dissipates. A child does not attempt to repress their upset. They scream and cry, letting it out fully, and then a few minutes later, they are laughing, playing, and on to another emotion. Expressing anger in a safe and constructive manner is key to you also experiencing joy and exuberance for life—just as a child is fully expressed. Hendrix says that "we fear that what is inside of us is dark, ugly, and overpowering. Yet once we gain the courage to wrestle with this fear and fully express our feelings, we learn an astonishing thing: what is hiding inside us is our own blocked life energy."

It is not unusual for you to be a little worried about your next argument, thinking, "Will all of the work I did go out the window? Will I remember to use I PAAVER in the midst of the upset?" I have heard similar concerns from participants at retreats, and that's why I want to make sure you are well prepared for your next argument. How do we know there will be another argument? Because you brought your partner to you to heal old wounds, and the way in which that occurs is your partner manages to find the wound and stick their fingers inside. Also, it is certain that disagreements will occur, because you are not the same people, and you have differing views, thoughts, and opinions.

If it is at all encouraging, John Gottman says that "most marital arguments cannot be solved." According to his research, those arguments are rooted in fundamental differences of lifestyle, personality, and values. Boiling it all down, Gottman says that "it is important to get to the bottom line of what is causing the conflict between you, not to solve it."[12] And the way that Harville Hendrix says it, and we worked on it in Chapter Six, "getting to the wound that we are seeking to be healed through our partnership." We can learn to go out of our way to provide our partner with what it is that they so desperately want—to heal that wound. And we can be compassionate, alert to the ways in which we may end up re-opening the wound through words or actions.

Some things to avoid in your next argument that come from the Gottman Love Lab:

1. Do not begin a discussion with criticism, sarcasm, or contempt—this is known as a "harsh start-up," and will not end well.

   An example of a harsh start-up would be, "You never think of anyone but yourself...," or "I can't believe that I'm the lucky one that gets to do the dishes AGAIN!" Or, "So help me God, I can't take another one of your excuses." It is beginning immediately by lashing out at your partner, either overtly or supposedly covertly. Think about the harsh start-ups that you have used with your partner, and you may want to jot them down to humble yourself. Again, notice I'm not suggesting you write down your partner's harsh start-ups. That wouldn't be being responsible, and would be you collecting evidence to be right about something.

2. Do not allow the Four Horsemen of the Apocalypse into the argument:

   Criticism: a global negativity or attack on your partner's character. You may want to complain about something, which is fine. But a complaint is specific, not a global attack on your partner's character. For example, you can say, "I cooked dinner, and now you want me to do the dishes too, and that feels like I have to do everything. It's unfair." That is very different than saying, "I have to do everything, and you do nothing. You are so selfish. Of course, I have to do the dishes even though I cooked dinner. It would be too much to actually expect support!" That is a global criticism of your partner's character, with contempt, which brings us to the next deadly Horseman...

   Contempt: sarcasm, name-calling, eye-rolling, hostile humor—anything that conveys disgust for your partner. The message with contempt is that you are superior to your partner, and that the way they think, do things, speak, or act is inferior to you. You convey more than judgment and disgust for who they are. It may be mocking them, using hostile humor, making faces, demeaning them. It may even be your tone of voice. When I get contemptuous, my tone of voice can get incredibly even with a teaching tone, like I need to be the one to illuminate my husband. Ick.

Defensiveness: "It isn't my fault; it's yours." Most couples play this game. It's boring. It's like watching an endless tennis volley where no one is really doing anything special—just hitting the ball back and forth. It's exhausting. Let's be clear: No one started the argument. It's been going since you got together and is the same old dance. It's a loop, with each of you having clearly identified roles. Dr. Susan Johnson spells it out nicely in *Hold Me Tight,* and Terry Real also beautifully explains the loop in *The New Rules of Marriage.*[13, 14] There is an adaptation of that spin at the end of this chapter, for you to dig in deeper.

Stonewalling: Tuning out, avoiding, ignoring, acting like you don't care—men are often the stonewallers in an argument. This could be purely anthropological, given that the amount of milk that a woman produces while breastfeeding is directly related to how relaxed she feels. And men, when hunting for game and protecting their families and children, needed to stay on alert far longer than women. Women learned to calm themselves and self-soothe more effectively than men. To this day, if there is a loud explosion nearby, men will have an elevated heart rate longer than women.[15] This is obviously a generalization and by no means true for everyone. What this means, if you are in a relationship with a man, is to be a little patient if he appears to be stonewalling. He may need some time away to process what is occurring and how he is feeling if the emotions become too intense and overwhelming. Sometimes space in the midst of arguments actually supports.

3. Flooding – when one person feels overwhelmed by negativity and goes to protecting.

   Sometimes women are great at verbal vomiting. We have a way of just barfing out everything at once. Meanwhile, if you've got a guy, he is sitting there looking shocked and overwhelmed, getting more and more quiet. ALERT: He's flooded. It was too much all at once, and for a male brain, this often results in not knowing what to focus on.

   Think about it; anthropologically, men were hunters. They needed to stay alert and have a single point of focus, or they could have been killed by the leopard who ran far faster than they did. Women were out gathering, scanning the savannah for berries, water sources, and other edibles. This still is in play. Traditionally, the female brain does much better at seeing an overview, while the masculine brain wants a point of focus. If you've got a guy, thin out your words. Take a breather before going into the other 74 things he's done wrong this week. Think Barn Owl focused on their prey. That's your guy.

4. In an argument, pay attention to your physiological responses. If your heart rate is elevated at or above around 100 BPM, it "means that you simply cannot process social interaction. When your heart rate gets up to 100 BPM in a relationship setting, that's called flooding. If you're not paying attention, flooding leads to erratic communication. Erratic communication leads to the Four Horsemen. The Four Horsemen lead to emotional disengagement and eventually to dissolution of the relationship.[16] Really, Gottman has tracked it. If you are sweating, beginning to feel hot, stop the argument and take a TIME OUT.

5. Failed Repair Attempts – attempts by one partner to de-escalate the tension.

John Gottman says that the failure to accept Repair Attempts predicts with 90% accuracy whether or not a relationship will last. He also says that there is a Repair Attempt made on average every three minutes for most couples. Repair Attempts are moves like:

- One partner doing something silly to break the tension, like sticking a tongue out or making a funny face
- Reaching out to hug your partner
- Saying, "I'm a boob; let's stop this."

Essentially, in an argument, it is your job to notice the Repair Attempts and to take them when they are made. A few years into our marriage, my husband and I had three dogs—a Labrador, a Lab-Rottweiler mix, and a blind Boxer-Shepherd. When we are in an argument, my husband has become adept at imitating one of the dogs. The Lab-Rottie had an under-bite and gives a pretty intense look, while the Black Lab is constantly excited about everything, and the blind Boxer-Shepherd gives a little cross-eyed look and sits like a sailor with her legs splayed open. The moment his face shifts into one of their expressions, the argument is set aside. Now we have four dogs, and all four are supporting our arguments in not getting too elevated.

Every couple has their own versions of Repair Attempts. Make them and take them. That goes along with letting go of being right. At the same time, if you are a person who does just about anything to avoid conflict, then you may attempt to use a Repair Attempt as a way to manipulate your way out of confrontation. In that case, it is not forwarding because you are holding back your true feelings and manipulating your partner. It needs to be true for you in order for you to make a Repair Attempt, not a manipulation.

6. Being entrenched in bad memories or negative interpretation of your partner.

You know these people. They are the ones who are eager to tell you about how horrible their partner is. They want to tell the recent story about how they were wronged. And when you attempt to bring up a positive quality about their partner, they meet you with yet another story about what a nightmare that person is. Is that person trying to convince you about what bad judgment they had in choosing to be with their partner? Are they wanting you to agree and feel sorry for them, even though they are clearly the one choosing it? It's a losing game. If you are this person, big warning: It will not end well. You will undoubtedly be right about whatever negative spin or interpretation you have about them. Whatever negative things you have decided about your partner, EVERYONE does not agree with you. There is a person or people who see that person as amazing, amusing, kind... something other than your pronouncement. Remember that chapter on LETTING GO....review it and do it.

I encourage you to read more about the Gottman Love Lab, and ways in which you are arguing that are damaging your relationship. For now, I feel that this is important enough information that I wanted to include it as red flags to get out of a heated discussion.

Some healthy parameters for you to express anger: First, if you are angry with your partner, make an appointment to express that anger. Yep, an actual appointment. If it is in the moment, you can say, "I'm upset about this; can we talk about it right now?" If the answer is no, then set an appointment. Grant requests for appointments as soon as possible, preferably immediately.

Second, both partners remain until the process is complete, unless it becomes too overwhelming for one (flooding), or the other becomes too angry to proceed (heart rate increase, blood pressure rising). In that case, a time-out is taken until both partners can resume, the one partner clearing their head and checking in with what they are feeling underneath the flooding, and the other partner getting some of the anger physically out of their body before resuming.

Third, neither partner causes bodily harm to himself/herself or their partner. Fourth, neither partner destroys ANY property. That means no throwing things, hitting walls, hurting yourself or others, including pulling hair, shoving, or making threats to hurt anything your partner values.

Yes, yelling is fair game in expressing anger, as is swearing. God knows I tend to swear like a sailor (no offense to sailors), in or out of arguments. Name calling is OFF-LIMITS. Those tend to stick.

Remind yourself in the midst of an argument that you wouldn't be arguing if you didn't care. You are feeling passion in the expression of your emotions precisely because you do care. And the expression of your truth will allow your partner to know you more fully and, in the end, create intimacy.

Yes, anger is a drug, and a damn strong one at that. In other words, you don't want to be using that drug with regularity, or you will become addicted to it. There is a great scene in the movie, *What the Bleep Do We Know?* where the viewer has an animated view of what occurs at a cellular level when anger floods into the system.[17] From a brain perspective, it is an elaborate game of tag. The moment you become angry, the amygdala activates and then plays tag with the hypothalamus. The hypothalamus releases corticotropin-releasing hormones, which triggers the pituitary gland. The pituitary gland releases adrenocorticotropic hormones that tag the adrenal gland. The adrenal glands release stress hormones like cortisol, adrenaline, and noradrenaline, a cocktail that poses a nightmare for your brain. For example, cortisol causes neurons to accept too much calcium, and a calcium overload can cause the cells to fire too rapidly, resulting in the death of those cells. The hippocampus and prefrontal cortex are most vulnerable to this calcium overload, resulting in an inability to plan for the future and make good decisions, as well as short-term memory loss and inability to form memories properly. Too much cortisol also suppresses serotonin production, meaning depression instead of happiness.

In terms of that nightmare cocktail flooding though your body, you can expect elevated heart rate, a rise in blood pressure, tension in your arteries, and an increase in blood glucose and fatty acid production. When those symptoms become chronic, they lead to the clogging of blood vessels, leading to stroke and heart attack. As that is occurring, cells are killed, thyroid function decreases, and cancers cells begin to rise. Blood flow decreases, and the metabolism slows down. Bone density lowers, eyesight decreases, and you are ripe for migraine headaches.[18] And the more that deadly game of tag is played in your brain, the more the cells within every part of your body become conditioned for that response. Meaning that each cell becomes addicted to the dangerous flood of chemicals they have been conditioned to receive.

So yes, anger can be healthy if expressed in a healthy way. It allows for expression when things feel unfair, or we feel unheard or frustrated by the conditions of life. And if we are constantly expressing anger, or it is taking over us, then it is probably a good idea to get some support with a therapist, coach, or counselor. Our partner may just be the wall to hit the ball against, when it is an inside job that is needed instead of the constant lashing out on our partner.

The Barn Owl is a great little example of passion, expressed sexually, and through anger. And perhaps the size of that little bird gives the message that even the smallest amount of passion can powerfully impact our relationships. BONUS SECRET: AS MADONNA SAID, EXPRESS YOURSELF, AND BE AWARE OF THE IMPACT OF YOUR EXPRESSION.[19]

You have read this book and have done incredibly hard work in journaling and exercises because you have a commitment to your relationship being extraordinary. By virtue of the fact that you found this book, you are committed to deep connection, passion, and intimacy. It takes work and commitment to be in a relationship and to grow with another person through life. It is easy to be on that mountaintop and be the source of love, joy, peace, and light, but it is another thing to do that when bills are coming in, someone promised to do something and didn't, or any number of day-to-day breakdowns that occur in being in a relationship. I believe it is a lifetime of practice to remain the source of love, peace, light, and joy in the face of whatever is occurring, experiencing our anger, sadness, and loss, but not being taken over by them. Likewise, experiencing our joy, passion, and freedom, and also letting them come and go as a process, rather than thinking anything is permanent.

Recently, my stepmother died. She was an amazingly powerful woman, and she was married three times. I think she got it right on the last one. About a year before she died and was well into the devastation of Lou Gehrig's disease, they renewed their wedding vows in front of family and close friends. The priest said something that hit me deeply—essentially saying that in the midst of much discord on our planet, with nations raging and people clinging to their own perspective, unwilling to be empathetic or see from another perspective, when people see a thriving, loving relationship, it is an example of what is possible in every relationship, even on a global scale. If two people can travel through their lives together, growing, changing, and adapting, and still love each other through those changes, what an incredible example and inspiration for everyone around them. Go forth with light bursting from your partnership!

THE BEES

1. Enter the realm of the soul. Bring to mind a sexual fantasy that you have had in your life. Maybe it has repeated itself through your life; maybe it has occurred only once or twice. Maybe the fantasy occurred while you were asleep, or maybe while you were awake, actively imagining it. Write it down, remembering as many of the symbols and details as possible.

2. Each partner, bring something to spice up your sex life and foreplay. DO NOT GO SHOPPING TOGETHER. This is for you to explore on your own what you believe would be interesting or fun to try. Perhaps it's playing with a sexual fantasy with special clothes, perhaps a sex toy you've heard about, or maybe a massage lotion. Let your imagination go. Have fun, and personally pack your item, or items, for a special date with your partner.

TAKE FLIGHT

First, this homework may occur over a night—and WOW, what a night!! Or, it may occur over two or three days, a week, a month, or a few months. Reminder: With sex, there is no "normal"; there is only what works for you and your partner: your choice. Don't feel pressured to get this all done in one sitting, or laying as the case may be.

Keep in mind that when your partner is sharing their sexual fantasy, it doesn't mean that they want it to happen. They probably do not. Instead, I ask you to be in exploration with your partner about the symbols or images. What might that symbol mean? Your job in communicating is to un-censor yourself, being revealed. Your job in listening is to openly hear, asking your partner questions to explore the symbols, which may or may not have anything to do with sex. Hear from a soul level.

Support each other lovingly as you do this exercise. Create a beautiful space for you to complete this work, with candles, soft music, or whatever will support you.

1. Choose a Partner A and a Partner B. Partner A will go first. You are going to set your journal aside and share, fully revealed and uncensored, your sexual fantasy. Partner B, listen from your soul, asking questions to better understand the images and symbols being presented by the unconscious. Be in exploration of what could be being communicated through this fantasy, and how you can bring that message alive in your relationship—not through enacting the fantasy, but by embracing the message. Ask questions, Partner B, and let Partner A do the leading. Take time to adequately explore, at least 15 minutes.

2. Now, Partner B, it is your turn to share a waking or sleeping sexual fantasy. Partner A, you are listening from your soul, asking questions to be in inquiry of the symbols, and letting Partner B do the leading. How can you bring the message of the fantasy into your lives and sexual expression? Take at least 15 minutes to be in inquiry.

3. Masturbate to orgasm in front of each other with no assistance from the other. Fully communicate what you enjoyed about doing it in front of your partner, what was challenging in the experience, and what turned you on. Allow the partner, who was witness, an opportunity to communicate their experience of watching. This is an exercise in being totally revealed, open, expressed, and seen by your partner. Do not masturbate simultaneously, but give full attention to your partner as they masturbate, and absorb their full attention as you masturbate.

4. Next, you each brought an item that you thought would be fun to spice up your foreplay and sex life. One at a time, you are to present your item to your partner and explain to your partner

what was appealing to you about that particular item. You are to share why you want to explore this part of your sexuality with your partner. Keep the relationship loop open in your communication. Ask questions to explore with your partner, with emotion. Your partner has full choice as to whether they want to engage in the exploration with you or not. If you are afraid of something about the toy or item, share your fears with your partner. Don't just go along, shoving your fear inside. Likewise, don't say no simply because of your own comfort zone, fears, or keeping power of intimacy in your relationship. Give at least 30 minutes of *play* to each partner's sexual item. Reminder: It is play, not homework, a "have to," or work.

5. According to tantric sex experts, self-awareness during sex is part of our sexual potential and a powerful goal of sex. They say this helps partners to focus their minds and emotions, channeling their energy and transforming their unity into ecstasy. Tonight, prior to having sex, sit in the yab-yum position, and place your right hand over your partner's heart. Your partner takes their right hand and places it over your heart. Imagine that you are sending out your love energy, through your heart, down your arm, and out your right hand into your partner. Take your other hand and place it over your partner's hand, pressing it into your heart. When coming together for tantric sex, the couple states intentions about what they want to happen through their lovemaking. This ritual usually starts by sitting in the yab-yum position, looking into each other's eyes, palms pressed together, and then declaring, for example: "I intend for this to be a beautiful exchange of our love for one another, feeling peace in our hearts, and sharing a deeper level of closeness than ever before." Your intention can be light-hearted: "I intend for us to laugh and celebrate tonight." Your intention can be an expression of love for the greater good for all. A couple could dedicate the lovemaking experience to a higher purpose: "I dedicate this time of being together for you achieving your dreams, for peace on our planet, and for people not as

blessed as we are in this moment to experience love in their lives." Each partner, set your intention or dedication for your lovemaking.[21]

6. Hold each other in silence for at least 10 minutes, rocking each other and tenderly caressing, without any sexual activity.

CHAPTER TWELVE

YOU'D HAVE TO BE A LOON

"Love, n. A temporary insanity curable by marriage."[1]
– Ambrose Bierce, *The Unabridged Devil's Dictionary*

*"People always fall in love with the most perfect aspects of each
other's personalities. Who wouldn't? Anybody can love the most
wonderful parts of another person. But that's not the clever trick.
The really clever trick is this: Can you accept the flaws? Can you look
at your partner's faults honestly and say, "I can work around that. I
can make something out of it?" Because the good stuff is always
going to be there, and it's always going to be pretty and sparkly, but
the crap underneath can ruin you."*[2]
– Elizabeth Gilbert, *Committed:
A Skeptic Makes Peace with Marriage*

*"To say that one waits a lifetime for his soulmate to come around is
a paradox. People eventually get sick of waiting, take a chance on
someone, and by the art of commitment become soulmates,
which takes a lifetime to perfect."*[3]
– Criss Jami, *Venus in Arms*

For many people, the idea of getting married is crazy. They would have to be certIflably looney to walk down the aisle and take the plunge. Given the statistics I've mentioned on divorce in this book, the odds are now against us. And yet billions of people willingly dive in, year after year. At this point, nearly seventeen years in, I can attest that it is not for the faint of heart or the faint of spirit. If it doesn't break you, it will most definitely grow you up: grow you up, with you getting out of petty self-absorption, needing to have the concern and welfare of another be bigger than your own; grow you spiritually, showing you every part of you that is attached, needy, fearful, angry, bitter—every part of you that pushes people away—then you have a chance to heal it; grow you psychologically, every limited or small thought made apparent for you to choose to keep or discard; grow you beyond who you know yourself to be.

And so the beautiful bird for this final chapter is the Loon of the Northwoods. I grew up in Northern Wisconsin, and the loon was a haunting companion in my childhood. It is the perfect bird to represent the insanity of love, the haunting quality of when we feel separated from our love, and the beauty of a love story that only you can write.

Loons do not mate for life. Recent studies of breeding pairs show that loons live 20 years or more, and over the course of their lifetime, they often get evicted from their territories. If the partner does not return in the spring, or is replaced by a rival loon, the loon then moves to a non-territorial space and finds a replacement mate. Since they live a long life and face repeated eviction with human encroachment, they have multiple mates over the course of their lifetime. But loons are genetically monogamous, raising their young together. They like their space, with small lakes having only one breeding pair, and larger lakes sometimes having more than one pair. After they mate, they stay close to each other, less than 65 feet apart, and if separated, make an effort to be close to each other again.[4]

The loon seems like a good example for this final chapter, going a little into my love story. I grew up in Lac du Flambeau, Wisconsin—truly God's country for me. Spring, summer, and fall were marked by the call of the loon, across the lake from where I lived. And when a pair would somehow lose each other, there is no sound quite as haunting and beautiful as their call to find each other again. It is lonely, melancholy, and haunting. To this day it is my favorite call of any bird, taking me back to my childhood.

I had the privilege of being a little white girl on a Chippewa reservation, which is a completely different book for another time. Needless to say, that experience shaped me and my brothers and sisters. I don't believe I would have chosen to do what I do in my life if not for the many ways I was impacted by that experience. I cherish the opportunities that I was given, and to be given a chance to experience what it means to be a minority in our nation; and it also came with a host of challenges that are commonplace to people who are the actual minorities in our mixing pot of America. Suffice it to say that as the youngest of eight children, and without consistent mothering, I was lonely, melancholy, and withdrawn, which is why the call of the loon struck a chord within my own heart.

How did I hear the call that hit that loneliness within my own heart? Let me give a little background as to how I met my husband, and the magical love story that unfolded. I met my husband because I declared that he would come into my life. He absolutely hates this story. He is beyond annoyed that he is the result of me making a declaration that I would find the man of my dreams. And he thinks that manifesting a declaration isn't very romantic. Maybe that's true, but it felt romantic to me.

I had been training self-development trainings for about seven years, when I started to hear whispers among the graduates of the workshops: "You can't have a successful relationship if you do transformational work," and "None of the trainers have really good relationships." And at that point, I had to admit, it was a little jarring, with accuracy. I had been in and out of a few relationships since doing the work of transformation, but I had been single for about four years and was clearly not looking for a relationship. I didn't date and was practiced at using an invisible shield to keep offers from even being made. I justified my choice of *singledom* by making it clear that I was absolutely elated in my life. I was beyond fulfilled by my career, and was lacking no intimacy, since it was being fulfilled through deep connection and a profound sense of oneness in my training work. I didn't date and didn't want to date. I think I had gotten spoiled by knowing people so profoundly and immediately through the work that I am blessed to do. I had no interest in superficialities, posing, or all the ways we traditionally go through the dating scene—definitely in America.

After realizing that there was a blind spot somewhere, and that I could use some assistance, I contacted a relationship coach and licensed psychotherapist for some concentrated work. I knew I wouldn't be able to pull the wool over his eyes, since he had worked with a few other people in my profession. Our first session was in August of 2001, and when I explained that I hadn't dated in years and had little interest, but thought it was an area where there could be a blind spot, he was quick to point out that I had no need for a relationship, since my intimacy needs were being met elsewhere. When he saw this so quickly, I knew that our collaboration would yield something. He then set a game for the next month: begin to take down my force field of invincibility, so that people would at least feel that I was available to ask out on a date. I was initially very resistant, making it abundantly clear that I didn't want to date just anyone and have a bunch of guys asking me out. He insisted that the goal was to get asked on dates, and that I did not have to accept the offer if I didn't want to. That first month of traveling from Washington, D.C. to Southern California, where I was doing most of my training work, was absolutely crazy. I was asked out on airplanes, in airports, the grocery store—by firefighters, policemen, and businessmen—you name it. I politely declined all of them. Step one complete.

September 2001, I wrote *the list.* Undoubtedly, some of you probably have created a list of the qualities or characteristics you wanted in a partner. I was quite clear on what I wanted: a man who was deep, spiritual but not religious, tapped into the messages of the universe, loving, kind, committed to growth, and funny. I was most clear that I also wanted a man who didn't want to date. I had no interest in dating at all. I had little patience for small talk. Even now, cocktail mingling and baby showers are agony to me, unless I can find one person to corner for a deep and substantial conversation. I didn't like the inauthenticity of presenting the best parts of yourself to another, like advertising for drugs that doesn't say the list of warnings clearly or loud enough. I simply wanted to fall in love and get married without having to do the dating. During that September, my focus shifted dramatically to the people in the World Trade Center, the Pentagon, and the vulnerability of our nation. I was reminded that life is urgent, and that people are what really matter at the end of the day.

I learned later that my husband was supposed to be in the Millennium Hotel, across from the World Trade Center, on September 11, 2001. He was supposed to be attending meetings that week, with the celebrity, Sean Combs—at that time known as P. Diddy. (Side note to Sean Combs: I've attempted to send you a thank you for being sick and not getting on that plane. I owe much to you.) You see, Sean Combs had partied too hard the night before, and in route to the airport, my husband was told that the meeting was canceled. He turned around, went home, and went back to bed. When he woke up a little later, he had about 67 phone messages from people who had thought he was undoubtedly injured or dead in the terrorist attacks. One of the calls was from his soon-to-be-ex-wife, Lori, who had just participated in a powerful transformational training that changed her life. She told him that she loved him, wanted the best for him, and she was clear that she wanted him to be in the next training. Even though they were getting a divorce, she wanted him to be happy and live the life he wanted to live. They had an intense phone call that day, and my husband was enrolled in training.

It was early October 2001, and I headed to California to conduct an intensive course on self-discovery, with a training company owned by a good friend, WorldWorks.[5] On the first night of the training, in the first row, my eye caught the eyes of an intent-looking Hispanic man. Our eyes locked for a little longer than they should have, and my very first thought was, "Thank God, you're back." The thought took me by surprise. I didn't even register what the man looked like, but I was clear that he had awakened some part of me I wasn't aware of, and that he felt incredibly familiar. He later shared that he had a similar thought and feeling in that moment. We felt like we *knew* each other. Maybe it was some part of our soul's calling out to each other. For those who believe in past lives, perhaps that was present. In fact, we have quite a story about that, maybe for the Epilogue.

On that first night, I called my partner in the work of transformation, and best friend, Lisa Kalmin. I stated that I had an attraction for someone who was in the training. To be clear, it was highly unusual for me to find anyone attractive while working with them. In fact, it had only occurred one other time, years before, and that time was a brief infatuation. I knew immediately that this was distinct from the crush I had enacted some years earlier. My friend and mentor asked if I could set aside my feelings long enough to actually serve this man, Gene, and I said that I could. And I successfully set it aside. For the remainder of the training, he was another participant, and I felt nothing specifically for him. But on Sunday, in the last hour of the workshop, the feelings came rushing back to me.

After that introductory course, Gene had painted me a card, thanking me. He was an artist and had a degree in fine arts, but he hadn't been painting at all. After his training, he picked up his paintbrush for the first time in about eight years and painted that card, a ship heading to sea at full sail. It was a snapshot from a meditative exercise in the training, evoking William Ernest Henley's poem, "Invictus"—"I am the master of my fate: I am the captain of my soul."[6] I was touched, but I knew I couldn't contact him since it wasn't a level relationship and, for me, it wouldn't be in integrity as a trainer to approach or make a pass at a student. My best friend laughed and joked that if he was going to be a viable option, he would need to continue to participate in the work of transformation. She was right. I wouldn't have given him credence unless he'd been willing to invest in himself and be open to continued work. And to be clear, my life is about learning, being open, and stepping into possibilities. If my partner wanted to hunker down with a closed mind, remaining certain in their current version of reality, it would be a set-up for disaster. Thankfully, Gene chose to go to the second-level training. When he completed *Breakthrough*, I began to get a glimpse of what was possible. Then he moved on to his three-month *Leadership Practice*. Every time I saw him, his hugs were a little longer than most participants, saying I was "an angel" to him. Was he simply loving me, like other participants who often put me on a pedestal after their training? Was he just grateful? Or was it something more? I kept vacillating between thinking that he reciprocated the feelings and questioning what I was feeling.

I knew I couldn't make the first move but had to allow him to contact me, which felt like absolute agony, given that Gene can be more introverted, and at times, self-doubting. Finally, an email came, then another that made it totally clear. Within days, we were on the phone from Virginia to California, burning up the lines for about six to eight hours a night. There was little chitchat but lots of diving deeply into our lives and who we were, wanted to be, and what mattered to us. We decided to meet in Chicago, Illinois, at Thanksgiving, for him to meet my family and to spend real one-on-one time with each other. When we finally met in O'Hare Airport, we dropped our bags at our feet, holding each other, suspended in time. Other travelers who were passing by were clapping and hooting because it was evident how grateful we were to be in that moment. Ironically, we both look back to that moment as the first time we were "alone" together, even though we were in one of the busiest airports in the world at one of the busiest times. At dinner, with much of my family that first night, Gene told them that we were going to be married. In January, he came to the East Coast to move me, and we ambled across the nation. In March, on my birthday, Gene officially proposed; and in December, we were married, in Keystone, Colorado. Whirlwind—and NO DATES!

I am giving a little background so that you have an idea of how my husband and I were almost like magnets, pulled towards each other because we both seemed to recognize a part of each other that few others had recognized prior. For as much as my husband survived by becoming artistic, internal, and accommodating, I survived by bravado, feigning greater confidence than I possessed, and ambition. Where Gene shrinks back from saying what is occurring for him, I rush in, like the bulls of Pamplona, sometimes saying far more than I should. Both Gene and I have a need for approval and validation to fill some whole of self-doubt. When I feel I fell short of that approval, I look to accomplish more and prove myself. When Gene falls short, he retreats into a shroud of self-doubt and depression, enacting what I often refuse to give space. It is a match made in heaven. We recognize the other the parts of ourselves that are still deeply wounded. He is the touchstone that calms my frenzied need for accomplishment, and I am the fire under his bum that spurs action when he'd rather remain in a cocoon.

Needless to say, that isn't what was presented on the surface, but thankfully, through much internal work, we could actually see what was occurring underneath the surface. This is the stuff that most people work to hide. But I trust that through some of the work you've done in this book, digging a little deeper, you have begun to discover that is where the real gold is.

Through the many humbling stories of our struggles, along with those of some other amazing and committed couples in this book, you already know that our marriage is far from perfect. Richard David Bach wrote, "You teach best what you most need to learn."[7] So, at some level, in writing this book and conducting Couples Retreats, I am doing my own work, keeping distinctions present, and holding myself accountable to a higher standard than I might if not writing this book. Thank you for doing this work alongside, and for your commitment to your relationship being a source of inspiration, for both spiritual and psychological growth.

We are like those loons, sometimes swimming in very different realms and worlds, calling to each other from afar. We like our space, and we also like to know that the other is near us, sharing the journey—not too close but available. And when we get too much distance, which by now we know has nothing to do with actual space between us, we find our way back to each other. Thankfully, we always have up until now, and I am praying that we continue to do so.

At some point, I needed to say that this book was done. Otherwise I could keep writing and writing, with no end in sight. There is much more to be said, and infinite sources of wisdom when it comes to your relationship. I hope that your time invested and work with your partner has been valuable. Here are some words to leave you with, which inspire me in my marriage and life, and are present in most of the journal work and exercises you have done, clearly reminding me of the loon and the space between us. Let this be a blessing on your union:

"Let there be spaces in your togetherness, And let the winds of the heavens dance between you. Love one another but make not a bond of love: Let it rather be a moving sea between the shores of your souls. Fill each other's cup but drink not from one cup. Give one another of your bread but eat not from the same loaf. Sing and dance together and be joyous, but let each one of you be alone, Even as the strings of a lute are alone though they quiver with the same music. Give your hearts, but not into each other's keeping. For only

the hand of Life can contain your hearts. And stand together, yet not too near together: For the pillars of the temple stand apart, And the oak tree and the cypress grow not in each other's shadow."[8]
– Khalil Gibran, *The Prophet*

I honor the commitment you are making to your partnership. I honor the time you have invested in your relationship, and I appreciate being on this amazing journey with you. Remember to unleash your passion AND to fight fairly. Use I PAAVER to really listen when there are upsets or disagreements. Love each other, and let your relationship be an example of what is possible in relationship: loving each other through challenges, differences between you, and remaining insanely committed to your partner and *love*.

About the Author

Over the past 27 years, Lynne Sheridan has trained tens of thousands of people around the world in achieving their dreams, no matter what the circumstance, obstacle, or consideration.

Through her work in transformation, Lynne is most inspired by the courage it takes people to go beyond their comfort zones, risking and letting go to become the best possible version of themselves. As a partner in Inspire Coaching and iNSPIRE BUSINESS SUCCESS, she works with individuals and corporate leadership teams in busting through limitations and achieving results and experiences that were previously only imagined, or even more thrilling, unimagined.

Lynne is a relationship expert, with a wealth of experience in working with couples to truly connect, with a depth of intimacy, understanding, and compassion through four levels of intensive Couples Retreats. She knows all too well the investment that it takes to be successful in business, but the price shouldn't be the loss of love—her intensive retreats come out of the vison for the genuine experience of life working across the board.

Lynne graduated from the University of Redlands, with a double degree in political science and creative writing. She has a certificate in transpersonal studies, from the Institute for Transpersonal Psychology, and a master's degree in counseling psychology, from Pacifica Graduate Institute. She also is a licensed marriage and family therapist, with a full-time practice in Orange, California.

Lynne is the wife of an amazing artist, and the mother of a nineteen-year old boy and a sixteen year old girl, who consistently serve as teachers to her, as well as a constant source of inspiration.

ENDNOTES

PROLOGUE:

1. *The Art of Loving: An Enquiry into the Nature of Love,* Erich Fromm, New York, N.Y.: Harper Brothers, 1956.
2. Bird Watchers Digest. Do Birds Mate for Life? Dawn Hewitt http://www.birdwatchersdigest.com/bwdsite/solve/faqs/do-birds-mate-for-life.php 1-28-17
3. Bird Watchers Digest. Do Birds Mate for Life? Dawn Hewitt http://www.birdwatchersdigest.com/bwdsite/solve/faqs/do-birds-mate-for-life.php 1-28-17
4. *Discourses, Fragments, Handbook*, Robin Hard (trans.), Oxford: Oxford University Press, 2014.
5. *Soul Mates,* Thomas Moore, New York, N.Y.: Harper Collins, 1994.
6. *When Men Batter Women*, Neil Jacobson and John Gottman PhD, New York, N.Y.: Simon & Schuster, 2007.
7. *Getting the Love You Want Workbook,* Harville Hendrix, New York, N.Y.: Henry Holt & Company, 1994.
8. *2017 New Year's Resolutions: The Most Popular and How to Stick to Them,* Nicole Spector, http://www.nbcnews.com/business/consumer/2017-new-year-s-resolutions-most-popular-how-stick-them-n701891
9. *Divorce Rate in the U.S. Drops to Nearly 40 Year Low*, Abigail Adams http://time.com/4575495/divorce-rate-nearly-40-year-low/
10. http://www.divorcestatistics.org, Divorce Resources, Feb. 3, 2017.
11. Percentage of Divorces in Selected Countries, 2002, http://www.infoplease.com/ipa/A0200806.html
12. *Letters to a Young Poet,* Rainer Maria Rilke, Germany, 1934.

CHAPTER ONE:

1. *The Scottish Himalayan Expedition,* W.H. Murray, London, England: J.M. Dent & Sons, 1951.
2. Audubon, Do Eagles Remain Faithful to One Mate Their Entire Lives? Alisa Opar, http://www.audubon.org/news/do-eagles-remain-faithful-one-mate-their-entire-lives February 2, 2017.
3. *Existentialism and Humanism,* Jean Paul Sartre, Les Editions Nagel, Methuen & Co 1948 English.
4. History Beta, http://findarticles.com/p/articles/mi_m3495/is_11_46/ai_80327062/ , Feb. 2, 2017.

CHAPTER TWO:

1. *"Steinsaltz edition of the Talmud"* Archived from *the original* on August 16, 2007, Feb.3, 2017.
2. *Basic facts about California Condors,* Defenders of Wildlife
3. Memories, Dreams and Reflections, Carl Jung, Vintage Reissue Edition, NY, NY, 1989.
4. *The Seven Principles for Making Marriage Work,* John Gottman, New York, N.Y.: Three Rivers Press, New York, NY., 2007.
5. *Blind Men and the Elephant,* John Godfrey Saxe, (1816-1887), http://www.allaboutphilosophy.org/blind-men-and-the-elephant.htm, Feb. 2, 2017.
6. *The Couple Is Telling You What You need to Know*, Toby & Norman Bobes, New York, N.Y.: W.W. Norton & Company, Inc. 2005

CHAPTER THREE:

1. *Wilhelm Meister's Lehrjahre,* Johann Wolfgang von Goethe, Johann Friedrich Unger Berlin, Germany: 1795-1796
2. *The Art of Loving: An Enquiry into the Nature of Love,* Erich Fromm, New York, N.Y.: Harper Brothers, 1956.
3. The Online Etymology Dictionary, http://www.etymonline.com/

index.php?term=victim, Feb. 2, 2017

4. *After the Affair,* Janis Abrahms Spring with Michael Spring, New York, NY, iUniverse, 2008.
5. *Friendship with God: An Uncommon Dialogue,* Neal Donald Walsch, New York, N.Y.: TarcherPerigee, Oct. 1, 2002.
6. *Eat, Pray, Love,* Elizabeth Gilbert, New York, N.Y.: Penguin, Feb. 16, 2006.

CHAPTER FOUR:

1. *All We Are Saying: The Last Major Interview with John Lennon and Yoko Ono* (2000) by John Lennon, Yōko Ono, David Sheff.
2. Ten High Flying Facts about the Puffin, http://www.worldwildlife.org/blogs/good-nature-travel/posts/ten-high-flying-facts-about-puffins
3. Animal Fun Fact Guide, http://www.animalfactguide.com/animal-facts/atlantic-puffin/, Feb. 3, 2017
4. Four Incredibly Cute Facts about the Atlantic Puffin, https://www.hurtigruten.us/must-read-articles/wildlife/4-incredibly-cute-facts-about-atlantic-puffin/2-19-16 published, Feb. 3, 2017
5. https://projectpuffin.audubon.org/birds/puffin-faqs, Feb. 2, 2020.
6. 3 Habits of Peak Performers. Carmine Gallo *Forbes Magazine.* https://www.forbes.com/sites/carminegallo/2016/05/24/3-daily-habits-of-peak-performers-according-to-michael-phelps-coach/#741f2644102c May 4, 2019.
7. The Brain Training Secrets of Olympic Athletes, Carolyn Gregoire, Feb. 14, 2014, The Huffington Post, http://www.huffingtonpost.com/2014/02/11/mind-hacks-from-olympic-a_n_4747755.html
8. *O, The Oprah Magazine*, The Way We Love Now, April 2010.
9. *O, The Oprah Magazine*, The Way We Love Now, April 2010.
10. Juhasz, Suzanne. "I dwell in Possibility: ED in the Subjunctive [sic] Mood." *Emily Dickinson Bulletin* 32 (1977): 105-109 Dwell in Possibility, Emily Dickenson

CHAPTER FIVE:

1. *Passionate Marriage: Keeping Love and Intimacy Alive in Committed Relationships,* David Schnarch, New York N.Y.: WW Norton & Co., 1997.
2. Reference, https://www.reference.com/pets-animals/scarlet-macaw-be8d81581a66a2f, Feb. 3, 2017
3. Anywhere, Scarlett Macaw, https://www.anywhere.com/flora-fauna/bird/scarlet-macaw, Feb. 3, 2017.
4. *Getting the Love You Want,* Hendrix H., Melbourne, Victoria: Schwarz & Wilkenson, 1998.
5. *Anatomy of Love,* Dr. Helen Fisher New York, NY, Ballentine Books, January 3, 1984.
6. *Babies in the womb can sense mom's emotions,* Kathleen Blanchard, 11-14-11, www.emaxhealth.com/1020/babies-womb-
9. *Pretty Woman.* Garry Marshall. Touchstone Pictures, 1990.
10. *Titanic.* James Cameron. Paramount Pictures, 1997.
11. *Say Anything.* Cameron Crowe. 20th Century Fox, 1987.
12. *Committed: A Skeptic Makes Peace with Marriage,* Elizabeth Gilbert, New York, N.Y.: Viking Press, January 2010.

CHAPTER SIX:

1. *Passionate Marriage: Keeping Love and Intimacy Alive in Committed Relationships,* David Schnarch, New York N.Y.: WW Norton & Co., 1997.
2. http://bioweb.uwlax.edu/bio203/s2009/beckwith_kayl/Interestingfacts.htm Canadian Goose, Kaylee Beckwith
3. *6 Honking Facts about Canada Geese,* Matt Soniak, Mental Floss http://mentalfloss.com/article/80243/6-honking-facts-about-canada-geese
4. *Birds in the Yard Month by Month,* Sharon Sorenson, Mechanicsburg, Pennsylvania: Stockpole Books. 2013.
5. *The Year of the Greylag Goose,* Konrad Lorenz, San Diego, CA, Harcourt Brace Jovanovich,1979.

6. *The Pig Who Sang to the Moon,* Jeffrey Moussaieff Masson, New York, NY, Random House, 2007.
7. "In my Life," *Rubber Soul,* The Beatles, EMI Studios, London England, 1965.
8. Rumi, Kabir Helminski, Coleman Barks, Daniel Liebert, Andrew Harvey, Muriel Maufroy, and Timothy Freke
9. https://en.wikipedia.org/wiki/Haystack_(food) May 4, 2019.
10. *The Comfort of Strangers,* Ian McEwan, Mishawaka, IN: Better World Books, 1981.
11. *Pandemonium,* Lauren Oliver, New York, N.Y.: Harper Collins, 2001.
12. https://en.wikipedia.org/wiki/Wabi-sabi, Feb. 2, 2020.

CHAPTER SEVEN:

1. *Are You Listening?* Ralph G. Nichols & Leonard A. Stevens, New York, N.Y.: McGraw Hill, 1957.
2. *"Dem Grimm Aeling," New Fairy Tales, First Book, First Collection. Hans Christian Anderson, C.A. Reitzel, Denmark,1843.*
3. Swan Lake, Pyotr Ilyich Tchaikovsky in 1875–76.
4. Birding information, Mute Swan, http://www.birdinginformation.com/birds/swans/mute-swan/, Feb. 3, 2017
5. *They famously mate for Life, but as one flighty pair find new lovers...the Truth about the Sex Life of Swans,* Colin Tudge, http://www.dailymail.co.uk/sciencetech/article-1246073/They-famously-mate-life-flighty-pair-new-lovers—truth-sex-lives-swans.html#ixzz4Xg2T9xtq July 1992, July 1992,
6. Parables of Leadership, W. Chan Kim and Renée A. Mauborgne: Harvard Business Review, July-August 1992.
7. Special Section, *Accounting for Narrative Therapy's Success, The Small and the Ordinary: The Daily Practice of a Postmodern Narrative Therapy,* Kathy Weingarten, Ph.D., Fam Proc. 37:3-15, 1998.
8. *Avatar,* James Cameron, 20th Century Fox, Dec. 10, 2009.

9. *Judge Softly.* Mary T. Lathrap. 1885.
10. *What the Bleep Do We Know?,* William Arnst, Roadside Attractions, April 23, 200411.   Millionaire Mind Intensive. https://millionairemindintensive.com May 4, 2019.

CHAPTER EIGHT:

1. Gandhi didn't actually ever say *"Be the change you want to see in the world." Here's the real Quote,* Joseph Ranseth, August 27, 2015 https://josephranseth.com/gandhi-didnt-say-be-the-change-you-want-to-see-in-the-world/
2. *Listen to the Mockingbird,* Doug Harbrecht, April1, 1994, https://www.nwf.org/News-and-Magazines/National-Wildlife/Birds/Archives/1992/Listen-to-the-Mockingbird.aspx
3. *Pilgrim at Tinker Creek,* Annie Dillard, New York, N.Y.: Banham, 1975.
4. *Conversations with God: An Uncommon Dialogue,* Neale Donald Walsch, New York, N.Y.: G. P. Putnam's Sons, 1996.
5. *Fear and Trembling,* Soren Keirkegaard, Denmark, 1843.
6. *Seven Spiritual Laws of Success,* Deepak Chopra, San Francisco, CA: New World Library, 1994.
7. *Isis Unveiled: A Master-Key to the Mysteries of Ancient and Modern Science and Theology,* Helena Blavatsky, 1877.
8. *The Secret,* Drew Heriot, Prime Time Productions, March 26, 2007.
9. *Jack Handey, Saturday Night Live* (1985–1998 and 2001–2002)
10. *Eye of the Storm, Blue Eyes, Brown Eyes Experiment,* Jane Elliot, teacher, William Peters, 1970, American Broadcasting Company.
11. *New York Subway Cello,* William Pendergast featuring Yoyo Ma, August 5, 2008, https://www.youtube.com/ watch?v=3YvWSr2gXbA
12. *Subtle Energies & Energy Medicine Journal,* Consciousness Interactions with Remote Biological Systems: Anomalous Intentionality Effects, William G. Brad, PhD, Vol. 2, No. 1, http://journals.sfu.ca/seemj/index.php/seemj/article/view/112, May 5, 2019.

13. *Subtle Energies & Energy Medicine Journal,* The Legacy Lives On, Lenore Wiand, PhD, Vol. 21, No. 2, http://journals.sfu.ca/seemj/index.php/seemj/article/viewFile/448/409, May 5, 2019.
14. McTaggart, L. (2002). *The field.* New York: Harper Collins.
15. *The Field: The Quest for the Secret Force of the Universe,* Lynne McTaggart, New York, N.Y.: Harper Perennial, 2002
16. *Man's Search for Meaning,* Victor Frankl, Vienna, Austria: Verlag fur Jugend, 1946.

CHAPTER NINE:

1. "Samuel Taylor Coleridge" poetryfoundation.org. 2 March, 2018. Retrieved 2 March, 2018.
2. https://www.phrases.org.uk/meanings/30800.html, 2 March, 2018. Retrieved 2 March, 2018.
3. *Pirates of the Caribbean: Dead Men Tell No Tales*, Walt Disney Studios, Release Date: May 26, 2017.
4. *Man's Search for Meaning,* Victor Frankl, Vienna, Austria, Beacon Press, 1946.
5. *Zen and the Art of Motorcycle Maintenance,* Robert Pirsig, New York, NY, William Morrow & Company, 1974.
6. *The General Theory of Employment, Interest and Money,* John Maynard Keynes, London, England, Palgrave McMillan, 1936.
7. Eliminate That Seven Times Statistic: How to Stay Away for Good, Sydney Martin, http://www.breakthesilencedv.org/beat-that-seven-times-statistic/ 15 January, 2015, Retrieved 2 March, 2018.
8. https://www.theguardian.com/commentisfree/2011/dec/17/abused-women-domestic-violence, 17 December, 2017, Retrieved 2 March, 2018.
9. http://www.thehotline.org/resources/statistics/, Retrieved 2 March, 2018
10. The Brain Can Work Against Abuse Victims, Rhonda Freeman, https://www.psychologytoday.com/blog/neurosagacity/201701/the-brain-can-work-against-abuse-victims, 18 January, 2017, Retrieved 3 March, 2018.

11. http://www.domesticabuseshelter.org/infodomesticviolence.htm, Retrieved 3 March, 2018.
12. *Why Won't You Apologize? Healing Big Betrayals and Little Hurts*, Harriet Lerner, New York, NY, Simon & Schuster, October, 2017.
13. Albatross, https://www.nationalgeographic.com/animals/birds/group/albatrosses/ Retrieved 3 March, 2018.
14. Albatrosses, http://factsanddetails.com/world/cat53/sub339/item2185.html, Retrieved 3 March, 2018.
15. Oldest Wild Bird in US Raises Chick https://www.theguardian.com/environment/2011/mar/10/oldest-bird-chicks, Retrieved 3 March, 2018.
16. *Moby Dick*, Herman Melville, New York, NY, Harper & Bros., 1851
17. https://www.youtube.com/watch?v=PnFKaaOSPmk, Retrieved 3 March, 2018.
18. Disorganization of Attachment Strategies in Infancy and Childhood, Kate Henninghausen, Karlen Lyons-Ruth, http://www.child-encyclopedia.com/attachment/according-experts/disorganization-attachment-strategies-infancy-and-childhood January, 2010, Retrieved 3 March, 2018.
19. Happy Parenting, Happy Kids, Dr. Joan D. Atwood, IUniverse, Bloomington, IN, 2019.
20. Parental Attachment Problems, Barit Brogaard, https://www.psychologytoday.com/blog/the-mysteries-love/201611/parental-attachment-problems, Retrieved 3 March, 2018.
21. https://en.wikipedia.org/wiki/Attachment_in_adults#cite_note-Mikulincer.2CFlorian.2CWeller, Retrieved 3, March, 2018.
22. Mirroring, http://parentingprocess.blogspot.com/2010/05/lets-consider-second-developmental.html, 9 May, 2010, Retrieved 3 March, 2018.
23. Yes, It's Your Parents' Fault, Kate Murphy, https://www.nytimes.com/2017/01/07/opinion/sunday/yes-its-your-parents-fault.html, Retrieved 3 March, 2018.
24. *Attached: The New Science of Adult Attachment and How it Can Help You Find—and Keep—Love*, Amir Levine, Rachel Heller,

Penguin Group, New York, NY, 5 January, 2012.

25. https://en.wikipedia.org/wiki/Attachment_in_adults#cite_note-Mikulincer.2CFlorian.2CWeller, Retrieved 3, March, 2018.
26. http://davidpuder.com/the-video-that-changed-my-life-the-still-face-experiment/, Dr. David Puder, Retrieved 3, March 2018.
27. Moving Towards a Secure Attachment Style: Can Repeated Security Priming Help? Omri Gillath, Emre Selcuk, and Phillip R. Shaver, http://users.metu.edu.tr/semre/files/GillathSelcukShaver08.pdf, 2008, Retrieved 3, March, 2018.
28. *Attachment and Loss,* John Bowlby, Perseus Group, New York, NY, 1982.
29. https://www.sfu.ac.at/wp-content/uploads/IPIntern012017OB.pdf
30. http://www.authenticityassociates.com/neural-plasticity-4-steps-to-change-your-brain/
31. Socratic Dialogue in Education of Children Diagnosed with Autism Spectrum Disorder, Ali Nouri, Dr. Ann S. Pihlgren, Dialogue in Education of Children Diagnosed with Autism Spectrum Disorder, http://igniteresearch.org/socratic-dialogue-in-education-of-children-diagnosed-with-autism-spectrum-disorder-asd/
32. https://www.drdansiegel.com and https://www.uclahealth.org/marc/, May 5, 2019.

CHAPTER TEN:

1. *Sense and Sensibility.* Jane Austen. 1811. Anon.
2. *The Bridge Across Forever.* Richard Bach. 1984. William Morrow & Co. Ltd. New York.
3. https://www.smithsonianmag.com/science-nature/14-fun-facts-about-lovebirds-180949742/#hxSoxR6xLv6AO82S.99 Jan. 17, 2019.
4. Parliament of Fouls. Geoffrey Chaucer. 1381-1382. Pre-printing press.
5. https://www.dove.com/us/en/dove-self-esteem-project.html January 17, 2019

6. Go West. Scenes from an American Homecoming. Peter Hessler. *The New Yorker.* April 18, 2010.
7. *Soul Mates.* Thomas Moore. Harper Collins. New York. 1994
8. https://www.drumondpark.com/rapidough/ January 17, 2019
9. *Seven Principles for Making a Marriage Work.* John Gottman. Three Rivers Press. NY, New York. 1998.
10. *Soul Mates.* Thomas Moore. Harper Collins. NY, New York. 1994
11. *The Book of Qualities.* J. Ruth Gendler. Harper. NY, New York. 1988.
12. https://www.radicalhonesty.com, January 17, 2019.
13. Rabbi Yehuda Berg. Daily Kabbalah Tune Up: Embarrassed to Say, Jan. 13, 2011.
14. Jerry McGuire. Cameron Crowe, TriStar Pictures, 1996.
15. Frozen. Walt Buck, Jennifer Lee, Walt Disney Animation, 2013.
16. "If You Leave Me Now." Chicago. Chicago X. July 31, 1976. Columbia Records. NY, New York.
17. *The Joshua Tree,* "With or Without You." U2, Danesmoate House, Dublin, Ireland, 1987.
18. "I Have Nothing." Whitney Houston. The Bodyguard Original Soundtrack Album. November 17, 1992. Arista Records.
19. Bowen M. (1974 in1978). "Toward the Differentiation of Self in One's Family of Origin." Ch 22 Family Therapy in Clinical practice. New York: Aronson.
20. How Politics in Trump's America Divides Families, *The Atlantic,* Kiley Bense, Nov. 26, 2018.
21. *Passionate Marriage.* David Schnarch. W. W. Norton & Company. April 27, 2009. NY, New York.
22. *The Dating Game.* Chuck Barris Productions. ABC Television. 1965.

CHAPTER ELEVEN:

1. *The Book of Martyrdom and Artifice: First Journals and Poems: 1937-1952,* Allen Ginsberg, Paperback, Boston, MA, 2008.
2. *Hey Nostradamus!* Douglas Coupland. Bloomsbury. New York, NY, July 1, 2003.
3. https://www.allaboutbirds.org/guide/Barn_Owl/lifehistory, May

5, 2019.
4. http://voices.nationalgeographic.com/2014/04/29/barn-owls-divorce-animals-science-mating/, May 5, 2019.
5. https://www.allaboutbirds.org/bird-cams-faq-barn-owl-nest/, May 5, 2019.
6. https://en.wikipedia.org/wiki/Barn_owl, May 5, 2019.
7. *Soul Mates,* Thomas Moore, New York, NY, Harper Perennial, 2016.
8. *The Collected Works of C. G. Jung, Archetypes and the Collective Unconscious,* Carl Jung, Part 1, Volume 9, Princeton University Press, 1969
9. *Soul Mates,* Thomas Moore, New York, NY, Harper Perennial, 2016.
10. *Behind Closed Doors: The Impact of Domestic Violence on Children.* UNICEF Child Protection Section Programme Division 3, New York, NY. July 14, 2019.
11. *Couples Companion for Getting the Love That You Want.* Harville Hendrix & Kelly Hunt. Pocket Books. New York, NY, 1991.
12. *The Seven Principles for Making a Marriage Work.* John Gottman & Nan Siver. Orion Publishing Group. New York, NY, 2018.
13. *Hold Me Tight.* Dr. Sue Johnson. Hachette Book Group. New York, NY. 2008.
14. *The New Rules of Marriage.* Terrence Real. Ballentine Books, New York, NY. 2007.
15. Journal of Personality and Social Psychology. Vol. 49, No. 1. Physiological and Affective Predictors of Change in Relational Satisfaction. Robert W. Levenson & John M. Gottman. American Psychological Association. 1985.
16. Manage Conflict, Part 4. Zach Brittle, LMHC. The Gottman Institute. https://www.gottman.com/blog/manage-conflict-part-4/, July 14, 2019.
17. *What the Bleep Do We Know?* William Arnst, Roadside Attractions, Los Angeles, June, 2004.
18. How Anger Affects the Brain and Body. National Institute for the Clinical Application of Behavioral Medicine.

https://www.nicabm.com/how-anger-affects-the-brain-and-body-infographic/, December 7, 2019.

19. "Like a Prayer," "Express Yourself," Madonna. Sire – Warner Brothers. May 9, 1988.
21. Tantric Sex 101: What It Is, Benefits, and How to Do It. Leslie Grace, R.N. https://www.mindbodygreen.com/0-23332/tantric-sex-101-what-it-is-how-to-do-it.html December 7, 2019.

CHAPTER TWELVE:

1. *The Unabridged Devil's Dictionary,* Ambrose Bierce, Great Britain, Arthur F. Bird, 1906.
2. *Committed: A Skeptic Makes Peace With Marriage,* Elizabeth Gilbert, New York, NY, Viking Press, 2010.
3. *Venus in Arms,* Criss Jami, United States, Criss Jami, 2012.
4. The Loon Project, https://loonproject.org/loon-breeding/, December 8, 2019.
5. https://worldworkstrainings.com/, Feb. 2, 2020.
6. *Invictus.* William Ernest Henley. 1875.
7. *Illusions: Adventures of a Reluctant Messiah,* Richard Bach, New York, NY, Dell Publishing, Random House, 1977.
8. *The Prophet,* Khalil Gibran, Knopf Books, New York, NY, 1923.